THE EROTOMANIAC

THE EROTOMANIAC

The Secret Life of Henry Spencer Ashbee

———

IAN GIBSON

DA CAPO PRESS

Cataloging-in-Publication data for this book is available from the Library of Congress.

First Da Capo Press edition 2001
Reprinted by arrangement with Faber and Faber Limited
ISBN 0-306-81064-6

Published by Da Capo Press
A Member of the Perseus Books Group
http://www.dacapopress.com

Da Capo Press books are available at special discounts for bulk purchases in the U.S. by corporations, institutions, and other organizations. For more information, please contact the Special Markets Department at the Perseus Books Group, 11 Cambridge Center, Cambridge, MA 02142, or call (617) 252-5298.

1 2 3 4 5 6 7 8 9——05 04 03 02 01

for Felicity Ashbee
with love and gratitude

Contents

———

List of Illustrations

Part I half title: H. S. Ashbee bookplate by Paul Avril
Part II half title: H. S. Ashbee bookplate by C. W. Sherborne

Introduction

Henry Spencer Ashbee, whose life coincided almost to the year with the reign of Queen Victoria, was a successful City merchant and, to all appearances, a pillar of society. Behind the scenes, however, he was engaged in the ambitious project of becoming the century's leading collector and bibliographer of erotic books. Ashbee emerges as the archetypal Victorian gentleman with a secret.

Given the prevailing puritanism of the nineteenth century, and the ban on all overt portrayal of sexuality, it is often difficult to distinguish between the genuine, pioneer sexologists of the time and those whose hidden agenda was to titillate. Ashbee was no exception to the rule, as is shown by the three voluminous erotic bibliographies he issued privately under the scatological pseudonym Pisanus Fraxi: *Index Librorum Prohibitorum* (1877), *Centuria Librorum Absconditorum* (1879) and *Catena Librorum Tacendorum* (1885).

The centre of erotic book production in London at the beginning of the Victorian period was Holywell Street, in whose 'literary garbage', wrote William Acton, 'illicit pleasure was depicted in all its most attractive and meretricious forms'. In 1857, when Ashbee was in his mid-twenties and presumably already interested in erotica, the Obscene Publications Act led to a clampdown that drove the trade underground.[1]

As the century progressed, and grew increasingly strait-laced, erotica publishing in English shifted to the Continent, particularly to Paris and Amsterdam, and there was a brisk trade in smuggling books into Britain, sometimes in diplomatic bags. It seems worth mentioning one of those most energetically engaged in this clandestine activity, Richard Monckton Milnes, Baron Houghton, who amassed a collection of erotica perhaps surpassed only by that of his friend Ashbee.

Milnes was educated at Trinity College, Cambridge, where he knew Tennyson, Arthur Henry Hallam and Thackeray. Politician and political commentator, as well as something of a poet, he rose to become a social power in London, with a reputation as 'the first wit in town and a maker of men'.[2]

Milnes was not just a collector of erotica. He also acted out his sexual fantasies. The Goncourt brothers, hearing rumours about his visits to a brothel in London with a Paris crony, Frederick Hankey (well known to Ashbee), made enquiries. It turned out that the establishment in question was run by a certain 'Mrs Jenkins' and provided facilities for flogging thirteen-year-old girls 'whom first', said Hankey, 'we made sit in class and then whipped – the little ones not too hard but the big ones very hard indeed'. The Goncourts expressed due indignation.[3]

It is now almost certain that Milnes was the author of an epic poem on flagellation, *The Rodiad*, composed in much the same vein as his friend Swinburne's unpublished *The Flogging Block*.[4]

Richard Burton, whom Ashbee also frequented, was the most famous member of Victorian London's clique of erotomaniacs, and headed what might be termed the Eastern Challenge to the existing sexual morality. To this end he and his fellow orientalist Foster Fitzgerald Arbuthnot set up the spoof Káma-Shástra Society (with Monckton Milnes as 'first invisible patron').[5] The aim was the translation, annotation and publication of the most venerable sex manuals of the Orient. Burton and Arbuthnot

cracked off with the *Káma-Shástra* (or *Ananga Ranga*) and the *Kama Sutra*, rendered from the original Sanskrit.[6]

The motive that drove Burton to devote endless energy to the divulgation of these and similar works was his conviction that Victorian sexual morality, based on a twisted, Manichaean interpretation of Christianity, was causing infinite and utterly unnecessary misery. Instead of puberty being an occasion for joyous celebration, for instance, it was cloaked in shame and anxiety. Anything to do with sex was taboo:

The mock virtue, the most immodest modesty of England and the United States in the Nineteenth century, pronounces the subject foul and loathsome; 'Society' sickens at all details; and hence it is said abroad that the English have the finest women in Europe and least know how to use them.[7]

Swinburne had met Burton in 1861 at one of Monckton Milnes's famous breakfast parties in Brook Street, and the two quickly became friends.[8] By 1865 the poet was calling the older man his 'tempter and favourite audience'.[9] As well as a shared interest in erotica, their hatred of Christianity served as a potent bond. Swinburne's was even more virulent than Burton's. His *Poems and Ballads* outraged the Victorian middle class (particularly the line 'Thou hast conquered, O pale Galilean; the world has grown grey from thy breath').[10]

In Swinburne's play *Atalanta*, God is upbraided by the Chorus for his cruelty. He is 'the Supreme Evil' who 'makes desire, and slays desire with shame'.[11]

It is a memorable line. Whether God is responsible or not, one of the functions of shame is certainly to slay desire – or to turn it into channels that make an uninhibited sex life impossible. (It had certainly made it impossible for Swinburne.) Victorian middle-class society was deeply ashamed about sex. And, by dint of that very condition, unable to articulate the true

nature of its deprivation, for, as Helen Merell Lynd has shown in *Shame and the Search for Identity*, the essence of shame is its incommunicability. Shame is an isolating emotion. It hides even from itself.

Ashbee's three erotic bibliographies, issued in limited editions, reached few people and were virtually forgotten until the new permissiveness led to a facsimile reprint in 1960. Eleven years later Steven Marcus put them firmly on the map in *The Other Victorians*, probing the author's psyche but not his life, about which little more was known at the time than the account appearing in the *Dictionary of National Biography*.

The *DNB* had not been able to draw on Ashbee's unpublished diaries. Put on the scent of these by James Pope-Hennessy's biography of Richard Monckton Milnes (1949–51), I eventually met Ashbee's granddaughter Felicity Ashbee, who with extraordinary generosity lent them to me. I read them with growing fascination.

Without the diaries this book would have been impossible. While not usually explicit about Ashbee's erotomania, they do shed light on it, as well as providing a host of details about his relations with Monckton Milnes, Burton and lesser-known members of their group. It seemed to me, after their perusal, that Ashbee deserved a monograph.

From the outset of my research I knew that Ashbee was a candidate for authorship of the anonymous sex marathon *My Secret Life*. Privately printed in eleven, small-format volumes on the Continent not long before his death in 1900, the book claims to be the reworking of the exhaustive erotic journal of a well-to-do Victorian who, over the decades, has had relations with many hundreds of women, mainly serving girls and prostitutes. Ashbee, certainly, could have written it. But did he?

The shadowy, Paris-based publisher Paul Harry Ferdinando, alias Charles Carrington, who was involved in hawking copies of

My Secret Life, maintained that Ashbee was indeed the author. But he chose not to provide any evidence. In his introduction to the 1966 Grove Press reprint of the book (another product of the new permissiveness), Gershon Legman took up the story and argued strongly for Ashbee's authorship, mainly on the grounds of certain stylistic similarities between *My Secret Life* and Pisanus Fraxi's three erotic bibliographies. Conclusive proof was still not forthcoming, although the circumstantial evidence had grown considerably.

In 1978 I visited Legman at his Provençal retreat in Valbonne. He was delighted to hear that I had access to the diaries and, more convinced than ever that Ashbee was the author of *My Secret Life*, encouraged me to continue with my research. But other pressures intervened and I had to shelve the project. Only now have I been able to take it up again. I have enjoyed assembling and sifting the evidence.

If Ashbee wrote *My Secret Life*, the book cannot be the true sexual history it claims to be (and which several scholars have claimed it to be) and becomes, instead, a fictional substitute for the real thing. Either way it is a major achievement. And, either way, Ashbee remains a remarkable Victorian.

PART I

Above: Pisanus Fraxi's signature from a covering letter sent with a copy of the *Centuria Librorum Absconditorum* in 1879.

Previous page: Ashbee's portrait in Paul Avril's bookplate (1890) was considered by one commentator to be a 'very good' likeness.

The Making of an Erotomaniac (1834–77)

———

Henry Spencer Ashbee was born on 21 April 1834 in Blackfriars
Road, Southwark, London, and baptized on 1 June following at
Boughton under Blean, in Kent.[1]

Both his parents were Kentish. Robert Ashbee, his father
(1804–1867), was the son of a farmer, John Ashbee, who owned a
substantial mansion near Faversham called Colkins (or The Clock-
house; see plate 2), built in 1697 by Thomas Stacey, the King's
Master Shipwright of Deptford.[2] It was a large family: John Ashbee
had nine children by his first wife, seven (of whom Robert
was the eldest) by his second.[3] Robert's wife, Frances Elizabeth
Spencer, was born at Deal in 1810. How she and Robert met is
not known. They were married on 29 June 1833 in St Andrew's
by the Wardrobe, Blackfriars (which doubled as the parish
church of St Anne's, destroyed in the Great Fire and never
replaced). Henry Spencer was to be the couple's only child.[4]

The Ashbees of Colkins were intensely proud of their Kentish
roots and loved to recall that freeholding yeomen ancestors of
theirs had played a leading role in the great rebellion of 1450
against Henry VI, when the Irish adventurer Jack Cade (or, as he
styled himself, Mortimer) led twenty thousand Kent men to
London and beheaded Lord Say, the King's treasurer. They were
fierce individualists, the Ashbees, and considered themselves a
match for anyone.[5]

In 1814, at the age of ten, Robert Ashbee distinguished himself as 'Best Speaker' at Lynsted School, a few miles from Colkins. The prize, later in the possession of his grandson, Arts and Crafts apostle Charles R. Ashbee, Henry Spencer's son, was a 'charmingly bound' copy of the poems of Robert Bloomfield, author of the celebrated *The Farmer's Boy* (1800), 'with "Bewick" or Luke Clennell's cuts' and the prizewinner's name tooled in gold on the cover. In later life Robert Ashbee retained his ability as a persuasive speaker, and was always to love books and poetry. In each respect Henry Spencer followed closely in the paternal footsteps.[6]

We are as in the dark about Robert Ashbee's movements before his wedding to Frances Elizabeth Spencer as we are concerning his whereabouts and profession over the next ten years. In the St Anne's, Blackfriars, marriage register he figures as 'Gentleman' and is listed as 'of this parish'. What was he doing in Blackfriars? We do not know. In view of his later, highly responsible, position as manager of the important Curtis's and Harvey gunpowder mills on Hounslow Heath, he must surely have had previous experience in the trade. But where? With Curtis's and Harvey themselves? Perhaps, but since the firms' records are no longer extant we have no documentary evidence to go on. It is more likely that Ashbee trained in Kent, where there were two gunpowder mills near by: John Hall and Son, at Faversham, and, two miles from Colkins, William Hall's establishment at Ospringe. But here too the search for documentation has been fruitless. Henry Spencer Ashbee must certainly have spent part of his childhood at Colkins. His Kentish background filled him with pride, as it did the rest of his family.[7]

It seems that Ashbee was incommunicative with his children about his father Robert's early life. Perhaps he did not know very much about it. According to a vague tradition recorded by his son Charles, grandfather Robert was living at Colkins when the

Corn Law was repealed in 1846, and took an immediate decision: '"There! They've passed the Bill; it'll be a glorious thing for the country, but it'll ruin all of us – and I'm off to South America!"' (ruin them, presumably, because the Ashbees lived off the land). Soon Robert was back, however, bringing with him a series of passable watercolours done 'in a kind of Richard Wilson convention'.[8] The dates, however, do not seem to fit, for, if *The Times* got it right in 1859, reporting on an explosion at the Curtis's and Harvey gunpowder works at Hounslow, Robert Ashbee had by that date been manager of the latter for fifteen years; since, that is, 1844, two years before the repeal of the Corn Law. When he visited South America is a mystery.[9]

Robert Ashbee lived with his wife and son in the manager's villa that went with the Curtis's and Harvey post (see plate 3). It backed on to the river Crane, the tributary of the Thames that fed the powder works and in which Henry Spencer was later to enjoy taking a plunge.[10] Today the area is changed almost beyond recognition, but several street names attest to its former importance: Curtis Road, Harvey Road, Powder Mill Lane . . . The shot tower figuring in the photograph has been preserved (the sole remaining trace of the extensive mills) in what is now Crane Park, a pleasant haven on the edge of Hounslow Heath that flanks Ellerman Avenue and is spoiled only by the roar of the jets approaching or taking off from Heathrow. A plaque affixed to the tower by the London Borough of Richmond upon Thames informs us (rather laboriously) that in the building 'lead bullets were made by dropping the molten metal from a height into water which "froze" the droplets into the spherical shape they assumed during their fall'.

Information about Henry Spencer Ashbee's childhood is disappointingly thin on the ground. Frederick Boase's claim in *Modern English Biography* (1908) that his first school was at Esher, some four miles from Hounslow, has not been

substantiated,[11] although an entry in Ashbee's diary for 1882 perhaps lends it some confirmation: 'The Old White Lady* just before entering Esher, quite familiar to me. Then Sandown Park which in my boyish days was an open medow [sic] with saddle back cows. The old school house, and the well, now railed in. Esher still a very pretty village.'[12]

What we do know for sure is that, in January 1848, when Henry Spencer was fourteen, his father enrolled him as a boarder at Kensington Proprietary Grammar School, situated at 26–28 Kensington Square, London.[13] The school had been founded in 1830 in union with the Corporation of King's College, London, for the purpose of 'providing an efficient course of education for youth, comprising religious and moral instruction in conformity with the principles of the Established Church, the Greek, Latin and Modern languages and literature, History, Geography, Mathematics and such other branches of knowledge and such accomplishments as it may be practicable and advantageous to introduce'.[14] The stress was on preparation for the active life, in particular the Army (one of the school's benefactors, Sir Henry Wilcock, offered an annual appointment to the East India Company's Military College at Addiscombe).[15] At a time when the teaching of modern languages in the public schools was negligible, Kensington Proprietary Grammar put great stress on French and German. It also taught Hindustani. By midsummer 1848, shortly after Ashbee was enrolled, other courses included Civil Drawing, Fortification and Military Drawing, Fencing and, of all things, Dancing. The school was proud of its large and constantly expanding library.[16] In 1850 the total number of pupils was 145.[17]

* The Old White Lady, a familiar Esher landmark, is a stone pillar some eight feet high in the Portsmouth Road, dating from 1750. On it are engraved the distances to Chertsey, Charing Cross, etc.

Kensington Proprietary School reinforced Henry Spencer's love of books, inherited from his father, and one imagines that he spent much time in the library. Musing at the end of his life on paintings inspired by poems and novels, he recalled:

In my boyhood I well remember that the Royal Academy, the only picture gallery I had the opportunity of visiting, was full of such paintings. On my return home I took the book from my father's shelves, & many a poem has been introduced to me in this manner. The poem was thus impressed on my mind, the picture still lingers in my memory.[18]

It appears that Henry Spencer left Kensington School at the age of sixteen after the 1850 midsummer examinations, when his father relinquished his position as a Proprietor.[19] The quarterly 'Order of Merit' lists published by the school during his stay show that he consistently obtained his best marks in Writing, became increasingly proficient at Mathematics and Arithmetic (winning a prize, admittedly in the second division), and was competent at French.[20]

Years later, in 1881, Ashbee was to come across one of his old schoolfellows in India. This was Major A. Lemesurer, chief inspector of the railway line at Bengalore, who recognized him immediately and exclaimed, 'You are the boy who used to give me such capital apples at Kensington School!'[21]

What did Ashbee do on finishing his school education? Whatever it was, he did not go up to Oxford or Cambridge. In the account of his father's household included in the 1851 Census, he is described as 'auctioneer and estate agent', with what justice it is impossible to say. Shortly afterwards he was apprenticed to Groucock, Copestakes, Moor and Co., at 5 Bow Church Yard, termed 'lace and sewed muslin manufacturers' in the 1846 edition of the *Post Office Directory of London*[22] and, in later directories, Manchester wholesalers and 'warehousemen'.[23]

Ashbee lived on the premises during the week, and by 1854,

now aged twenty, was keeping a diary. It confirms him as a voracious reader and shows that he was a haphazard speller. The opening entries read:

6 July 1854. Thursday. Walked to Business from Mr Lee's House, arrived at 5 B.C.Y. [Bow Church Yard] about 9 o'clock. – Stayed in during the evening & read.

7 Friday. Up early. – Shower Bath. – Read. – Went with Father to the Cristal Palace at Sydenham, was delighted – ravished with the beauty of that enchanting place. The Building itself is noble & shows now to much better advantage than it did when in Hyde Park, this is not only to be attributed to its now standing on a hill but also to the addition of two extra transepts, etc. The principal objects of interest in the interior are the various courts of Archetecture & Sculpture, which are both enchanting to the casual visitor & instructive to the student. The beautifully scented Orange Trees & Flowers of which some of the latter are suspended in pretty baskets nearly level with the first galery, the equal & pleasingly strong (but not too powerful) light pervading the whole building & the pleasing arrangement of the various objects of attraction, make it a perfect Eliysium, a resort fit for the Houris. – Returned to 5 B.C.Y. & read during the evening.

8 Saturday. Did not rise early. – Took Aunt Fanny Ashbee down to Hounslow. – Spent the evening in walking in the Garden, enjoying the smell of the flowers etc. Father read aloud two or three Ballads.

9 Sunday. Walked with Father & Aunt to Hanworth Church, heard a good Sermon from Mr. Cresswell on the 5th of Ecclesiastes 4 & 5 verses. Walked back; did not take a drive in the afternoon as it rained very sharply.

From succeeding entries we learn that Henry Spencer habitually spends his weekends at the family home in Hounslow and is an opera lover (he greatly enjoys Grisi and her husband's performances in *Lucrezia Borgia* at Covent Garden). He reads constantly in both French and English. Having finished a certain

Madame Ancelot's *Isabelle ou Deux Jours d'Espérience* [*sic*] ('not bad but nearly like all that I have hitherto read of her'), he embarks on the same author's play *Clémence ou la Fille de l'Avocat*, and soon afterwards is immersed in Gleig's *Battle of Waterloo*, 'in order that I may the better appreciate the view of the plain on which the battle was fought when I go over to Belgium'. His father contributes to his enthusiasm for Waterloo by reading aloud Byron's description of the battle in *Childe Harold*. The Ashbees are typically Victorian self-improvers: the maximum value must be extracted from everything.

The trip to Belgium (a holiday, not a business visit) lasted from 22 July until 7 August 1854. Henry Spencer was accompanied by another Groucock, Copestakes and Moor apprentice, a young man called Marshall. The weather was hot and clammy, and Ostend, where they landed, proved titillating. It is our first glimpse of the future authority on erotica:

I myself never saw such a sight as the water presented, men & women promiscuously mingled together bathing & romping in the water without any regard to the natural reserve existing between the sexes; we were ourselves, part of the time we were in the water, close by, that is within five yards of a party of two girls & one young man who were helping each other to flounder about in gallant style. After we had finished bathing ourselves we watched for some time the other bathers; we saw one girl come out of the water & walk into her machine, there was a young man waiting for her on the sand and he stood for some ten minutes upon the step of her machine smoking a cigar & rubbing her hair, with the most perfect nonchlance, whilst she was in a perfect state of nidity & apparently enjoying the operation vastly; nor were we less amused to see some of the girls, after bathing, parade upon the Digue with a towel pinned over their backs, & their hair quite loose & dischevelled laid over it to dry in the sun, whilst they used merely a parasol to protect their heads from its burning rays; or to see two women belonging to the baths strip stark naked & redress in one of the

machines with the door & windows wide open; after thus enjoying ourselves we repaired to a café & had a glass of capital beer.[24]

Things, clearly, were freer in Belgium than in England. A few days later, at Brussels, Ashbee and Marshall have another adventure. A wily guide ('commissioner') has told them that there are some good tableaux vivants to be seen in the city, and they duly set off with him:

The carriage drew up before a very respectable house, the commissioner rang the bell, & we were ushered into a very beautiful furnished appartment, where we had not been seated three minutes before a half a dozen very pretty girls came running in & seated themselves around us, laughed, chatted & frollickd about in the most enticing & amorous manner, we immediately saw what the case was, we had been sent into a brothel. I ordered a bottle of wine & after a half an hour's chat & romp with the girls we left, heartily laughing at the neat joke our commissioner had played upon us. We were of course invited to stay the night. I did not stay for reasons best kept to myself.[25]

Throughout the diary Ashbee's tendency will be, precisely, to keep to himself the private aspects of his activities. The passages quoted reveal a mixture of sexual curiosity and prudishness which comes out strongly later in the journal. The *Mannekin Pis* elicits a similarly ambiguous response. 'It cannot fail to strike a stranger,' comments Ashbee, 'more especially an Englishman whose idea of decency is generally very refined, & perchance sometimes too rigid.'[26]

Ashbee has a roving eye for a pretty girl, certainly. In a Brussels park a large crowd gathers to listen to a military band. 'I do not ever remember having seen so numerous a collection of beautiful & beautifully dressed women,' he comments.[27]

Ashbee and Marshall's fortnight in Belgium is a hectic affair. Waterloo, much prepared for, is visited, so too Ghent, Bruges, Malines, Liège, Namur (which provokes a facetious reference to

Sterne's Uncle Toby and his comments on fortifications) and Antwerp, their port of re-embarkation, where 'the women were fine, & some very good looking'.[28]

Henry Spencer is an ardent scrutinizer of churches and other monuments, and diligently notes down details of ceilings, statues, arches and, above all, paintings. While none too fond of the Roman Catholic Church (there are scornful references to the 'flummery' and 'messing about' of priests at the altar), he responds enthusiastically to the beauty of the liturgy, to the Latin and the music. He is alive, too, to scenery. As for books, he indulges in the purchase of a four-volume, unbound edition of Rousseau's *Confessions*. A handsome young man, to judge from a photograph taken when he was twenty-six (see plate 1), he was not averse to cutting something of a figure, buying a 'blue blouse', which he thinks, perhaps hopes, will 'astonish' people in London.

Back home he takes the train down to Hounslow every Saturday as before. At Hanworth church the Reverend Cresswell's sermons are proving repetitious, and Robert Ashbee continues to indulge in his proclivity for reading aloud, revelling particularly in Taylor's *Holy Living and Holy Dying*. During the week, Henry Spencer enjoys dropping into a tavern of an evening for a ditty or two, sometimes 'up west', sometimes 'down east', and sings in a choir at St Martin's Hall that this year performs, among other works, Handel's oratorio *Judas Maccabeus* and *Messiah*. He brushes up his French (much praised in Belgium) at an advanced evening class at the YMCA; diligently attends lectures at Exeter Hall; spends a strenuous fortnight doing business in Cornwall; sets up a society at Groucock, Copestakes and Moor for the reading aloud of the best English plays; and expresses passionate admiration for Shakespeare, claiming in his diary that he has read *Hamlet* '100's of times'. Reading is the supreme joy. 'I have gone on regularly since my last entry with Les

Confessions, Wyatt's Poems, The Plea for Religion (on Sunday),* & Hamlet,' he records on 18 October 1854, 'snatching as I always do every minute from the time allowed either for dinner or tea etc., so much do I love reading.' The diary shows that his preferences are plays and biographies: there is no indication of much interest in fiction, contemporary or otherwise.

After 21 December 1854 the diary falls silent until 6 May 1855, when a commentary on Wycherley's play *Love in a Wood*, which Ashbee has just finished reading, contains once again an uneasy compound of puritanism and sexual curiosity. Despite the work's merits, there runs through it 'a vein of loose immorality & foppish vice, which prevents from more general perusal the plays of that period, although the moral of Love in a Wood is not actually & altogether wrong, for Gripe is severely punished for his letchery, & Lady Flippant marrys Addlepot, her aversion, & is thus rendered unhappy for life.' The play's 'immorality', Ashbee allows further, is 'easily accounted for', as it is in most Restoration works: 'It is but the reflection of the reaction which naturally enough took place in the public feeling after the austerity & too rigid piety of the Puritans.' 'The scenes in St James's Park are truthful,' he adds, 'but revolting to morality & reflect little credit upon the ladies and gentlemen of that period.'

Then comes a further hiatus until 21 July 1855, when Ashbee resumes what he terms his 'log-book' to chronicle another fortnight's holiday with Marshall, this time in Holland and Germany. They visit Rotterdam, The Hague, Amsterdam and Utrecht, then travel up the Rhine from Arnhem to Düsseldorf. Cologne (which he notes is distinctly malodorous – Ashbee will always have a nose for bad smells) and Mayence [Mainz] are surveyed, then in quick succession Frankfurt and Hamburg, to

* By one Simpson.

which latter destination the two are impelled mainly by a desire to inspect the famous gaming houses:

Never did I see a more surprising & disgusting sight, old and young of both sexes sitting at the tables with flushed cheeks & fevered brows, the utmost excitement depicted on every feature, playing, & watching the dice as if their lives depended on the number turned up; I was much grieved to see very many English at the tables.[29]

Next it is the turn of Heidelberg and Mannheim, the account petering out on 4 August 1855 at Aix-la-Chapelle, as if Ashbee were too bored to continue writing up his adventures.

The diary then breaks off. Ashbee takes it up again almost a year later, on 23 May 1856, to record that he has just arrived in Paris and is staying with a Monsieur Rollin at 23 Place de l'Esplanade, 'for three months to study, and make myself perfect in the French language'. Maddeningly, no further details of the stay are provided. Almost thirty years later an entry suggests that Ashbee enjoyed himself:

Thence to Bullier, where in my youthful days I passed so many gay evenings when the establishment had the name of 'Closerie des Lilas'. Then only grisettes, girls of the quartier in bonnets blancs, where [were] the only frequenters with the students; later, the garden was frequented by lorettes & gentlemen from the other side of the Seine; now a non-descript class of women, of a lower order than either grisettes or lorettes & an equally low class of young men & calicos, 'possess it merely'.[30]

It seems fair to assume that Ashbee sowed his wild oats liber-ally during those three months in Paris, far from the prying eyes of his family and his business associates back home. Henry Mayhew's *London Labour and the London Poor*, published four years later, carried an illustration of the Closerie des Lilas in its chapter on prostitution.[31] It seems impossible that Ashbee failed to see it there, although there is no reference to Mayhew's famous work anywhere in his writings.

The next entry comes on 15 September 1858, when we find Ashbee on board ship bound for Oporto. Now twenty-four, his fortunes have improved considerably during the last year and a half with the firm, and he has been much on the move:

In that time what changes have taken place; many of my friends are dead, others married, others entirely separated from me.* My father & mother, thank God, are both as well perhaps better than they were then. And I how I am changed! Then delighted to see a little of the world in a fortnight's holiday; now a traveller for my house, I have seen nearly the whole of Europe. Why have I not noted & put to paper the observations I have made during my first business journey on the Continent? Why have I not endeavoured to store up for a future day the information which my travelling cannot fail to have presented to me? I do not know. Is it that I am too idle? This may partly account for it; but on looking back upon the foregoing pages I have been disgusted with the shallowness of my remarks & the want of thought visible throughout my journal. The fact is I want habits of reflection; the pursuit of business is I fancy for one thing against quiet thought, & the learning of languages which has lately occupied my spare time does certainly not foster it [. . .] My calling however as foreign traveller demands a certain acquaintance with modern languages & I have therefore been forced to make them my study. I must endeavour this journey to make deeper reflections, & observe less superficially what passes before me.

Unable to land at Oporto, Ashbee disembarks bad-humouredly in Lisbon. He had begun to learn Spanish three weeks before leaving London, and has been at his grammar book during the voyage. The Victorian entrepreneur in person, he feels certain that, once in Spain itself, he cannot fail, 'with a little industry', to pick the language up rapidly. Meanwhile he makes his way back to Oporto and does his first business of the trip. He had hoped to take a steamer from Lisbon to Gibraltar, but there

* Who these people were it seems impossible to ascertain.

14

is a week's delay and, finding himself bored by the Portuguese capital, he sets off for the Rock overland. Persuaded to take a diligence from Badajoz to Seville, he swears he will never repeat the experience: the road is atrocious.

Ashbee's reaction to the Rock is foreseeably conventional – 'What native of Britain can look at Gibraltar without feeling how great is his nation & without being thankful that he is an Englishman?' – but he is even more impressed by a troupe of Andalusian singers and dancers from Seville. Their performance in a Gibraltar theatre astonishes him:

How different from the cold meaningless pirouettes of the London, Paris & Petersburg stages. Here you have soul! Here you have love! Here you have poetry! The object of the dancer is not to show how high she can jump & how many times she can kick her heels together in one leap, nor how many times she can turn round upon one toe without losing her balance & falling headlong into the orchestra: but to speak a silent poetry with every limb, what limb does not speak, the foot, the hips, the neck, the head, the eye, ah! the eye how it rolls! how it flashes fire! how it elec-trifyes one! The head, the arms, even the fan & robe 'speak with most miraculous organ'. Here is true dancing! Here is the poetry of motion! An Andalucian girl dances, other balet girls jiggle. – One dance particu-larly pleased [me], it is called the 'Olé' and is thoroughly Spanish. The air is lame & melancholy but the dance all grace, all poetry, all variety. – 'El Torero y la Malagueña' also pleased me very much.[32]

Ashbee is enchanted with Cadiz, where he spends ten days. Byron was right about its lovely girls (in *Childe Harold*), and 'the race is by no means extinct'. 'I think that more pretty women can be seen here in a week than in other towns in a month,' he records confidently. 'There is something exceptional about them. Their eyes, hair, walk, dress, every thing about them is per se, every-thing is charming & attractive.' In Cadiz he has another oppor-tunity to see Spanish dancing and is confirmed in his enthusiasm: 'The more I become acquainted with the national dances of

Spain the more I like, appreciate and understand them. xxx.'[33]

In the first month of his diary (July 1854) Ashbee appends a cryptic x three times to entries in which he says he has been out for a walk in London. When he gets back from his trip to Belgium it recurs: 'Took some tea & went out for a walk down Green Lane etc. x.'; 'I was tired but took a walk as far as the viaduct. Etc. x.'[34] It then disappears until this visit to Spain, where we find it ten times, accompanied by one xx, one xxx (as just seen) and one xxxx, with a particularly high incidence in Andalusia. That the mark has a sexual significance seems evident, and my hunch is that it stands for masturbation. The above passage and others in the diary show that Ashbee was very excited indeed by the Andalusian women dancers he saw along his way. In fact, he never forgot them and they were to remain in his mind as the supreme expression of female sexual appeal. Not surprisingly, he fantasizes about spending the rest of his life 'amidst such beauty'.[35]

Seville is his next port of call. Ashbee loves the giant, dark cathedral and the delicacy of the Moorish Alcázar. But again it is the women who particularly enchant him. He now sees gypsy dancing for the first time, or what today we would call flamenco:

What a strange people these Gitanos & Gitanas are, & how remarkable are their dances. I do not however find as much grace in them as I expected from accounts by Borrow* & others, their dances are original & peculiar but possess little grace; they are more to excite than to charm & are lacivious to a degree; they consist in an excessive wriggling of the hips & middle of the body while the arms are held up in the air or the hands clapped in time with the guitar. The movement of the feet & legs is slight sometimes time is kept with the former as well as with the hands. The player of the guitar generally sings at the same time &

* George Borrow's *The Zincali, or An Account of the Gypsies of Spain* had been published in 1841, two years before his more famous *The Bible in Spain*.

frequently the dancer at the hight of the dance sings herself or cryes & sighs in the most exciting manner; it is then that cryes of Ole Salero Viva la Gracia etc. burst from the spectators. The proper way to see the Gitanas dance is upon a table, then every movement can be observed every posture scrutinized every expression apreciated. This is how the Gitanos & Spaniards enjoy the amusement. The night before last with some of my friends Sevillanos I had the treat myself. The Gitanas danced to perfection, & sang as well but as they have by no means sweet voices & as I could understand but very little of their songs, I did not enjoy them so much as the dancers. Spanish women as well have generally unpleasant voices, which is strange, when one finds in the sister kingdom as it were Italy such pleasant & soft ones.[36]

Ashbee himself enjoyed dancing, having perhaps been initiated at Kensington School. In Seville he is not content to be a mere spectator:

If the Gitana dances are enchanting the national Boleros of Andalucia are much more so. I dined last evening with Juan Lequia Elias; during dinner two Gitanos played the guitar & sang to us, after the meal was over we had some dancing in which after being instructed by the young ladies there I joined & they also danced the Boleros of Andalucia. I was enchanted. The way they played the castinets & the grace they displayed in the dances pleased me beyond measure. They danced with a spirit & at the same time an artlessness only to be found in Spain. – x[37]

Another x! Ashbee is mesmerized, too, by the paintings of Murillo, with Velázquez one of Seville's most famous sons. On 11 November 1858 he notes in his journal:

Have just returned from a second visit to the pictures of Murillo. How glorious they are! All nature, & only nature which after all is the perfection of art. On these living canvasses one sees the very people, the very faces with all the expression which one meets here every day in the streets: the same beggars who appear to be uttering their eternal 'por Dios Señor'. The same lovely women, hair, eyes, expression perfect. In

looking at Murillo's virgins one has always in the mind's eye the living form of some lovely Andalucian girl he has seen before, & of which the virgin of the picture appears to be the portrait. And what could Murillo do better than copy the lovely creatures he saw day after day? Could he improve upon his models? He could not it would have been 'to paint the lily'. Rubens also painted the women he found around him, but his types were too gross too florid; he might perhaps have done well to have spiritualised somewhat instead of copying exactly. But Murillo had the perfect angel incarnate in the perfect women before him, he could but paint absolutely & unaltered what he saw and make himself immortal. – And then his art, no one however uneducated his eye can fail to admire Murillo's pictures, the warmth of colour, the masterly arrangement of the faces; it is the highest art, it is nature in art, & speaks therefore to nature's children.

From Seville Ashbee makes the dreary journey up through the seemingly endless plains of La Mancha to Madrid. In the capital he catches a throat infection which keeps him in bed for ten days. It is made worse, in his view, by a doctor of homoeo-pathic persuasion ('if one falls sick in Spain he has nothing to do but die'). He then travels to Barcelona via Valencia and, still under the weather, decides to strike out for England as quickly as possible ('when one is sick there is no place like home').

Ashbee is impressed by the industriousness of Barcelona com-pared to indolent Madrid, his reaction being similar to that of the English travellers who have immediately preceded him, notably Richard Ford, author of the great *A Hand-book for Travellers in Spain and Readers at Home* (1845). On 13 December 1858 he makes the last entry of the trip:

Barcelona is a very fine city, the houses regular & well built & the public promenades delightful. The main street & boulevard is much like Unter den Linden at Berlin. The Teatro de Liceo is one of the largest in Europe & is well decorated for its size. There is more movement in the streets at Barcelona than at Madrid, or rather it is a

different kind of movement. At Madrid the movement is one of idleness, people loiter about appearing to have nothing to do; here every one seems to be employed, every one seems to be about his business.

The diary then falls silent, inexplicably, for fifteen years, the next entry, on the following page, being dated 15 October 1873. The resumed journal contains some flashbacks, which enable us to fill in occasional gaps, but in general we must turn elsewhere for information about this crucial period from which Ashbee emerges as a confirmed erotomaniac.

Robert Ashbee had been briefly in the public eye in March 1850, when a tremendous explosion at the Curtis's and Harvey gunpowder works in Hounslow caused eight deaths and much injury.[38] In March 1859, shortly after the last entry in Henry Spencer's diary, there was another explosion at the mills. This time nine men were killed and many more injured. Robert Ashbee, according to a report in *The Times*, was in London when the accident occurred, seeing one of the proprietors. There was no suggestion that there had been any negligence on his part.[39]

Robert Ashbee was in the habit of going up to London for another reason. Over a century later it transpired that he had a young mistress in Chelsea, Frances Marion Purchase, who gave him a daughter, Frances Marion, in February 1857, and a son, Robert George, in Novmber 1858. So much for Taylor's *Holy Living and Holy Dying*. Did Henry Spencer ever discover that by the mid-1850s his father was running a second household? It is tempting to surmise that perhaps he did, if only after the latter's death, and that the revelation came as a nasty surprise.[40]

We have no concrete information about Ashbee's movements between 1858, when the diary falls silent, and 1862, although from his later remarks we can be sure that he continued to travel widely in Europe for his firm during these years. On 27 June 1862

he was married at Hamburg to Elizabeth Josephine Jenny Lavy, the daughter of a wealthy merchant, Edward Otto Charles Lavy, much respected in the Free City for his probity and business acumen, and an English mother, Marian Benjamin, the daughter of a London businessman, presumably Jewish, called Abraham Benjamin.[41]

Henry Spencer Ashbee was twenty-eight when he and Elizabeth married, she twenty-one. Presumably they met during a business trip of Ashbee's to Hamburg, described in a contemporary account as 'one of the great centres of trade at present existing in the world'.[42] According to family tradition, the honeymoon was spent in Paris.[43]

The Lavys of Hamburg were Anglophile, liberal-minded and Jewish (but not Orthodox), and two of Elizabeth's sisters also married Englishmen.[44] Charles Lavy (as Edward Otto Charles was always known in the family) must have approved of Ashbee, for his reaction to the marriage was to found an independent, London branch of his firm with Henry Spencer as senior partner. It is likely that Elizabeth also brought money to the union. Suddenly Ashbee's fortunes had changed beyond expectation.

The first premises of Charles Lavy and Company were at 9 Bow Lane, a stone's throw from Groucock, Copestakes, Moor and Co. in Bow Church Yard, where Henry Spencer had begun. A year later the firm moved to 7 New Basinghall Street.[45] It exported machinery, Sheffield goods and textiles to Europe, an enterprise for which Ashbee was admirably suited. Business flourished and soon he was well on the way to being rich.[46]

The couple's first house was in Spring Grove, a desirable new estate straddling the parishes of Heston and Isleworth and in almost open country. The main reason for the choice was, probably, to be close to Robert Ashbee, still manager of Curtis's and Harvey at nearby Hounslow, whose wife Frances had died that March at the age of fifty, one assumes in ignorance of her

husband's double life.[47] The estate was just a few paces from Spring Grove and Isleworth station, on the loop line from Waterloo, with fast and effortless access to the City. We can be certain that, during the two years the family lived in Spring Grove, Ashbee used it habitually to ply between his home and his business.

It has not proved possible to identify the house that Ashbee apparently rented, rather than bought, from the developer (Henry Daniel Davies). The latter figures in the contemporary records as proprietor at this time of several Spring Grove villas, among them Eversley House and Thornbury House: perhaps it was one of these that Ashbee took.[48]

On 17 May 1863 Elizabeth Lavy gave Ashbee a son, Charles Robert, later of Arts and Crafts fame, who was baptized at St Mary's Church, Spring Grove, on 13 October.[49]

In 1865, with business thriving, Ashbee decided to move into town and installed himself with his family as 46 Upper Bedford Place, Bloomsbury, just off Russell Square, where he was to remain for twenty years. It is difficult to avoid the suspicion that the choice of Upper Bedford Place was not unrelated to the propinquity of the British Museum Reading Room, only a few minutes away on foot, for Ashbee was by now a confirmed bibliophile.

On 3 February 1866 the Ashbees' second child, Frances Mary, was born in the new family home.[50]

The following year, on 5 October 1867, Robert Ashbee died while with Henry Spencer on Whitton Common.[51] It seems that by this time Elizabeth Lavy had come to feel a deep affection for her father-in-law. Charles Ashbee, then four, remembered being given a last glimpse of his grandfather:

I must have been very small for they had to lift me up to see what was set in the middle of the long room, the light streaming in, though the

blinds were half-drawn. Two strong arms, those of some tutelary deity, they may have been my father's, it was not my mother who did it – held me, as you might hold a kitten in mid-air, and I saw what looked to me like a waxen face, cold and rather splendidly chiselled, very stately, but of a world for me utterly passed away. The eyes were closed. The face was hard, a sort of enamelled beauty but not unkind. There may have been a touch of mockery about the mouth, I am not sure.[52]

Robert Ashbee left £100 to his sister Frances and the residue to Henry Spencer, sole executor of the will.[53]

The year 1867 saw not only the death of Robert Ashbee but the setting up of a Paris branch of Charles Lavy, with the active participation of Henry Spencer, at 38 Rue des Jeûneurs, in the second *arrondissement* not far from Montmartre.[54]

Ashbee's professional sojourns in Paris facilitated his acquisition of erotic books, a passion that now consumed him and that seems to have been due in considerable measure to the influence of the bibliographer Joseph Octave Delepierre (1802–1879), the Belgian Consul in London, whom he had first met when he applied for a visa to Belgium in the 1850s (see plate 7). As conversant with English literature as with French and Flemish, Delepierre was deep into erotica. The publisher Nicholas Trübner, his son-in-law, later referred tactfully to Delepierre's bibliographical interests: 'The follies of man,' he wrote, 'his mental and moral aberrations, singularities of literature, enigmas of life and manners, and the like, had a strange fascination for his mind, and were treated by him in preference to subjects of more general interest, for which his natural taste, his vast reading, his versatility, and powers of analysis equally fitted him.'[55]

Ashbee approved of this pen portrait. 'A kindred taste in literature' had led to his own lasting friendship with the Consul, he wrote at Delepierre's death – without explaining what that 'kindred taste' was, or how their relationship had developed.[56] It

was Delepierre, according to Ashbee on another occasion, who suggested to the Belgian bookseller, publisher of erotica and bibliographer Jules Gay that he compile what was to become the monumental *Bibliographie des Ouvrages relatifs à l'Amour, aux Femmes, au Mariage, et des Livres Facétieux, Pantagruéliques, Satyriques, etc.*, the first edition of which appeared at Paris in 1861. In Ashbee's view, anybody capable of inspiring such an achievement was worthy of all respect. 'Delepierre actually began the labour,' he added, 'and his MS. entitled: *Pornodidascaliana, ou Bibliographie Curieuse d'ouvrages dans le genre badin, érotique et gaillard, Roma 3581*, is now before me.' That Delepierre put Ashbee in touch with like-minded devotees of erotica in Brussels and Paris seems beyond reasonable doubt.[57]

From the 1850s France was much freer from literary censorship than Britain, which was to grow increasingly repressive over the following decades. Ashbee shared Dickens's view that English sexual prudery was a calamity. With a substantial income that allowed him to buy whatever books he fancied, he was now putting together what was to become one of the largest collections of erotic books in the world. Not only that: he had conceived the idea of producing a vast, descriptive bibliography of such works. The task was to occupy him for twenty years.

But where to keep his erotica? He could not have housed such material at 46 Upper Bedford Place, all outward respectability, where his wife might have stumbled on it and had an unpleasant shock. (It is unlikely that Elizabeth Lavy had much, if any, inkling of her husband's hidden proclivities until years later.) The solution was to take chambers at 4 Gray's Inn Square, Holborn, three-quarters of a mile away from his house (near but not too near), an all-male preserve that afforded suitable secrecy. Here at 'The Inn', as he liked to call it, secure on his own territory, Ashbee was to foregather for almost thirty years with his bibliophile and erotomaniac friends. Meanwhile his collection of

'top-shelf' books swelled to thousands of volumes in six or seven languages.

Because of the absence of a diary, we have very little precise information about Ashbee's life at this time. We do know that he continued to travel extensively in Europe; that on 31 May 1869 his third child, Agnes Jenny, was born at 46 Upper Bedford Place;[58] and that in 1871 he visited Berlin, witnessing the entrance of the troops after the Franco-German war.[59] Agnes Jenny was followed, on 1 February 1873, by the Ashbees' last child, Elsa.[60] During the same year the London branch of Charles Lavy became silk mercers and moved to 1 Coleman Street.[61]

Then, in October 1873, Ashbee resumed his diary. The first entry records that he has just made the acquaintance of John Davenport, linguist and pioneer sexologist, deemed rather unfairly by Steven Marcus 'a semi-learned pornographic hack'.[62] Davenport was about to issue ('privately printed') a book entitled *Aphrodisiacs and Anti-aphrodisiacs: Three Essays on the Powers of Reproduction; with some account of the Judicial 'Congress' as Practised in France during the Seventeenth Century.* Ashbee considered it 'an able and erudite work, well written, and fairly exhaustive of the subject it treats of'.[63] Davenport, now in his eighties (he had been born in London in 1789), was badly run down physically and financially, and virtually on the bread line. 'Poor old man,' writes Ashbee, 'he had indeed described himself correctly in his letter to me.' Soon Davenport was attending the dinners Ashbee now held every Tuesday at Upper Bedford Place – and enjoying them heartily. 'It is really heart-rending to see so erudite & clever a man in such poverty – almost as it were starving,' Ashbee wrote in his diary on 12 November 1873. 'He eat & drank as if he had not partaken of a good meal for several days; poorly, even miserably dressed, deaf, absent, & infirm, he is nevertheless quite the gentleman.' Ashbee undertook to defray the costs of Davenport's next entreprise, an ambitious work

entitled *Curiositates Eroticae Physiologiae; or, Tabooed Subjects Freely Treated. In Six Essays, viz.: 1. Generation. 2. Chastity and Modesty. 3. Marriage. 4. Circumcision. 5. Eunuchism. 6. Hermaphrodism, and followed by a closing Essay on Death.* He entrusted the manuscript to a small London printer, James Henry Gaball, in March 1874, and the book appeared the following year.[64]

At almost exactly the same time that Ashbee resumed his diary he made his public début as a bibliophile, sending a tiny entry, signed 'H.S.A.', to that curious Victorian institution *Notes and Queries*, with whose editor, John Doran, and sub-editor, Henry Frederick Turle, he was soon on good terms. His contribution appeared on 11 October 1873:

'LONDON BY NIGHT.' By The Author of *Skittles, Anonyma*, &c. With Illustrations by William Gray. London: William Oliver, 3, Amen Corner, E.C. Fancy paper cover, with 'Evans and Co., Fleet Street', on it. Large 8vo. pp. vii and 176. – Wanted information as to the year of publication and authorship of the above. The book is called a 'Descriptive Novel', which it in reality is, and a work of merit in its way.

With its reference to Sade's *Justine*, Ashbee's second entry (22 November 1873), again signed 'H.S.A.', was more indicative of his true interests. This time it was an answer to someone else's query:

GILLES DE LAVAL, SEIGNEUR DE RETZ. – In the *Histoire de la Bretagne*, par Dom Lobisieau, will be found an account of this monster of iniquity; the Marquis de Sade (*arcades ambo*) mentions him at vol. i, p. 223, of *Justine*, edition of 1791.

Over the next four years Ashbee sent some forty contributions to *Notes and Queries* (see bibliography). Half were signed 'H.S.A.', the others either 'Apis' ('Bee' in Latin) or 'Fraxinus' ('Ash'). Amused by the punning potential of his surname, Ashbee had several rebus bookplates made over the years in which the

bee and ash motifs were charmingly exploited. The best was that executed by his friend Paul Avril in 1890 (see page 1), in which, according to one commentator, the portrait of the bibliophile was a 'very good' likeness.[65]

Ashbee was so pleased with 'Apis' and 'Fraxinus' that they were pressed into further, more complex, service for the monumental bibliography of erotica on which he was now engaged. In Victorian England he could not possibly have issued this under his own name: to do so would have been to court not only social obloquy but criminal proceedings. A *nom de plume*, therefore, was essential. He could have opted for an anodyne one, but chose not to do so. Instead, availing himself of *fraxinus* and *apis*, he came up with the anagram PISANUS FRAXI (see page 2), which had the advantage of proposing a scatological joke in its first element ('piss anus'). The radical ambiguity of Henry Spencer Ashbee's life, its Jekyll and Hyde quality, is perfectly expressed in the pseudonym with which he chose to present himself to the world, at once the thinnest of disguises, a scholarly hoax, a dangerous flaunting of Victorian convention and an admission of acute personal fascination with the affairs of the flesh.

The years leading up to the publication in 1877 of the *Index Librorum Prohibitorum*, Ashbee's first volume of erotic bibliography, were ones of intense activity, with frequent business trips to Paris (where the French expressed amazement at his boundless energy), one to St Petersburg and Moscow in January 1874 (returning via Warsaw, Berlin and Brussels), and another, in the summer of 1875 (with his family), to Hamburg, where, while not socializing with the Lavys, Ashbee slipped off to the public library. There he corrected the copy he had made previously of a manuscript of *Sodom*, a ribald play attributed to the Earl of Rochester.[66]

The diary tells of family holidays at a relative's house in Worthing (Heene Terrace); the convivial Tuesday dinner parties

at 46 Upper Bedford Place (enlivened by music, pool and bil-
liards, and sometimes by spirited recitations by Ashbee himself);
the renewal of Italian lessons; and frequent visits with his wife
to the theatre and the opera. What it does not tell us about is
Ashbee's secret life, although occasionally there is a tiny clue.

Ashbee was now a leading authority on the collecting and
printing of erotica in London, Paris and Brussels (epicentre of
erotica publishing in Europe since the 1860s).[67] While most of
his book-loving cronies in London were probably not into this
field (George William Reid, Keeper of the British Museum's
Print Room, for instance, or Robert Samuel Turner, or the
publisher Nicholas Trübner, or the octogenarian artist George
Cruikshank, who, now reformed, had become a rabid tee-
totaller), several of them most certainly were. In the first place,
the Belgian Consul Joseph Octave Delepierre, who, as we saw,
was a crucial influence when Ashbee was embarking on his
career as a bibliographer of erotica in the early 1860s. By the
time Henry Spencer resumed his diary in 1873, Delepierre was a
regular visitor not only to 4 Gray's Inn Square, but a frequent
guest at the Tuesday dinner parties at 46 Upper Bedford Place.[68]

Another collaborator was the young publisher John Camden
Hotten, who in 1866 had courageously taken Swinburne's *Poems
and Ballads* on board after Payne of Moxon's had 'dropped him
like a hot brick' in the face of widespread hostility from the
philistines.[69] Also to his credit, Hotten played an important role
in introducing contemporary American poets such as Whitman
and Lowell to the English reading public. According to Ashbee,
he 'was almost the only respectable English publisher of tabooed
literature, and in this he took great delight'. Hotten did a special
line in flagellant books. Among his productions was the series of
works wittily and misleadingly entitled *Library Illustrative of
Social Progress. From the Original Editions Collected by the late
Henry Thomas Buckle, Author of 'A History of Civilization in*

England' (described by Steven Marcus as 'a kind of masterpiece of senseless obfuscation'[70]). Hotten's 'private library of erotic literature was extensive and was, at his death, purchased *en bloc* by a London amateur', Ashbee wrote in the *Index Librorum Prohibitorum* after the publisher's death in June 1873 at the age of forty-one. The 'amateur' was Ashbee himself, as his diary shows.[71]

Another leading figure in this coterie of erotomaniac cronies was the protean personage described by Ashbee in his diary as 'J. C. Redie, alias James Campbell, alias C. Vernon Wilson (see plate 8)'.[72] For Peter Mendes, James Campbell Reddie (as we can agree to call him) was 'surely the pivotal figure in the world of Victorian pornography, as collector, translator, author and transmitter of texts from authors to publishers'.[73] As translator, Campbell Reddie turned out, among other things, 'infelicitous' versions of French baudy books for William Dugdale,[74] perhaps the principal Victorian purveyor of erotica in the 1860s. Dugdale was repeatedly imprisoned for his activities and died in a house of correction in 1868. 'One of the most prolific publishers of filthy books,' Pisanus Fraxi terms him hypocritically.[75]

It is not clear when Ashbee first met James Campbell Reddie, but they were undoubtedly on close terms by the early 1870s. He 'read with ease Latin, French and Italian, and although not familiar with German, few erotic books in that language were unknown to him', writes Pisanus Fraxi:

So thorough indeed was his knowledge of this particular branch, that hardly an obscene book in any language had escaped his attention. His industry was unflagging. Each book, or different edition, as he acquired it, was at once collated, confronted with every available authority upon it, and compared page by page, word by word, with any other procurable issue of the same work. Of very scarce books, which he might not be able to acquire, he frequently made copies with his own hand. By this it may be judged how exact and thorough he was, and how

completely he had mastered his subject. James Campbell viewed erotic literature from a philosophic point of view – as illustrating more clearly than any other human nature and its attendant foibles [. . .] His enthusiasm for the bibliography of erotic literature was so great that, had his funds been sufficient to warrant his incurring the risk which such an undertaking must always involve, he would probably have given to the world a compilation of his own, which could not have failed to be a masterpiece of exact and comprehensive research.[76]

Exact and comprehensive research: no doubt, but Campbell Reddie also clearly enjoyed writing erotica himself.

He was the author of *The Adventures of a Schoolboy; or the Freaks of Youthful Passion* (1866),[77] *The Amatory Experiences of a Surgeon* (published posthumously);[78] and, probably, of *The New Ladies' Tickler; or The Adventures of Lady Lovesport and the Audacious Harry* (1866).[79] Like many of his confrères, Campbell Reddie was interested in flagellation. Of *The New Ladies' Tickler* Pisanus Fraxi says: 'This is a well written book, worthy of a less silly title, and better illustrations. Although it contains a great many flagellation scenes, there are other episodes of a more generally interesting character, all of which are forcibly told and are very voluptuous.'[80] *The Amatory Experiences of a Surgeon* appeared under a witty rubric: 'Printed for the Nihilists, Moscow, 1871'. For Gershon Legman, this was 'an allusion – perhaps unconscious – to the important social-revolutionary impact of the underground movement towards sexual freedom throughout the nineteenth century'.[81] Be that as it may, the book contained passages that would not be everyone's cup of tea:

I gave myself up without reserve to the pleasure of love. All my patients who shewed the least susceptibility were overcome by my potent argument, and vigorously fucked. Satiety, that enemy to the indulgence of the soft enjoyment, now attacked me, I wanted a change. I longed for an unripe beauty, a young girl, a child even – I found a lovely little girl of thirteen years of age, who had been under my care for a spinal affliction.[82]

Swinburne evidently appreciated Campbell Reddie's efforts as a publisher. 'Have you heard that Campbell is going to publish a popular "Justine"?' he wrote to Simeon Solomon. 'We are coming to a sense of what is right.'[83]

Brussels was now 'an important publishing place for forbidden literature', as Ashbee recalled nostalgically in a footnote to his poem 'The Baffled Collector' (1891), and boasted a plethora of bookshops, both second hand and modern.[84] His main contact in the city, inevitably, was Jules Gay, the compiler of the massive *Bibliographie des Ouvrages relatifs à l'Amour, aux Femmes, au Mariage, et des Livres Facétieux, Pantagruéliques, Satyriques, etc.* In its enlarged second edition (1864) this work greatly inspired Ashbee's own endeavours in the field of erotic bibliography (his interleaved and annotated copy of the work is in the British Library). Gay had frequent problems with both the Belgian and the French police after the halcyon days of the 1860s. In September 1875 Ashbee was briefly in Brussels. 'Old Jules Gay the publisher has returned there,' he wrote in his diary, 'and he called on me Sunday afternoon, and told me all his troubles and the unjust seizure which he has suffered at St. Remo.'[85]

Paris was the centre of Ashbee's erotomaniac activities on the Continent, not least because of the branch of Charles Lavy at Rue des Jeûneurs and the frequent visits this entailed – and justified. By the 1870s Ashbee had fallen in there with an eccentric Englishman, Frederick Hankey, the son of General Frederick Hankey, one-time Governor of the Ionian Islands, and a Greek mother. Born in Corfu, Hankey had become a captain in the Guards, retiring from active service in the 1840s and setting up house in Paris, where he was soon devoting himself to his twin passions: erotic books and the world of prostitution.[86] One of his activities consisted in supplying erotica to Swinburne, Richard Monckton Milnes and Richard Burton (to whom he was introduced by Milnes in 1860).[87] In each case their needs were

of a predominantly sado-masochistic nature. An entry in one of Monckton Milnes's commonplace books for 1860 reads:

Burton of Hankey: 'There is no accounting for tastes in superstition. Hankey would like to have a Bible bound with bits of skin stripped off live from the cunts of a hundred little girls and yet he could not be persuaded to try the sensation of f . . . g a Muscovy duck while its head was cut off' [. . .] Hankey's line of cruel enjoyment and his strong sense of the wickedness of killing animals for food. His extreme desire to see a girl hanged and have the skin of her backside tanned to bind his 'Justine' with.[88]

On 7 April 1862 Hankey had been visited by those two indefatigable chroniclers of Parisian literary life, the Goncourt brothers, who recorded in their diary (habitually couched in the singular):

Today I visited a madman, a monster, one of those men who live on the edge of the abyss. Through him, as through a torn veil, I had a glimpse of an appalling aspect, a terrible side to a wealthy, blasé aristocracy – the English aristocracy – who bring ferocious cruelty to love and whose licentiousness can only be aroused by the woman's suffering.[89]

Burton had promised Hankey to try and bring him from Africa the skin stripped from a sacrificial victim, and the latter could not prevent himself from boasting to the Goncourts about the offer. But the famous explorer and linguist failed to produce, writing to Milnes from Dahomey: 'I have been here 3 days and am generally disappointed. Not a man killed, not a fellow tortured. The canoe floating in blood is a myth of myths. Poor Hankey must still wait for his peau de femme.'[90]

Another visitor to Hankey's 'Enfer' was the Londoner William Simpson Potter, who specialized in 'erotic pictures, engravings, photographs and bric-à-brac generally'[91] and was co-author of a celebrated erotic novel called *The Romance of Lust*.[92] In a letter to Milnes dated 17 June 1865, Potter told him that he

had just returned from Paris with 'some little things which I shall be happy to show' and went on: 'I left Hankey in his usual fever constantly acquiring some addition to his Bibliothèque Érotique in rare editions of his favourite authors.'[93] Ashbee also knew Potter, although there is no reference to him in his diaries.[94]

During a visit to Paris Swinburne had been much taken with two erotic sculptures by James Pradier in Hankey's collection. Writing to George Powell on 29 July 1869 he said he hoped to be able to introduce him in Paris to a friend of his, '*the* Sadique collector of European fame':

His erotic collection of books, engravings, etc., is unrivalled upon earth – unequalled, I should imagine, in heaven. Nothing low, nothing that is not good and genuine in the way of art and literature is admitted. There is every edition of every work of our dear and honoured Marquis. There is a Sapphic group by Pradier of two girls in the very act – one has her tongue up où vous savez, her head and massive hair buried, plunging, diving between the other's thighs.[95]

Ashbee saw Hankey frequently during his visits to Paris, and, like Swinburne, appreciated his Pradier group. On 8 April 1875, a few days before dashing down to Bordeaux to meet the great bibliographer Gustave Brunet, a close friend of Delepierre, he wrote in his diary:

Spent the afternoon and evening with Mr F. Hankey among his unique volumes. His collection is small, but each vol is a gem either of rarity or choice binding. Hankey himself is a remarkable man, quite a study, he appears to me like a second de Sade *without the intellect*. He has given himself up body and soul to the erotic mania, thinks of nothing else, cares for nothing else, lives for nothing else. Nothing is bawdy enough for him, whether in expression, thought or design. Besides his books all of which are erotic, this is a sine qua non with him, he has two of the most charming erotic statues which exist, and is further surrounded with ceintures de chasteté, dildos, and every other obscene object possible to be procured.

Hankey himself I should take to be about 50 years old, lean, tall, with yellow hair, a white skin, and soft blue eyes, a good forhead, and yet his expression is entirely devoid of energy or determination. In his youth he must have been good looking, but efeminate, much as the Marquis de Sade is pictured to have been. Hankey's debaucheries are telling upon him, and he complains much of his health, he is not I think destined to make old bones. His apartments are situated in the best part of Paris, 2 Rue Laffitte, look out on the Boulevard, and face the Caffé Anglais and Opéra Comique, but in spite of their excellent situation they are not convenient, and as kept by Hankey and his mistress are entirely wanting in comfort.

Hankey was Ashbee's main source for information on London's flagellant brothels, and, as we shall see, the latter's view of the *vice anglais* in general was deeply influenced by the erotomaniac Englishman whose professed sadism had so affected the Goncourt brothers. In *The Romantic Agony*, Mario Praz has studied the development of that stock figure in French novels of the nineteenth century, the English sadist. Hankey was not his prototype, but that he influenced the model there can be no doubt.

It was apparently at Hankey's that, in November 1873, Ashbee first met Eugène Paillet, a French authority on erotica with whom he was soon on excellent terms, and Alfred Bégis, who collaborated with Hankey on an erotic play entitled *L'École des biches*.[96] Bégis showed Ashbee his 'interesting collection of autographs, & documents connected with the Marquis de Sade'.[97] Paillet, by profession a *juge d'instruction*, was to claim that it was Hankey's collection that first gave Ashbee the idea of compiling his bibliographies. Perhaps there was some truth in this, although Jules Gay's huge work was also influential. Fundamental, too, as we saw, was Ashbee's friendship with Octave Delepierre.[98]

Meanwhile, on the domestic front, the Ashbee family appeared to be thriving. On 27 June 1875 Henry Spencer confided to his

diary: 'My wedding day, 13 years married, do not think it possible for any man to have a better wife, or nicer children, am perfectly happy. Drove my dear wife and children to Bushy Park where we picknicked. Glorious weather, spent a most pleasant & enjoyable day, were quite alone.' The park in question was one of the haunts most favoured by Ashbee in his role as Victorian pillar of society and paterfamilias. His son Charles wrote later:

When spring came, and the chestnuts blossomed, my father would don a smart top hat, stick a cigar in his mouth, mount the box of his landau and drive us to Bushy Park. The ritual was of spring and carefully observed; the hamper with picnic under the chestnut trees, the state apartments in Hampton Court Palace, the Maze, the swans, the deer, and the drive back in the evening. He always drove himself. He affected a somewhat rakish bucolic manner on those occasions, the Kentish sap rising.[99]

Ashbee looked good, too. He was now about forty, but Ralph Thomas, a *Notes and Queries* friend, recalled that he always had the appearance of a man ten years younger. According to Thomas (who in 1868 had brought out a *Handbook of Fictitious Names* under the anagram Olphar Hamst),[100] Henry Spencer was 'the image in every way' of the warrior in Paolo Veronese's *Respect, an Allegorical Group*, in the National Gallery.[101]

There are frequent references at this time in Ashbee's diary to 'my Charlie', and he seems to have been pleased with his son's progress, first at home under a German governess, then at the (unidentified) preparatory school to which he was sent in 1873 at the age of ten. Charles, according to his biographer Alan Crawford 'a dreamy and puny child' (although his parents had made of him a good rider and swimmer),[102] was enrolled in 1877 at Wellington College, where he stayed until 1882. Ralph Thomas congratulated Ashbee on sending his son to a public school (Wellington was one of the newest and most

expensive),[103] but Charles was a misfit and hated the bullying, the 'tedious conformity', the compulsory sports and the philistinism. One day, when he could take no more pummelling, he successfully stood up to one of his schoolboy tormentors. 'My father said you should always go for a bully and get him on the nose if you can,' he explained to one of the three kindly teachers who saved him from despair at Wellington.[104]

Charles loathed the school's headmaster, the Reverend E. C. Wickham, not least because he was the son-in-law of William Gladstone, for whose chest-thumping oratory, he, like his father, had nothing but scorn. Wickham imposed insufferably boring and holier-than-thou sermons on his charges, and every so often Gladstone would come down to the school and, in his own high-flown vein, emulate him. In revenge, Charles, soon a rebel, apparently played some memorable practical jokes on 'Old Oystermouth', as slimy, unctuous, puritanical Wickham was nicknamed by the boys. Wellington set Charles well on the way to becoming a Socialist . . . and eventually to clashing with his father, who did not believe in the right to strike, in giving money to the poor (it would only be spent on drink) or in 'over-educating' women.[105]

Charles Ashbee was to leave an interesting account of his father's attitude to religion. The Ashbees of Kent had always been easy-going Anglicans. But Henry Spencer went a bit further:

Our conventions were pagan and never sabbatical. The Church was always kept at arm's length, still more so any form of dissent. My parents had no use for the old religious wrangle. But it was well, thought they, to observe how, in such matters, the human mind moved, and what were the conventions of others. So for many years it was our custom to visit the London churches and conventicles, High, Broad, Low, Roman, Positivist, Dissent in any form, no matter how the word of God was spluttered or intoned. Observe it all but be yourself unbound. The parcel of good tidings, however done up, might contain some grain

of Truth; that was the idea. And over the Sunday dinner – roast beef and Yorkshire – the mission and the minister were mercilessly torn.[106]

One Sunday Ashbee and Charley entered a Salvation Army centre. An officer asked them if they were saved. 'I don't think so,' replied Ashbee courteously, 'but I don't think I want to be.'[107]

Ashbee decided to confide the *Index Librorum Prohibitorum* to the printer James Henry Gaball, who was then resident in New Park Road, Brixton Hill.[108] 'I gave him the first few pages of my M.S., so the book is started,' he wrote in his diary on 21 June 1875. On 30 July following, on board ship for Hamburg, he recorded that the printer had called the previous evening at 46 Upper Bedford Place:

I returned him the first sheet of my 'Index' corrected for press, he left me rough proof of the second sheet, which I corrected during the evening & posted to him. As my book contains so much matter in foreign languages, Gaball who knows English only makes many blunders, & gives me much labour in correcting the press, each sheet, I can plainly see, will have to go several times through my hands before it is fit for 'press'. Well I suppose I should hardly fare better in the hands of a foreign printer.

That was probably true, but it was no consolation for Gaball's continuous blunders. Early the following year Ashbee left on record why he had not been keeping up his journal:

My life for the last two months has been passed very quietly & regularly, which accounts for the absence of entries in my diary; every evening nearly has been spent at home working at my book, of which the correction of the press is terrible labour, for as it comprises so many languages which the printer, Gaball, does not understand, the blunders are interminable, & every sheet has to be gone through 4 or 5 times.[109]

James Campbell Reddie and Ralph Thomas had been lending Ashbee a hand with the proofs, also a certain Dr Brett (or Brette),

of Christ's Hospital. But none of them knew German or Spanish. And to make matters worse Gaball had changed his address three times since beginning work on the book. The printer was to be pitied, certainly, not only on account of the troublesome foreign languages but because he had to cope with the liberal use demanded by Ashbee of different typefaces and colours. 'I must get another man to do the next vol.,' the entry ends. 'Altogether I have been working too hard, & feel the necessity of a change.'[110] The companion volume in question, on which Ashbee was already busily engaged, was to be entitled *Centuria Librorum Absconditorum*.

The agony of correction continued throughout 1876, interspersed with trips to the Continent, sporadically recorded in the diary. In Brussels Ashbee saw Jules Gay again in June, and called in on Hartcupp, 'the publisher and translator of a good deal of trash which he is now issuing from Brussels and Paris'.[111] (Much of the 'trash' was flagellant in character.)[112] A few weeks later Hartcupp fell foul of the police when, at the instigation of the British Ambassador, who had received complaints from London, his house was raided. 'Several of his publications have in consequence become scarce,' Ashbee reported a year later.[113] As regards Brussels booksellers, Ashbee frequented the establishments of Daffis, Rouquette and Blanche.[114]

In August 1876 Ashbee left his family on holiday in Blankenberghe, a place he detested, and returned alone to London, settling in at his Gray's Inn Square chambers while modifications were effected at 46 Upper Bedford Place. There he entertained bookworm friends who included the architect Alexander Graham and, over from Paris, Eugène Paillet.[115]

At the end of October 1876 Ashbee spent a hectic nine days in Paris, putting up as he so often did at the Hôtel Marguerit. Business sessions at Rue des Jeûneurs; visits to Hankey (where he meets another distinguished collector of erotica, Prince Augustin Galitzin),[116] the erotica publisher Auguste Poulet-

Malassis, formerly based in Brussels (who shows him his fine collection of drawings and etchings by Félicien Rops), Bégis (still hot on the trail of Sade) and the opera; book-buying at Rouquette's and Daffis's; a night outside Paris at the country estate of a French merchant; a call on Jules Adolphe Chauvet, author of the frontispiece to the *Index Librorum Prohibitorum* (from whom he now orders a set of drawings); dinners with Paillet, who produces his rare copy of Restif de la Bretonne's *Anti-Justine*; an evening ('alone', unusually) in Montparnasse at the Closerie des Lilas, scene of his youthful revels . . . one wonders what was the secret of Ashbee's stamina.[117]

Back in London, he continued to labour at the proofs of the *Index Librorum Prohibitorum*. For the next six months the diary is sporadic, with considerable gaps. We catch glimpses of Ashbee visiting his old friend Joseph Octave Delepierre, now unwell; attending Robert Samuel Turner's bibliophiliac Saturdays at Albany, and frequenting two editors, John Doran of *Notes and Queries* and Norman McColl of the *Athenaeum*.[118] 'Passed the last sheet of my "Index" for press,' his diary records on Sunday, 15 April 1877. This does not quite tally with the 'Concluding Note' to the volume, which states that the book left the printer's hands on 30 March 1877.[119]

On 11 May John Davenport died at his 'miserable room' at 15 Alfred Street, Tottenham Court Road. 'The old man retained the use of his intellect till the last moment,' wrote Ashbee, '& passed away quietly & without a struggle.'[120] It must have saddened him greatly that Davenport did not live to see the *Index Librorum Prohibitorum* in print. The following day Ashbee received his first finished copy from the binder (whose name, aptly, was Roger De Coverley).[121] He hurried around at once to 35 Howley Place, Maida Hill West, to give it to Delepierre. A fitting gesture, for it was probably Delepierre who more than anyone else had turned Ashbee into an erotic bibliomaniac.[122]

The Index Librorum Prohibitorum *(1877)*

Between them, Ashbee and Gaball had gone to no end of trouble: the *Index Librorum Prohibitorum* ('Index of Books Worthy of Being Prohibited') is a thing of beauty. The 250 copies must have cost Ashbee a fortune.[1] Printed in large quarto on heavy toned paper, and displaying a handsome array of different typefaces and decorative fleurons, with the titles of the books noticed highlighted in red, the weighty volume comprises the frontispiece commissioned by Ashbee from Jules Adolphe Chauvet, a page of epigraphs, a brief preface, a 68-page introduction in which 800 lines of text are all but engulfed by 1,400 of footnotes and source references, three photo-lithographic plates, 436 pages of bibliography proper devoted to some 150 books in English, French, German, Italian, Spanish and Latin, arranged in alphabetical order of titles, 38 pages of 'Authorities Consulted' (almost 300 of them), an exhaustive, two-column index occupying no fewer than 58 pages, a 'Concluding Note', and five-and-a-half pages of errata. In all, 544 pages. The binding was suitably sumptuous: 'Red pigskin spine, stamped in gold with title, author's name, and London 1877; red moiré cloth printed with a black repeating pattern perhaps of vines, over boards, on the sides. Top gilt. Head and foot bands.'[2]

The title-page, with its mocking allusion to the Vatican's *Index*

Librorum Prohibitorum, first drawn up in 1559, sets the tone of ambivalence that pervades the work from beginning to end:*

INDEX
LIBRORUM PROHIBITORUM:

BEING

𝔑𝔬𝔱𝔢𝔰
𝔅𝔦𝔬- 𝔅𝔦𝔟𝔩𝔦𝔬- 𝔍𝔠𝔬𝔫𝔬- 𝔤𝔯𝔞𝔭𝔥𝔦𝔠𝔞𝔩 𝔞𝔫𝔡 𝔠𝔯𝔦𝔱𝔦𝔠𝔞𝔩,

ON

ℭ𝔲𝔯𝔦𝔬𝔲𝔰 𝔞𝔫𝔡 𝔘𝔫𝔠𝔬𝔪𝔪𝔬𝔫 𝔅𝔬𝔬𝔨𝔰

BY

PISANUS FRAXI

... Quis enim non vicus abundat
Tristibus obscoenis? Juv., Sat. 2

[device]

LONDON:
𝔓𝔯𝔦𝔳𝔞𝔱𝔢𝔩𝔶 𝔓𝔯𝔦𝔫𝔱𝔢𝔡:
MDCCCLXXVII

Aping a practice habitual in the bawdy book trade, with its tangle of euphemism, fake names, incorrect dates and spurious imprints, Pisanus Fraxi presents the volumes under consideration as 'curious and uncommon' rather than 'erotic' or 'obscene'. The quotation from Juvenal, that most bowdlerized of men, continues the joke, the word *obscoenis* leaping off the page although the Latin poet may not have used it in our sense of 'obscene' ('every back street abounds with solemn-faced hum-

* Pisanus Fraxi comments, tongue-in-cheek, in his introduction: 'The title may perhaps not seem altogether well chosen. "*Index Librorum Prohibitorum*" is of very ancient date, and has been frequently employed, particularly by the Church of Rome. A title which would indicate clearly, and yet without offence the books which these pages embrace was not easy to devise. The few English words with which I qualify the Latin heading will, I trust, obviate any confusion or ambiguity' (pp. lxiv–lxv).

buggers,' reads a modern translation).[3] Was Ashbee aware that Juvenal's satire is an attack on homosexuals? Perhaps. At all events it is the word *obscoenis* that seems to have caught his eye. It paves the way for a quotation on the epigraphs page from Molière's *La Critique de l'école des femmes*:

CLIMÈNE: There's an obscenity that goes too far.
ÉLISE: What's that word you've just used, madam?
CLIMÈNE: Obscenity, madam.
ÉLISE: My God! Obscenity. I don't know what it means; but it strikes me as the prettiest word in the world.

Immediately following on the same page, a quotation in support of the reading of *erotic* books is adduced from the introduction to *L'Anti-Justine*, by Restif de la Bretonne (1734–1806):

Fontenelle used to say: 'No unhappiness can resist an hour's reading.' Now, of all reading, the most engaging is that of erotic works, particularly when accompanied by expressive imagery.

Dangerous, if delightful, reading matter 'worthy of being prohibited', the blurring of the boundary between the obscene and the erotic, between genuine investigation into sexual mores and mere prurience or titillation . . . this is the ambiguous terrain through which Pisanus Fraxi proposes to guide the reader in the *Index Librorum Prohibitorum*.

Ashbee had rejected J.-A. Chauvet's first design for the frontispiece, specifying exactly what he wanted in its place.[4] The definitive etching (see plate 13a) represents a bookcase containing some of the more significant volumes analysed in the *Index*. Two columns festooned with the names of authors of 'forbidden books' sustain a pediment on top of which a group of putti are busily fustigating one of their fellows affixed to a ladder. Beneath them leers a repellent horned devil (one can almost smell the sulphur) while, further below, another cupid helps an infant faun, bedecked in priest's hat and collar, to commit condemned

works to a bonfire. The base of the bookstand bears the legend EI BLOT FOR LYST, a slightly misquoted Danish saying meaning 'Not only for Pleasure'.

Having set the stage, and the mood, with frontispiece, title-page and epigraphs, Pisanus Fraxi states his intentions in a succinct 'Preface':

Far from deprecating criticism, or spurning the opinion of friends, I court, on the contrary, their judgements, and solicit their corrections. My objects are – truth, the extension of bibliographical studies, and the accurate description of the works noticed in the following pages.

To strangers, into whose hands my book may fall, I would say, in extenuation of my numerous shortcomings, that I am not an author by profession; but being actively engaged in pursuits of an entirely different nature, have sought recreation in compiling this work during my few leisure hours. 'Dulce est desipere in loco.'

Whatever reception this compilation may meet with at the hands of the few bibliophiles and students for whom it is intended, I may say that the pleasure I have experienced in making it has already amply rewarded me for my labour. 'The struggle for knowledge (aptly observes the Marquis of Halifax) hath a pleasure in it like that of wrestling with a fine woman.'[5]

One can imagine the glint in Ashbee's eye as he transcribed that simile.

In his lengthy 'Introduction' Pisanus Fraxi gets down quickly to brass tacks. From a sexual point of view, England is intolerant and intolerable:

That English erotic literature should never have had its bibliographer is not difficult to understand. First and foremost the English nation possesses an ultra-squeamishness and hyper-prudery peculiar to itself, sufficient alone to deter any author of position and talent from taking in hand so tabooed a subject.[6]

Thanks to this lamentable situation, in England only the 'veriest

grubbians' have 'put their pens at the disposal of Venus and Priapus', whereas, 'in France, in Italy and even in Germany some of the most esteemed authors have not hesitated to write licentious books'. John Cleland, the author of *Fanny Hill*, is the greatest exception to the rule, but 'he is, after all, but a star of very inferior magnitude'. England's 'ultra-squeamishness and hyper-prudery' have made it impossible for genuine writers to explore 'the truth' about human sexuality.[7]

Pisanus Fraxi wants to right the balance, to contravene current attitudes on sex (in his view merely circumstantial) and to argue the case for greater openness and tolerance. He is so immersed in the study of erotica, however, and so obviously turned on by it (despite his claim that the 'true student' of the subject is impervious to titillation),[8] that at times he seems unable to distinguish fact from fantasy. Indeed, he would even have us believe that, for the 'historian' or 'psychologist', the study of erotica can be more profitable than that of books 'in many other and better cultivated fields of literature'. This is special pleading.[9]

After a quick review of the current state of the erotica trade in Europe (where things have disimproved recently), Pisanus Fraxi proceeds to enumerate 'the peculiar lech, favourite passion, or pet crime' which has been ascribed, 'in a somewhat arbitrary manner it must be acknowledged', to the inhabitants of different countries.[10] Sodomy has found a permanent home in Turkey and Italy, whence it has spread to France. In England it 'has also had its votaries', although, Pisanus Fraxi assures us, 'to a much more limited extent'.[11] Tribadism (lesbianism) is, 'we are told', chiefly indulged in by Turkish and French women. And there has always been a lot of it in nunneries.[12] Abortion is much practised in France, 'and to a greater extent than is generally supposed in England; although the palm must be given to the Americans'.[13] Corpse profanation? It is found, 'as some affirm', in Italy, and even in

France.[14] Bestiality, 'so dear to the Romans', is undoubtedly still perpetrated in Italy, especially (as one might expect) 'among the rural population'.[15] A taste for 'Black Women' 'is perhaps peculiar to the French', specimens of 'these coloured beauties' being found in several Paris brothels and even in the provinces.[16]

And what of England? It comes as no surprise to find Pisanus Fraxi insisting that 'the propensity which the English most cherish is undoubtedly Flagellation'. Here there can be no question of hearsay:

That the rod has been used in all Roman Catholic countries by the priests as an instrument to serve their own lubricity is of course not to be denied; and although the subject has been most seriously and scientifically treated by a Dutch doctor;* yet this vice has certainly struck deeper root in England than elsewhere, and only here, I opine, can be found men who experience a pleasure rather in receiving than in administering the birch. Nevertheless this is a fact, and did not discretion forbid, it would be easy to name men of the highest positions in diplomacy, literature, the army, etc., who, at the present day, indulge in this idiosyncracy, and to point out the haunts they frequent.

Books innumerable in the English language are devoted to this subject alone; no English bawdy book is free from descriptions of flagellation, and numerous separate plates exist, depicting whipping scenes; it has caused the separation of man and wife; the genteelest female schools have been made subservient to the passions of its votaries; and formerly it was spoken of without reserve on the public stage [. . .] Although their productions have not been printed, it is well known that some of our most eminent poets and novelists of the present day have employed their pens on the subject.[17]

* Johann Heinrich Meibom (1590–1655), better known as Meibomius, Professor of Medicine at the University of Helmstedt. Meibom's treatise, *De Flagrorum Usu in Re Veneria & Lumborum Renumque Officio* ('On the Use of Rods in Venereal Matters and in the Office of the Loins and Reins'), was first published at Leyden in 1629, went through numerous editions and was repeatedly translated into German, French and English. See plate 10.

Ashbee knew that the root cause of British flagellomania was the system of corporal punishment habitual in the public schools, and imitated by the others lower down the scale. He also knew that 'the genteelest female schools' of Britain had *not* 'been made subservient to the passions of its votaries'. It is here that we begin to sense that he not being as objective as he claims. In his following remarks, Pisanus Fraxi refers to the flagellant correspondence columns that not only filled such Victorian clandestine periodicals as the *Ramblers* and the *Bon Ton Magazine* but those of popular publications designed for home consumption such as the *Englishwoman's Domestic Magazine* and the *Family Herald*. Such columns, as the journalist and novelist George Augustus Sala pointed out at the time, were 'gross fables [. . .] cunningly devised as decoy-ducks to draw forth genuine communications from [female] correspondents writing in good faith'.[18] A few did write, but the hundreds of letters purporting to come from mothers and schoolmistresses, with details of their *modi operandi*, were obvious fabrications devised by male flagellomaniacs. Pisanus Fraxi cannot have been unaware of this.[19]

At this point in his introduction Pisanus Fraxi appropriates a communication sent to him by 'a gentleman still living, a passionate devotee of the birch, and one who is worthy of all confidence in matters connected with flagellation'.[20] The 'gentleman' is Frederick Hankey, Ashbee's Paris crony, and the document is preserved in the latter's interleaved and annotated copy of the *Index Librorum Prohibitorum* in the British Library. The original reads:

Mr. F. Hankey of 2 rue Laffitte Paris has requested that the following details might be sent to Mr. Ashbee.

The first establishment known by me over the last fifty years where the practice of the rod was carried on to a great extent was held by Mrs. Collett in Tavistock Court, Covent Garden, from whence she removed

into the neighbourhood of Portland Place – and then to Bedford St., Russell Square, where she died – George the 4th is known to have been in her house – She brought up a niece in the same line, and who as Mrs. Mitchell carried on a great business in the same line, in various places, and finally in St. Mary's Square, Kennington, where she died –

Then came Mrs. James who had been maid in the family of Lord Clanricarde – she had a house in Carlisle St. but eventually retired from business with a good fortune, a villa at Notting Hill, and a house in Quebec Street – with pictures and jewels without end. No one ever surpassed in this particular line Mrs. Theresa Berkley who lived and died in Charlotte St., Portland Place, no. 28 – A few days after her death her brother who had been a missionary for 30 years in Australia arrived, and found that she had bequeathed to him 12,500 pounds in the funds, besides other property – but when he learnt the source from which it had been derived he renounced all claim and immediately went back to Australia – In default the property was to go to Dr. Vance of Savile Row, her medical attendant, but he also refused to administer, the whole was escheated to the crown – She never destroyed a letter, and Dr. Vance as executor received several boxes full, which he allowed the writer of this to examine. They were of the most extraordinary character, from the highest personages, male and female, in the land –

Mrs. Potter carried on a good business a few years ago near Tottenham Court Road, but being sentenced to imprisonment for getting some young girl birched by one of her customers was ruined –

There were several others whose names and addresses I forget – all made fortunes –

The only establishment I know of now is in the Regent's Park, a lovely little villa presided over by a well-educated lady, well versed in the birchen mysteries.

Her clientele is small but select, consisting of a few persons belonging to the higher order of society –

The birch at most of these places was provided by one Mrs. Potter, living at Walworth –

In my experience I have known personally several ladies of high

rank who had an extraordinary passion for administering the rod, and that with merciless severity – I knew too the wife of a clergyman, young and pretty, who carried the taste to excess – I have known only one who liked to receive it, and she was quite of the lowest order – when excited by drink she would allow herself to be birched until the bottom was utterly raw, and the rods saturated in blood, she crying out during the operation, 'Harder, harder', and blaspheming if it was not well laid in – At the establishment I have named in Regent's Park, there come two very young girls who go through all the phases of a school-mistress and whip fearfully severely –

The programmes sent by 'pupils' are extraordinary – some like to be whipped as children across the knee – some on the back of a servant, others to be strapped down –

A friend of Hankey who had been a governess in a [?] family in England, used the rod most cleverly – she is French, but is going to be married next week, and to the loss of the lovers of discipline.

I could give many anecdotes connected with this business.

I write in poste haste, starting today for Paris.

Delighted by Hankey's account, Ashbee drew heavily on it in the *Index*, modifying it slightly and adding one or two details of his own:

Mrs. Collett was a noted whipper, and George the IV is known to have visited her; she had an establishment in Tavistock Court, Covent Garden, whence she removed to the neighbourhood of Portland Place, and afterwards to Bedford Street, Russell Square, where she died. She brought up her niece in the same line, who, as Mrs. Mitchell, carried on a successful business in various places, among others at No. 22 (afterwards 44) Waterloo Road, and finally at St. Mary's Square, Kennington, where she died. Then came Mrs. James, who had been maid in the family of Lord Clanricarde; she had a house at No. 7 Carlisle Street, Soho; she retired from business with a good fortune, and dwelt at Notting Hill in luxury, her house being decorated with pictures, and her person covered with jewels. There were, further: Mrs. Emma Lee, real name Richardson, of No. 50 Margaret Street,

Regent Street; Mrs. Phillips, of No. 11 Upper Belgrave Place, Pimlico; Mrs. Shepherd, of No. 25 Gilbert Street; Mrs. Sarah Potter, alias Stewart, of various addresses, who died in 1873; and, were it not indiscreet, I might add the names of one or two other ladies who still carry on their calling. But the queen of her profession was undoubtedly Mrs. Theresa Berkley, of No. 28 Charlotte Street, Portland Place; she was a perfect mistress of her art, understood how to satisfy her clients, and was, moreover, a thorough women of business, for she amassed during her career a considerable sum of money.[21]

'And, were it not indiscreet, I might add the names of one or two other ladies who still carry on their calling': thus Pisanus Fraxi paraphrases Hankey's observations on 'the lovely villa' in Regent's Park (probably the one frequented by Swinburne),[22] ascribing to himself first-hand knowledge of some current practitioners. Again, we cannot but feel that he is covertly acknowledging his personal interest in the subject.

As the reader can see, Pisanus Fraxi has reserved Hankey's account of the notorious Theresa Berkley till last, altering the arrangement of the sadistic Englishman's original communication. He does so in order to be able to link it smoothly to that provided by the erotica publisher William Dugdale in his preface to a work of the purest flagellant fiction, *Venus Schoolmistress; or, Birchen Sports*.[23] According to Dugdale, quoted at length by Ashbee, Theresa Berkley

possessed the first grand requisite of a courtizan, viz., lewdness; for without a woman is positively lecherous she cannot long keep up the affectation of it, and it will soon be perceived that she only moves her hands or her buttocks to the tune of pounds, shillings and pence. She could assume great urbanity and good humour; she would study every lech, whim, caprice, and desire of her customer, and had the disposition to gratify them, if her avarice was rewarded in return. Her instruments of torture were more numerous than those of any other governess. Her supply of birch was extensive, and kept in water, so that

it was always green and pliant: she had shafts with a dozen whip thongs on each of them; a dozen different sizes of cat-o'-nine-tails, some with needle points worked into them; various kinds of thin bending canes; leather straps like coach traces; battledoors, made of thick sole-leather, with inch nails run through to docket, and currycomb tough hides rendered callous by many years flagellation. Holly brushes, furze brushes; a prickly evergreen, called butchers bush; and during the summer, glass and China vases filled with a constant supply of green nettles, with which she often restored the dead to life. Thus, at her shop, whoever went with plenty of money, could be birched, whipped, fustigated, scourged, needle-pricked, half-hung, holly-brushed, furse-brushed, butcher-brushed, stinging-nettled, curry-combed, phleboto-mized, and tortured till he had a belly full.

For those whose *lech* it was to flog a woman, she would herself sub-mit to a certain extent; but if they were gluttons at it, she had women in attendance who would take any number of lashes the flogger pleased, provided he forked out an *advalorem* duty. Among these were Miss Ring, Hannah Jones, Sally Taylor, One-eyed Peg, Bauld-Cunted Poll, and a black girl, called Ebony Bet.

The machine represented in the frontispiece to this work* was invented for Mrs. Berkley to flog gentlemen upon, in the spring of 1828. It is capable of being opened to a considerable extent, so as to bring the body to any angle that might be desirable. There is a print in Mrs. Berkley's memoirs, representing a man upon it quite naked. A women is sitting in a chair exactly under it, with her bosom, belly, and bush exposed: she is *manualizing* his *embolon*, whilst Mrs. Berkley is birch-ing his posteriors. The female acting as *frictrix* was intended for Fisher, a fine, tall, dark haired girl, all must remember who visited Charlotte Street at that day, as well as the good humoured blonde, Willis; the plump, tight, frisky, and merry arsed Thurlow; Grenville, with the enormous bubbies; Bentinc, with breadth of hip and splendour of buttock; Olive, the gipsy, whose brown skin, wicked black eye, and medicean form, would melt an anchorite; the mild and amiable Palmer,

* Dugdale's plate is reproduced by Ashbee.

49

with luxuriant and *well fledged* mount, from whose tufted honors many a noble lord has stolen a sprig; and Pryce, the pleasing and complaisant, who, if birch was a question, could both give and take.

When the new flogging machine was invented, the designer told her it would bring her into notice, and go by her name after her death; and it did cause her to be talked of, and brought her a great deal of business. She died in September, 1836, having funded ten thousand pounds during the eight years she had been a governess. The original horse is among the models of the Society of Arts at the Adelphi, and was presented by Dr. Vance, her executor * * * * [. . .].

Mrs. Berkley had also in her second floor, a hook and pulley attached to the ceiling, by which she could draw a man up by his hands. This operation is also represented in her memoirs. Many persons feel disappointed at her promised memoirs being so long delayed, but the publication was suspended at the request of Dr. Vance, of Cork Street, her executor. His recent death, however, will enable the firm, who hold the copyright of her autobiography, speedily to put it to press.[24]

After imposing on the reader such a lengthy extract from Dugdale's preface to *Venus Schoolmistress*, Pisanus Fraxi remarks: 'This account of Mrs. Berkley is, it must be acknowledged, curious, and, being substantially true, I have ventured to give it in full'.[25] 'Curious' it certainly is; perhaps even 'substantially true'. But, if Pisanus Fraxi has 'ventured' to give it in full, the real reason is, surely, that he himself is excited by the subject.

Pisanus Fraxi now formulates his conclusion on English flagellomania in a short paragraph blatant in its illogicality:

Many of these women, there can be little doubt, took an interest, if not a pleasure, in their vocation. It is a well known fact that women are, and always have been, even more fond of wielding the rod than men, and this passion pervades the higher, rather than the lower classes.[26]

For the first sentence, despite its provisos ('there can be little doubt', 'if not a pleasure'), there was some justification: it was in the interests of flagellant prostitutes to pretend to enjoy what was

required of them by their clients, to act their part with conviction. For the following claim there was no evidence whatsoever. The 'well known fact' was a mere fantasy, its true nature being ratified by the footnotes added in support: Hankey's zany account of flagellant women he claimed to have known, cited above, and a sixteen-line quotation from Brantôme's notoriously unreliable and fictitious *Vies des dames galantes*. Commenting on Pisanus Fraxi's allegation about woman's flagellant propensities, Steven Marcus notes: 'There is no evidence in support of this contention, there never was any, and if Ashbee had been able to disentangle himself from the material that he reproduces in his pages he would have been able without much effort to make this out.'[27] In the 'pre-psychological' age, though, such disentanglement was wellnigh impossible for anyone hooked on the flagellant fantasy, with its inherent burden of shame and incommunicability. Ashbee, in my view, was such a person.

The rest of the introduction is occupied with explaining the method employed in the bibliography. Readers of a compilation such as his, Pisanus Fraxi avers, want *'facts and facts only'*.[28] He will cast his net wide, providing accounts of books 'in every branch of literature' (which is not true), deliberately selecting 'works as various as possible, in order to show through what widely spread ramifications erotic literature extends, and what a vast field has to be traversed'.[29] His information will always be based on volumes he has perused personally, and for any second-hand information he will always give his authority.[30]

Pre-empting the charge that his commentaries are obscene, Pisanus Fraxi insists that 'in treating of obscene books it is self-evident that obscenities cannot be avoided', adding immediately that in his own text he will never be caught using an 'impure word when one less distasteful but equally expressive can be found'.[31] And, anyway, nobody is going to be aroused by reading the book:

The passions are not excited. Although the citations I produce are frequently licentious, being as a matter of course those which I have considered the most remarkable or most pungent in the books from which they are extracted; yet I give only so much as is necessary to form a correct estimate of the style of the writer, of the nature of the book, or the course of the tale, not sufficient to enflame the passions. This could only be accomplished by the perusal of the books in their entirety, by the reader giving himself up to the author.

My extracts on the contrary will, I trust and believe, have a totally opposite effect, and as a rule will inspire so hearty a disgust for the books they are taken from, that the reader will have learned enough about them from my pages, and will be more than satisfied to have nothing further to do with them. As little, it is my belief, will my book excite the passions of my readers, as would the naked body of a woman, extended on the dissecting table, produce concupiscence in the minds of the students assembled to witness an operation performed upon her.[32]

This is balderdash, since Pisanus Fraxi knows that many of the passages quoted are indeed capable of 'exciting' or 'enflaming' the passions. Does he really expect the reader to believe that he has gone to all this trouble (years of work and painstaking annotation) in order to make him feel *disgust* for the books described? Marcus comments: 'It is difficult to decide to what extent the divisions in Ashbee's consciousness are the result of ordinary hypocrisy or of unconscious contradictions'.[33] But perhaps they are neither. Ashbee may simply be intent on ridiculing, sending up or even taking revenge on a society in which 'ultra-squeamishness and hyper-prudery' are the order of the day. To use one of his favourite words when discussing erotica publishing, the disgust he claims to feel for these books is a *supercherie*.

The principal message transmitted by Pisanus Fraxi's commentaries on the hundred and fifty or so books noticed in the *Index Librorum Prohibitorum* is that heterosexual copulation is a

normal, desirable activity encouraged by Mother Nature, and
that, in matters of the flesh, Victorian England is ludicrously,
'unnaturally' puritanical. That he revels in his subject is evident
from the gusto of his plot summaries, the inordinate amount of
space afforded to a book such as *The Ups and Downs of Life* by
Edward Sellon (which Pisanus Fraxi wants us to believe is true
autobiography) and the choice of quotations. There is no evi-
dence whatsoever here of 'disgust':

Knowing her lover's principles, and that the more 'ausgelassen' she is
the more she will please him, she does not for a moment hesitate, but
stripping to the skin she takes the youth's member in her mouth, while
the giant enjoys her from behind, in each hole alternately, until she is so
exhausted that she has to be put to bed and allowed some time to
recruit her overtaxed forces. Her lover, be it understood, stands by and
witnesses the scene with the greatest interest and satisfaction.

St. Léger determines to punish both friend and mistress. The lady he
takes as 'maîtresse en titre' for a couple of months, and then suddenly
abandons her. His friend he corrects in a more severe manner, for he
having married Sophie, St. Léger manages to seduce her on the nuptial
evening between the wedding and bedding (hence the title of the book).

The various 'leches' to which men of pleasure are addicted are
reviewed, the gambols of young girls in boarding schools are peeped at,
and indeed the little treatise is pretty exhaustive of its subject.

Lucy and Kate mutually relate their amorous experiences each night
as they retire together to rest; distant at first, and coy as far as Kate is
concerned, they gradually warm into complete confidence, and end by
narrating their separate deflorations with every minute and voluptuous
detail. Their conversations are interspersed with caresses which at
fitting moments grow into thorough tribadism.

8vo.; pp. 62; 8 plates in all, fairly drawn and coloured, the frontispiece
is a fancy design, a winged arse in clouds.

This book is cleverly written and contains some very lascivious

episodes. That at the beginning of the work, in which the hero is seduced, corrupted and sodomised by his tutor, is forcible and original. Towards the end there is a scene with an amorous old lady, which is curious and very powerfully told.[34]

In tune with his introduction, Pisanus Fraxi, while admitting the concept of 'obscene' or 'indecent', never attempts to define it or to indicate the boundary that separates it from the merely 'erotic'. Referring equally to illustrations or passages in books, we find him using again and again, indiscriminately, phrases such as: 'It is free, but scarcely obscene'; 'Although scenes pretty free are described, objectionable words and expressions are invariably avoided'; 'Although the scenes are very free, anything contrary to nature is either eschewed or vituperated'; 'The scenes are very natural and lascivious'; 'A series of sketches of manners of the time, satirical, and at times amorous, never obscene or even immodest'; 'They are free, but not obscene'; 'Sometimes free, but never indecent'; 'The plate is not indecent, but only suggestive'; 'But although entirely erotic, it is never crapulous or disgusting'; 'They are nearly all free, but not obscene'; 'None of these doggerel pieces are positively obscene, but are highly suggestive'.[35] What Pisanus Fraxi seems to be suggesting is that, if the art is good (writing or drawing), the sex depicted is legitimate. It is more a question of aesthetics than of morals.

For Pisanus Fraxi, Victorian England has got it grossly wrong where the ancients got it right (and the French still do), and he is full of praise for his friend John Davenport, whose *Aphrodisiacs and Anti-aphrodisiacs* contains a disquisition on 'Ancient Phallic Worship' in which it is argued that copulation not only once afforded no embarrassment to humanity, but was revered (the Round Towers of Ireland are adduced as evidence!).[36] Davenport's posthumous *Curiositates Eroticae Physiologiae; or, Tabooed Subjects Freely Treated* (1875), which Ashbee financed, is singled out for special applause. A substantial extract from its preface is

provided. Davenport fulminates against current notions of modesty, deprecates English cant, hypocrisy and sexual euphemism (and by inference Christianity), and makes a plea for a more natural life of the affections. It could be Pisanus Fraxi himself writing:

Of all the subjects included under the term *Physiology*, there is not one so interesting, curious, and important as that *of human generation and its subsidiary branches*. A few works of the kind have, it is true, been published at long intervals, but their language has, in deference to a *pseudo* modesty, been so veiled and disguised as to render these works spiritless, jejune, and destitute of all interest, the inevitable consequence being that the wearied and impatient reader casts the volume aside in utter disappointment.

Fastidiousness such as this was despised by the ancients, who, as they regarded the productive powers of nature, and, consequently, the reproductive organs and functions themselves, with the greatest awe and reverence, so they could afford to *call a spade a spade*.

Now the moderns, on the contrary, influenced, we suppose, by *outré* and ridiculous notions of delicacy, look upon the same parts with aversion and disgust, as if they had been the work of some filthy and obscene spirit, rather than that they had been fashioned by the Almighty hand of a pure and divine Demiurgos.

An exaggerated delicacy must always be regarded as suspicious, it being found that the possession of a virtue is the less, in an inverse ratio to the boast of having it.

Thus Dean Swift remarked that the greater the squeamishness of a man's ears, the nastier were his ideas and thoughts.

Now, if this observation be true, as we believe it is, what is to be said of those would be *linguistic purists* who recommend mutilating the brave old English work *cock*, and thus metamorphose it into *co.*, on account of its indecency, a sentence which is to be extended to all the unfortunate words compounded of it, as Turncock, which must be read Turnco, &c., &c. . . .[37]

Ashbee greatly admired Richard Burton, whom he had not

yet met in person, and the *Index Librorum Prohibitorum* carries an extensive, eighteen-page account (one of the longest in the book) of Burton and Arbuthnot's translation of the *Káma-Shástra*. Ashbee had been in correspondence with Arbuthnot, who wrote to him:

The first impression on roughly running through the writings of the old Indian Sages is that Europeans and modern society generally would be greatly benefited by some such treatises. It is difficult to get Englishmen to acknowledge that matrimonial happiness may in some cases be attained by a careful study of the passions of a wife, that is to say admitting that a wife be allowed to feel passion. Many a life has been wasted and the best feelings of a young woman outraged by the rough exercise of what truly become the husband's 'rights', and all the innate delicate sentiments and illusions of the virgin bride are ruthlessly trampled on when the curtains close around the couch on what is vulgarly called the 'first night'.[38]

Pisanus Fraxi was astonished by the *Káma-Shástra*. 'A very remarkable book', it contained 'among many things almost incomprehensible to an European, much matter which would repay his careful study'.[39] Which was indeed the case. What sets the *Káma-Shástra* apart from all nineteenth-century Western books dealing with sex is that its purpose is to promote 'conjugal fidelity and satisfaction' by helping married couples to improve their love-making. In England at the time there was no official recognition of the female orgasm. Thus, Dr William Acton, one of the great unintentional anxiety-makers of the age, felt entitled to articulate the following statement in his best-selling *The Functions and Disorders of the Reproductive Organs* (1857), the leading Victorian sex manual:

As a general rule, a modest woman seldom desires any sexual gratification for herself. She submits to her husband, but only to please him; and, but for the desire of maternity, would far rather be relieved from

his attentions. No nervous or feeble young man need, therefore, be deterred from marriage by any exaggerated notion of the duties required from him. The married woman has no wish to be treated on the footing of a mistress.[40]

In a society so hidebound by sexual repression, ignorance and hypocrisy, so terrified of masturbation and its alleged consequences (blindness, insanity . . .), with the stress on muscular Christianity and the benefits of restraint (and, if possible, abstinence), the revelations of the *Káma-Shástra* could obviously not be brought to the attention of the nation's readership at large. For example, the advice to a woman concerning what Pisanus Fraxi terms 'the management of her Yóní during coition':

The wife will remember that without an especial exertion of will on her part, the husband's pleasure will not be perfect. To this end she must ever strive to close and constrict the Yóní until it holds the Lingam, as, with a finger opening and shutting at her pleasure, and finally, acting as the hand of the Gopála-girl, who milks the cow. This can be learned only by long practice, and especially by throwing the will into the part to be affected, even as men endeavour to sharpen their hearing, and their sense of touch. While so doing, she will mentally repeat 'Kámadeva! Kámadeva!' in order that a blessing may rest upon the undertaking. And she will be pleased to hear that the art once learned, is never lost. Her husband will then value her above all women, nor would he exchange her for the most beautiful Rání (queen) in the three worlds. So lovely and pleasant to man is she who constricts.[41]

On the evidence of the *Káma-Shástra*, the Indian Angel of the House was very much more accommodating than her British counterpart.

As the introduction has led us to expect, with its account of flagellant brothels and prostitutes, Pisanus Fraxi devotes a large amount of space in the body of the *Index* to describing English flagellant books. In particular he persists in his determination to

establish that women, given the opportunity, positively enjoy beating. But the only extra 'evidence' he can adduce comes in fictional works such as *The Romance of Chastisement*, in which it is stated: 'As a rule, women do not readily resort to rods. Some are too tender-hearted, others too chaste or too timid – but their scruples overcome and vengeance safe, they know no measure in the cruel sport that, under the name of duty, gives the rein to passion and gratifies two lusts at every lunge.'[42]

If William Acton was certain that male children can be affected sexually by flagellation, resulting in impotence in later life unless there is recourse to it in reality or fantasy, so too was Pisanus Fraxi, who quotes approvingly from *Venus Schoolmistress*, already plundered in his introduction:

Many persons not sufficiently acquainted with human nature, and the ways of the world, are apt to imagine that the *lech* for Flagellation must be confined either to the aged, or to those who are exhausted through too great a devotion to venery: but such is not the fact, for there are quite as many young men, and men in the prime and vigour of life, who are influenced by this passion as there are amongst the aged and debilitated.

It is very true that there are innumerable old generals, admirals, colonels, and captains, as well as bishops, judges, barristers, lords, commoners, and physicians, who periodically go to be whipped, merely because it warms their blood, and keeps up a little agreeable excitement in their systems long after the power of enjoying the opposite sex has failed them; but it is equally true, that hundreds of young men through having been educated at institutions where the masters were fond of administering birch discipline, and recollecting certain sensations produced by it, have imbibed a passion for it, and have longed to receive the same chastisement from the hands of a fine woman. To the truth of this statement, two of the most experienced governesses now retired from business, Mrs. Chalmers and Mrs. Noyeau, can bear ample testimony, and that the propensity follows such parties through life, inasmuch, as however vigorous and capable they may be of subagitating a

woman to her heart's content, yet they care little for the act, unless accompanied by the seasoning of their favourite sauce.[43]

Surely it must be clear by now that Ashbee, alias Pisanus Fraxi, was yet another Victorian flagellomaniac?

One of the most remarkable aspects of the *Index Librorum Prohibitorum* is its voluminous, two-column 'General, Alphabetical and Analytical Index', which occupies no fewer than fifty-eight pages. Authors, publishers, titles of all the works reviewed (or mentioned in passing), places of publication (real or spurious), the names of characters in the books noticed, the subjects treated . . . it's all here, meticulously set out in different typefaces (with authors' names in small capitals, subjects in Antique, and titles in Old English). The index is humorous at times, too, 'facts' contained in the fictions being mixed indiscriminately with reliable information, and some amusing cross-references essayed:

BACKSIDES can blush, 352.
ABBYSSINIA. Arab women are able to constrict the muscles of the vagina, 290 (note).
BIJOUX INDISCRETS. See DILDOES.
COITION. See COPULATION. (Under the latter, one entry reads: 'Monotony condemned'.)

Nine columns are devoted to Ashbee's pet subject of BIBLIOGRAPHY, which includes entries such as:

An infant science, ix.
Unremunerative and thankless, ix.
Compared to a potato field, ix (note 2).
No satisfactory catalogue of erotic literature exists, xvi.
Reasons why English erotic literature has been neglected, xvii.
English writers and artists (erotic) inferior to Foreigners, xviii.
The more a book is prohibited the more it is sought, xxvi.

Improper books compared to poisons; should be treated as such, xxvii.
Authors allowed to quote obscene passages, liv.
Obscene words used, but only when unavoidable, lxviii.
Obscenity is in the mind, not in words, lxviii (note 110).
Immoral authors not commended, lxix.
The passions are not excited, lxx.
A disgust for bad books will be inspired, lxx.
Length of the introduction apologised for, lxxvi.

The index must have taken Ashbee many months of painstaking work. It is an earnest of his obsessive need to classify, arrange, order and pin down. Moreover, it confirms that in his mind the terms 'obscene' and 'erotic' are interchangeable. One cross-reference reads 'OBSCENE LITERATURE. See EROTIC LITERATURE', and under individual countries we find:

AUSTRIA. Book trade (obscene) in, xxx.
BELGIUM. Book trade (obscene) in, xxxi.
FRANCE. Book trade (erotic) in, xxix.
GERMANY. Book trade (erotic) in, xxx.
INDIA. Obscene books published in, 277 (note).
ITALY. State of book trade (obscene) there, xxxi.
SPAIN. Book trade (obscene) there, xxxi.

Ashbee is writing some ten years before the appearance of Richard von Krafft-Ebing's revolutionary *Psychopathia Sexualis* (1886). Krafft-Ebing was a distinguished professor of psychiatry, not a pedlar in erotica, and his hundreds of detailed clinical histories were unlike anything the world had ever seen before. The book, which began as a slim plaquette, grew in size with each successive edition (like Acton's *Functions and Disorders of the Reproductive Organs*), and was soon translated into other languages. It unfolded an extraordinary panorama of bizarre sexual behaviour, and the fact that the juicier bits were given in (transparent) Latin did not affect sales:

Occasionally he would obtain a prostitute, undress himself completely (while she was not to take off a thing), and have her tread upon him, whip him, and beat him. *Qua re summa libidinum affectus pedem feminae lambit quod solum eum libidinosum facere potest; tum ejaculationem assequitur.* Then disgust at the morally-debasing situation occurred, and he retired as quickly as possible.[44]

Krafft-Ebing not only put the already existing term 'sadism' firmly on the psychological map, but himself coined its opposite, 'masochism' (from Leopold von Sacher-Masoch, author of *Venus in Furs*). His case histories made it clear that the so-called sexual deviations, and not least flagellomania, first manifest themselves in childhood. His assumption that such deviations are hereditary in origin was soon to be contested by psychoanalysis, but nobody could deny that Krafft-Ebing had made a major contribution to the understanding of human sexuality.

The impact of *Psychopathia Sexualis* was immense, and it comes as no surprise to learn that it was among Oscar Wilde's favourite reading (if we can credit Lord Alfred Douglas). But it arrived on the scene just too late to influence the *Index Librorum Prohibitorum* and its two successors.[45]

Ashbee emerges from the *Index* as a genuine searcher after sexual truth despite his hang-up on flagellation and his tendency, when discussing it, to veer, perhaps unconsciously, into fantasy, particularly where women are concerned. That he detests the 'ultra-squeamishness and hyper-prudery' of contemporary British society there can surely be no doubt. Nor that, to his way of thinking, the repression of the sexual instinct is a sure recipe for misery. The *Index Librorum Prohibitorum*, with its vast corpus of documentation, is one of the most deliberately subversive books ever written in the English language.

From the Centuria *to the* Catena
(1877–85)

The *Index Librorum Prohibitorum* could not be reviewed in any conventional English publication without calling down fire and brimstone on the heads of those responsible, so Ashbee himself, in a fine display of bravado, made a point of obliquely bringing it to the attention of the curious in the 26 May 1877 issue of *Notes and Queries*, only two weeks after printing was completed. Referring to *An Essay on Women*, ninety-four lines of bawdy doggerel attributed to John Wilkes, Lord Mayor of London (1727–1797), 'H.S.A.' explained that for several years he had been endeavouring to track down a copy of 'the *original* edition of this historically interesting poem', adding in a matter-of-course way that he had just found listed in the *Index Librorum Prohibitorum*: *being Notes Bio-, Biblio-, Iconographical and Critical* (London, 1877) 'no less than fourteen different editions and versions' of the work. After quoting the *Index* on the subject (without facilitating the author's pseudonym, or any further details), 'H.S.A.' enquired, 'Have all the copies which Wilkes struck off at his own private press ceased now to exist, and, if so, can any of your contributors afford information as to their destruction?' It is difficult to believe that Henry Frederick Turle, sub-editor of *Notes and Queries*, whom Ashbee now saw frequently (as his diary shows) was not a party to the joke.

During the two years spent preparing the *Index* for the press Ashbee had also been hard at work on the sequel. On 30 June 1877 he handed Gaball the first instalment of the *Centuria Librorum Absconditorum* ('A Hundred Books Worthy of Being Hidden Away'). Like the *Index*, it was to be two years in the making.

As 'Apis' and 'Fraxinus', Ashbee continued to make frequent appearances in the columns of *Notes and Queries*. On 14 July 1877, joining in a debate on a volume entitled *Tableaux des moeurs du temps*, 'Apis' commented that only one copy of the first edition was known to exist. It belonged to 'Mr. H***** of Paris' (Frederick Hankey). He then went on to say that there was a copy of another edition 'in the library of a bibliophile in London'. A fortnight later one J. Borrajo (Ashbee himself in yet another disguise?) enquired, 'Can Apis, without breach of confidence, tell me who Mr. H***** of Paris and the bibliophile of London are?' 'Apis' replied on 18 August that he regretted having 'to decline Mr. J. Borrajo's further inquiry'. He then pointed out that on page 129 of the *Index Librorum Prohibitorum; being Notes Bio- Biblio- Icono- graphical and Critical on Curious and Uncommon Books* (London, MDCCCLXXVII) was to be found a notice of twelve plates done for the *Tableaux des moeurs* by Louis Jaugey. Once again no indication of author or publisher was supplied. It was all very tongue in cheek.[1]

Ashbee's diary for this period is sporadic and dull. The journal contains no political comment, no references to the public life of the nation, no information about his business activities, no psychological insights. It simply lists some of the people he has met or been frequenting, some of the places he has been to and, in considerable detail, the operas and plays he has seen. We learn disappointingly little about his family life. Thus, on 3 September 1877, he notes laconically after visiting Ashbee relatives near Faversham: 'Returned from Westwood where I have been spending 10 days with Charley. Elizabeth has not left town this summer.'

Hardly a penetrating comment on the relationship of father and son (who, now aged fourteen, was just about to be sent as a boarder to Wellington College).[2]

Just occasionally the diary gives us a tiny peep into Ashbee's 'secret' activities. On 25 July 1877, for example, we learn that for £300 (a huge sum then) he has bought the lion's share of the collection of erotica put together by his friend James Campbell Reddie, recently departed for Bath. (At the same time Campbell presented Ashbee with the manuscript, in three volumes, of his *Bibliographical Notes on Books*, which were to prove invaluable to him in preparing the second and third volumes of his own great biographical venture.)[3] At the end of October 1877, in Paris for ten days, Ashbee records that at last he has met the famous artist Félicien Rops, who has promised to do the frontispiece for the *Centuria Librorum Absconditorum* (charging a handsome price, no doubt). He has also been introduced by Eugène Paillet to Baron Roger Portalis, another noted authority on books 'uncommon and curious', and has fallen in with a certain Major Ricketts, who was to remain one of the more shadowy figures in Ashbee's entourage of erotomaniacs.[4]

In December 1877 we find Henry Spencer in Hamburg for Christmas, accompanied by his 'whole family', the German governess and an English servant called Hesta Jones. 'Papa' Charles Lavy, his father-in-law and benefactor, is at the quay to meet them.[5] Back in London, Ashbee attends the funeral at Kensal Green of his old artist friend George Cruikshank. Among the literary men present are Lord Houghton and George Augustus Sala. Ten days earlier Ashbee had lost another 'dear friend', John Doran, editor of *Notes and Queries*. 'They were not however *ejusdem farinae*,' he wrote in his diary. 'Doran a generous but moderate liver, Cruikshank a teatoteller, always preaching total abstinence. Doran once said to me about Cruikshank "Why, he is constantly drunk with the pride of never drinking!"'[6]

Every Tuesday, when Ashbee is not travelling, the dinner parties continue at 46 Upper Bedford Place. One of the new guests is the distinguished (but impecunious) Spanish Arabist, scholar and bibliographer Pascual de Gayangos (1809–1897). Author of *Mohammadan Dynasties in Spain* (London, 1841–43), this engaging Andalusian from Seville had been a friend of the great Hispanist Richard Ford, who thirty years earlier, in his celebrated *A Hand-Book for Travellers in Spain, and Readers at Home* (1845), had termed him 'by far the first Hispano-Arabic scholar of his day'.[7] In 1871 Gayangos edited one of the most famous ribald texts in the Spanish language, Francisco Delicado's *La lozana andaluza* (1528), and was now completing a *Catalogue of the Manuscripts in the Spanish Language in the British Museum*. The learned Arabist, who contributed articles on Spain to the *Athenaeum*, rekindled Ashbee's interest in the country, encouraged him to explore Spanish erotica, and also, it seems, stimulated him to read Cervantes, who was soon to become a passion. Years earlier Gayangos had helped a young Richard Burton, then floundering at Oxford, with his first steps in Arabic.[8]

On 5 April 1878 Ashbee met Richard Monckton Milnes (see plate 5) for the first time, the encounter taking place at Robert Samuel Turner's rooms in Albany. Fred Hankey and his mistress, over from Paris, were also present. About Milnes's flagellant proclivities Ashbee was well informed thanks to Hankey. He owned the manuscript of *The Rodiad*, and knew that Milnes was its author. Two years earlier 'Apis' had referred to the poem in *Notes and Queries* (21 October 1876):

'THE RODIAD' – This poem, which is by no means devoid of merit, was not written by George Colman the younger. I do not know who was the author, although I possess the original MS., and could give its history. J. C. Hotten printed *The Rodiad* in a neat little vol., which did not of course get into the hands of the trade generally; but curiously enough

he misspelt the author's name, giving it as Col*e*man instead of Colman. The whole thing then is a *supercherie*.

Ashbee was no doubt fascinated to meet Monckton Milnes, who was soon visiting 4 Gray's Inn Square. On 8 June 1878 he recorded in his diary: 'Lord Houghton came for the *second* time to the Inn, and brought with him E. Bellamy whom he introduced to me.'

In Houghton's letters to Richard Burton, Henry Edward Vaux Bellamy (*c.* 1837–1889) is 'invariably mentioned' in association with the flagellomaniacs Hankey and General Studholme Hodgson.[9] The latter, it appears, was one of the authors of the notorious *An Experimental Lecture on Flagellation* by 'Colonel Spanker', issued according to Pisanus Fraxi in 1878–79.[10] Ashbee now began to frequent Bellamy and Hodgson assiduously, but the diary adds few personal details about either man.

Monckton Milnes seems to have liked Ashbee, and before long admitted him to membership of his select Philobiblon Society, founded in 1853.[11] 'My dear Lord Houghton,' Ashbee wrote to him on 7 October 1878:

My friend judge Paillet of Paris is here, & would, I am certain, like to be introduced to you. He & a few other friends will dine with me next Friday (11 Inst.). I should be pleased if you would honour us with your company. 6.30 for 7 o'ck. You will understand, & pardon this short notice.

The M.S. which you left in my hands is very curious & interesting. I hope to make good use of it.

Believe me
Yours very truly
H. S. Ashbee.[12]

It is not possible to identify the manuscript in question, although it seems fair to assume that it was of an erotic character. In December Ashbee dined with Houghton 'at his hotel in

Clifford Street',[13] and before long the latter was a frequent guest
at the increasingly cosmopolitan and polyglot Tuesday dinners
in Upper Bedford Place. Charles Ashbee recalled one of these
visits . . . and the deference Houghton, by then known as a Keats
scholar, showed to his mother:

The poet politician came to dinner one night late from some debate in
the House of Lords. He was excited and full of fire. It was the literary
side of him that appealed to us, not the political, and I don't remember
what the talk was about. But I do remember how he went down on one
knee to the little mother, called her 'my beautiful lady', and kissed her
hand. She was disturbed at the poetic licence, but my father laughed at
her scruples and said the poet had drunk too well. To me it seemed
perfectly appropriate, especially as she was wearing my favourite dress
of black velvet with a crimson camellia in her black hair. My early read-
ings of Keats are inseparably bound up with this scene, and it was Lord
Houghton that first led me on that search for the immortals.[14]

Between the summer of 1877 and early 1878 neither 'H.S.A.',
'Apis' nor 'Fraxinus' appeared in the columns of *Notes and
Queries*. Why they had fallen silent is not clear. On 8 February
1878 Ashbee resumed his collaboration, sending over his own
name, now embellished with a recently acquired 'F.S.A.' (Fellow
of the Society of Art), an enquiry about George Cruikshank.
Throughout the year and into 1879 some thirteen further entries
appeared, attributed to 'Apis', 'Fraxinus', 'H.S.A.' and 'H. S.
Ashbee' and often relating covertly to the *Centuria Librorum
Absconditorum*, on which he continued hard at work when not in
Paris. On 6 April 1879 his diary records that he 'corrected and
sent to press' the last sheets of the volume. Soon afterwards the
journal, now increasingly sporadic, broke off. It was not resumed
until late the following November.

The format of the *Centuria Librorum Absconditorum* follows
almost exactly that of the *Index*, although the epigraphs now

occupy six pages instead of one, the books are no longer arranged alphabetically but according to subject, and the index is even more comprehensive. Pisanus Fraxi explains in his 'Preliminary Remarks' that, if the previous volume concentrated on 'a few items' – the complete works of Edward Sellon and John Davenport, the *Essay on Women* by John Wilkes and numerous books on flagellation and sodomy – pride of place in the *Centuria* will be afforded to the medical works of the famous German doctor Martin Schurig, who died in 1736 ('Of all the learned physicians or surgeons who have written upon the physical connection of the sexes, no one has treated the subject so thoroughly, or brought together so many curious, interesting and extraordinary details'),[15] books connected with Roman Catholicism, and the erotic drawings and etchings of Thomas Rowlandson.

In his early diary, Ashbee had expressed dislike of the Roman Catholic priesthood while visiting the Continent. Now he detests them. 'Every reflecting mind', he muses, 'must find it difficult to understand how, in the present nineteenth century, a system so false, prurient, and polluted, can still be believed in, can find devotees ready to lay down their lives in its support, and even make converts of men of knowledge, experience, and bright parts.'[16] Loathe Roman Catholicism he may, but in the *Centuria* the confessors' manuals and various accounts of immoral priests, spurious or otherwise, provide him with much pungent material for extracts and analysis. *The Confessional Unmasked*; *The Priest, the Woman and the Confessional*; *Frauds of Romish Monks and Priests*; *The Nunns Complaint Against the Fryars*; *The Awful Disclosures of Maria Monk*; *Reasons Humbly Offer'd for a Law to enact the Castration of Popish Ecclesiastics*; *The Cloisters Laid Open* . . . these are the sort of tawdry works to which Pisanus Fraxi now addresses himself, for hundreds of pages. It is hard to justify the claim, made in the 'Preliminary Remarks', that

in the *Centuria* 'less rubbish will be found' than in the *Index*.[17] The book comes to life only when the author embarks on a lengthy account of *Sodom*, the outrageously ribald play attributed to the Earl of Rochester; provides a detailed list and description of Rowlandson's erotic etchings, or, in the 'Additions' section, launches once more into a lengthy discourse on flagellation. The rest is drudgery all the way.

In the new pages on flagellation, the stress, as before, is on establishing that women enjoy wielding the rod even more than men.[18] 'Women, as I have elsewhere remarked, delight in administering the birch,' insists Pisanus Fraxi, 'and innumerable are the tales of schoolmistresses whipping their pupils, mothers, and especially mothers-in-law their children, and taking grim pleasure in the operation. Indeed women are more cruel and relentless than men, especially to those of their own sex.'[19] As proof, Pisanus Fraxi adduces a statement by the Marquis de Sade, two flagellant plates, an obviously spurious account 'by a gentleman whose name I am not at liberty to divulge, but whose veracity may be relied upon',[20] extracts from two equally ficti- tious accounts 'made by a gentleman who took a special interest in all matters connected with the Rod',[21] and details of two recent English court cases in which women have been accused of cruelty towards their charges. Pisanus Fraxi concludes, 'Evidence there is then, more than sufficient, to show that women take delight in chastising others, that they are more prone to it, and more insa- tiable and obdurate, than the sterner sex.'[22] But the evidence was not 'more than sufficient', as Ashbee well knew.

Ashbee's diary continues to register the surface comings and goings of his life at this time, but never his innermost thoughts or feelings. At the end of November 1879 a typical entry reads:

Returned this morning from Paris, where I have been spending a week, after having been a few days in Brussels. In Paris this time I lunched

with Paul Lacroix ['Le Bibliophile Jacob'] & met at his table Baron Pichon, whom I met some time ago at Turner's here, & M. Reed (?), editor of 'L'Intermédiaire'; dined at Paillet's, & was introduced to M. A. Piet, & others; dined two days ago at Baron Roger Portalis's, met nearly the same company. Was asked to become a member of the Société des Amis des Livres.[23]

Les Amis des Livres was a group of thirty or so manic biblio-philes, some of them interested in erotica. For an Englishman to be invited to become a corresponding member of the company was a considerable honour, and soon Ashbee was attending their dinners regularly. Not only that: he sometimes crossed the Channel solely to be present on such occasions. 'There was only one Englishman capable of such heroism,' Paillet recalled.[24] Ashbee showed his gratitude to his Parisian friends by publish-ing a charming article on their activities in the *Bibliographer*, entitled 'A Dinner of French Bibliophiles'.

In January 1880 a review of the *Index* and the *Centuria*, by Fernand Drujon (a member of Les Amis des Livres), appeared in the inaugural issue of the Parisian journal *Le Livre*, which sported a section on English books. Drujon had been struck by the inordi-nate amount of space devoted by Pisanus Fraxi to flagellation, and commented:

Let us only say that the author declares that *flagellation* is the element of pleasure most appreciated by the English, furnishing, with a special plate in support, the most detailed remarks on the subject. God forbid that we should allow ourselves to criticize the learned author of the *Index* under consideration! We cannot refrain from saying, however, that in his Introduction he has given a great deal of space to this subject – a subject which, in our view, would figure much more opportunely in a manual of ethnography or legal medicine.

Drujon seems to have been in no doubt, reading between the lines, that Pisanus Fraxi, like so many of his countrymen, was afflicted with, or partial to, 'le vice anglais'.[25]

The *Saturday Review* severely upbraided *Le Livre* for pub-
lishing Drujon's review, commenting that, if the editor wished
his journal to circulate in Britain, 'we should recommend him
not in future to insert, under the title of "Bibliography in
England", articles on privately printed catalogues of obscene
books which have no right whatsoever to the title of literature'.
The remark, like the anti-French bias, was typical of the journal
in question.[26]

George Saintsbury, in the *Academy*, was even more offended.
Assuring his readers that he was not one to burn incense before
the shrine of the Reverend Thomas Bowdler, he none the less
insisted:

But when we open an article on English bibliography we do not expect
it to contain an elaborate notice of a catalogue of obscene books, upon
which it seems somebody or other, who has the grace to write under a
pseudonym, has wasted good paper and handsome typography. The
reproach of this sort of thing is already heavy on Continental biblio-
philism. But in England there is absolutely no excuse for it. The French
reviewer himself admits that his pseudonymous muck-raker has gone
out of his way to collect details which have nothing whatever to do with
bibliography.* It is, moreover, a notorious fact (and we can again cite
M. Drujon in our support) that such work in England rarely or never
possesses the slightest literary value. It is simply the product of a dis-
eased imagination, as in Payne Knight's case;† or else of deliberate and
mercenary catering for unhealthy tastes, as in the immense majority of
cases. In neither instance, perhaps – certainly not in the latter – can the
product be considered worthy the attention of the bibliographer.[27]

Ashbee was probably amused to be called 'a pseudonymous
muck-raker', and may have wondered if the authors had any
inkling of the true identity of Pisanus Fraxi.

* I.e., the attention lavished by Pisanus Fraxi on flagellation.
† Richard Payne Knight (1750–1824), author of *An Account of the Worship of Priapus*,
noticed by Ashbee in *ILP*, pp. 3–9.

A week later, on 18 February 1880, he lunched with the Rabelais Club at the Grosvenor Restaurant, finding the gathering 'very slow and un-rabelaisian'. Then he was off once again to Paris, where he complained that London theatres 'were superior in point of comfort'.[28] On 25 February he was present when a bust of Victor Hugo was crowned in the Théâtre Français, and Sarah Bernhardt, whom he greatly admired, recited a eulogy of the great man by the poet François Coppée. On 1 March, still in Paris, he met the editor of *Le Livre*, Octave Uzanne, for the first time, and the following evening (another first encounter) his reviewer Fernand Drujon, with whom he coincided at a dinner given by Les Amis des Livres. Ashbee may have been tickled by the fact that, if Eugène Paillet was a judge, Drujon, author of a *Catalogue des Ouvrages, Écrits et Dessins de toute nature Poursuivis, Supprimés ou Condamnés depuis le 21 Octobre 1814 jusqu'au 31 Juillet 1877, etc.*, was 'head of the *Premier Bureau* at the Paris *Préfecture de Police*'.[29]

By April Ashbee was back in England, riding down to Kent and Sussex with Charles and once more spending a few days with his relatives at Westwood Court. To all appearances he was the epitome of the conventional Victorian gentleman.[30]

On 24 July 1880 Ashbee wrote to Lord Houghton from 1 Coleman Street to commiserate over the latter's loss of a bag or purse in Paris, and to supply him with the names and addresses of some of his bibliophile acquaintances in the French capital: Drujon, Major Ricketts ('do not speak of him to Hankey as they are not friends'), Uzanne, Paillet, Baron Roger Portalis, Paul Lacroix and Hankey's chum Alfred Bégis (who has 'a remarkable collection of documents etc. concerning "Le joli Marquis" de Sade'). Ashbee wished that he could be with Milnes in France, but it was impossible: he was about to go with his family to see the Passion Play at Oberammegau. As a poor substitute, he provided Houghton with the names of two of the employees in the

Paris branch of his business whom his lordship had met recently at Upper Bedford Place: they would be only too delighted to be of service.[31]

Meanwhile, if the *Centuria Librorum Absconditorum* had been receiving some critical attention in France, in England it might not have existed. With one exception. In his book *Rowlandson the Caricaturist* (1880), Ashbee's acquaintance Joseph Grego had this to say about the volume:

A selection of subjects, treated by Rowlandson with more freedom than is consonant with the taste of the latter half of the nineteenth century, is also given by PISANUS FRAXI, in his elaborate and exhaustive work CENTURIA LIBRORUM ABSCONDITORUM (1879). Pisanus Fraxi has set down (pp. 346–398) descriptions of over one hundred and twenty subjects of more or less erotic tendency. The major part of the etchings included by this authority are of necessity inadmissible in the present work, owing to their licentious suggestiveness; but a few of the subjects described in the 'Centuria Librorum Absconditorum', restricted exclusively to social caricatures by Rowlandson, the originals of which may be consulted in the Print Room and Library of the British Museum, are also instanced in the foregoing pages.[32]

Ashbee took note of the allusion to Pisanus Fraxi's efforts on behalf of a Rowlandson practically unmentionable in 1880. And no doubt he was delighted to find the *Centuria* described as an 'elaborate and exhaustive work'.[33]

On 20 October 1880, now in his forty-sixth year, Ashbee set out alone from London on a world tour which was to occupy him until the following July. He had decided to turn his hand to travel writing, and, with a book in view, kept a detailed, almost day-by-day journal of what he did and saw.

The tour took him, successively, to Egypt, India, Ceylon, Penang, Singapore, Java, Siam, Hong Kong, Canton, Shanghai (see plate 4), Peking, Japan and, finally, the United States. The

diary shows that part of the reason for the trip was business: at each port of call, after picking up his mail, Ashbee contacts his local agent, who, after the work is concluded, often acts as his guide to the locality's antiquities, temples and other notable monuments. While few details are provided as to the exact nature of the business done or discussed along the way, the impression is that Charles Lavy and Co. is thriving.

The diary confirms Ashbee as the archetypal confident Victorian. Immensely proud of being British and of the Empire, he is in no doubt as to his country's superiority over all other comers, whether Chinese, Indian, American or anything else. For the Chinese he expresses particular dislike. Dirty and treacherous, a love of birds is 'one of the few pleasant traits in their character'. 'Were such scepticism admitted,' he writes, 'I should almost be inclined to doubt that Adam was the common father of the Chinese and ourselves.' On occasion, when irritated by a 'native', Ashbee is capable of resorting to violence. At the Yung-ho-kung temple in Peking, for example, he has some trouble while trying to spy on the priests at their devotions:

The difficulty we had at every door, the constant & exhorbitant demands of the gate keepers, their insulting demeanour rendered our visit a most disagreable one, & we were glad to get out of the place without having visited all its curiosities. I could not help striking one old man with my riding whip, & was on the point of knocking down another. Dr Gorman* fairly siezed one of the impertinent rascals by the throat.[34]

When Ashbee rewrote this passage back home for an article, he embellished his original account somewhat:

As I was watching these fanatics the gate-keeper stood before me, and with unmistakable gesticulations intimated his order that I should leave

* Ashbee's companion that day.

the place. I was, however, too much interested in the proceedings of the lamas to depart before the termination of their ceremonies. My companions had already left. The janitor's motions became more demonstrative, and it seemed that he was not undisposed to employ force. By this time my interpreter was at my elbow. 'Tell this man', said I, speaking aside to my guide, but looking the Mongol rascal full in the face, and clenching my fist at the same time, 'that if he dares to touch me I will knock him down.'[35]

Intent on gathering material for his book, Ashbee is obsessive about visiting (or, as he says, 'doing') all the local sights, allowing nothing and nobody to deter him, noting down with plodding precision every detail of temples, pagodas and monuments, checking to see what the guidebooks say, and often, not without satisfaction, finding the latter sadly deficient. 'Quote Doolittle, incorrect as to size,' we read on one page. On another, Mr Murray is scorned for not mentioning a building in Bangalore clearly deserving of inclusion.

Ashbee is curious, as one would expect, about the religious beliefs and the customs of the societies he visits, and is intolerant of the Christian missionaries who meddle with them. 'How terrible that we should sully the infantine naiveté of this people by the introduction of our false modesty,' he observes of the Japanese (the one race for whom he expresses admiration), 'and force on them the unnatural restraints and ridiculous prejudices of an overwrought and unnatural civilization.' Since he is writing with the general public in mind, there are only some vague hints concerning oriental sexual mores. In India, he finds some of the carvings and sculptures 'very obscene', 'quite obscene', 'quite indecent' and even 'lewd in the extreme', but enlightens the reader no further. He shows some interest in the Hindu nautch girls, pointing out that they are prostitutes but adding no other details. At Mysore, he professes shock on finding that the raja's throne room contains 'tawdry French engravings and native ones

of the most indecent character'. Two doors to the same chamber boast 'more or less free' Hindu designs, and the guide tells Ashbee that some 'entirely obscene' panels were recently replaced with others 'less objectionable'.[36]

This is Ashbee writing, not Pisanus Fraxi, so he is careful not to suggest that he has derived pleasure from viewing Indian erotic art. His interest in the breasts of the local women, however, keeps breaking through. In Java he finds that 'the women in the towns attach their sarongs above their breasts, and support them by means of these protuberances, in the country they are not so particular and do not hesitate to expose their bosom completely'. At Bangkok, the women 'have good breasts which they seldom cover except when walking out, when they place a strip of cloth over them very gracefully'. In Japan, the 'better class' women 'wear no under linen, and the gown, generally open in front, exposes the bosom to view generally. They never wear stays, and the breasts are generally good, and well formed.' In his 'General Remarks' on Japan, a passage on bathing recalls his remarks on Belgian beach machines in his first, youthful diary:

No reserve is displayed by women in bath houses or open baths, & they do not object to be looked at when naked. Saw 3 women at Kiga in bath. [. . .] Freedom of girls in tea houses, & exposure in baths of those parts of the body which in Europe are usually hidden, must not be looked upon as proof of either immorality or want of modesty. [. . .] Open bathing has been so much a custom from time immemorial that exposure of the body is thought no more of than exposure of face or neck. Much scandalised would be the unsophisticated girls of Japan on seeing ladies with their bosoms systematically laid out at an European court reception, or at the false breasts, dress improvers, or skin tight jackets affected in Paris and London, where the object of the wearers seems to be to exaggerate, or obtrude those part of the person which they suppose excite the desires of the opposite sex. Such indecency or indelicacy cannot be laid to the charge of the daughters of nature of the empire of the rising sun, who, if they innocently allow their bosoms or

legs to be seen in performing their daily avocations, never wilfully or designedly appeal to a man's passions through extravagant or indecent clothing.[37]

On 26 May 1881, in Tokyo, Ashbee notes laconically in his diary, 'After dinner, went out with young Dresser and his friend to see John Kino.' 'This was not a mysterious Japanese citizen,' Guy Langham, Ashbee's grandson, has explained, 'but a strip-tease dance, Japanese version.'[38] Unfortunately, Ashbee adds no details of the performance, which probably took place in the Yoshiwara, Tokyo's famed red-light district, evoked in his 'General Remarks' on Japan:

Yoshiwara is frequented by all Japanese, of whatever class, with scarcely an exception, & it is not uncommon for a Jap lady in conversation to ask a young guest when he was last there, & how he enjoyed himself, as a French lady might enquire of a friend concerning his coffee. At certain seasons, everybody visits the Y., & respectable men conduct their wives & children there to enjoy an evening's dancing & singing. It is in fact looked on like a coffee house, or music hall. There is such an establishment of greater or less extent in every Jap town & village almost. One of the best and largest, perhaps the largest, is the Kuhan Nog at Yokohama, having the expressive sign of Arbor Vitae; singing & dancing every night; three houses, 2 for Europeans & 1 for Japs. In spite of what Griffis says girls from these houses are not infrequently taken as second wives by wealthy Japs, or even as first wives by young men, less well to do.[39]

One or two comments made during his tour reveal that, during the missing years of his journal, Ashbee visited Scandinavia, Malta (which he is reminded of when visiting the island of Enoshima, in Japan), and Italy (a view of the Japanese coast conjures up the Bay of Naples, and there are also allusions to Rome, Milan and gondolas in Venice).

Very little correspondence has come to light from these months, although the diary shows that Ashbee received and

wrote numerous communications during the trip. One exception is the letter he sent to Monckton Milnes from Java on 18 February 1881. It shows that the latter has put him up for membership of the Royal Geographical Society (of which Richard Burton was a founder member):[40]

Dear Lord Houghton,

Although separated from you by so many miles of land and water, I am nevertheless reminded that your kindness has not ceased. My wife writes me that you have proposed my name for the Geographical Society, for which attention accept my thanks. She adds that she has paid the subscription, so that matter is I suppose entirely in order.

You see by the heading of this letter that I am almost in the middle of my intended journey. From here I go to Jahore to see the Maharajah, who has given me an invitation, then to Siam to witness the ceremony of the cremation of the empress, thence to China, and Japan.

I went very thoroughly, for a globe-trotter, through India, especially the south, which is not so much visited as the north, and spent many days and nights in bullock carts. 'Ye gentlemen of England who sit at home at ease,' or take pleasant excursions to the Continent, do not know what travelling is, you must come to the East and experience the heat, dust, and discomfort which every move involves, and then you will know what real travelling is. But I am not going to worry you with a letter of complaints, nor am I going to trouble you with a long epistle describing the wonders I have seen, and which soon make one forget the inconvenience which one experienced in getting to and at them. This must be left, should you wish to hear of my pilgrimage, till my return, when I hope you will let me see you frequently, as I promise not to inflict too many of my adventures upon you.[41]

Having met a few objectionable Americans along his way, Ashbee was predisposed to dislike the United States, and had time to ponder on his forthcoming tribulations during the crossing from Yokohama to San Francisco. On 22 June 1881, shortly after embarking, he wrote to his bibliophile friend Ralph Thomas. He was missing England:

The voyage is of more than a fortnight's duration, out of sight of land the whole way and only an occasional bird or whale visible, so you can understand that one is driven to think of friends at home and to find a relief and pleasure in writing to them. I long to get back to my home again, and trust that in about a month after the arrival of this letter I shall be in London once more.[42]

On 27 June Ashbee landed in San Francisco and, after lunching at the Palace Hotel ('$4 per diem, a very big showy place'), made his way to the Post Office 'where I found many letters, and a telegram announcing birth of a child, death of Barber and Mrs. Nicholson'.* The child was a new son, who died almost immediately afterwards and was buried in the Ashbee family tomb at Kensal Green.[43] Years later the laconic diary entry was to strike Ashbee's family as a demonstration of his selfishness and lack of sensitivity.

Ashbee is struck by the brutal contrast between San Francisco and subtle, enigmatic Japan, and claims to see more prostitutes in a day than in the previous eight months of his voyage. 'I am truly once more within the pale and reach of European vice and progress, power and misery,' he comments. As he makes his way across the continent his worst impressions are confirmed. In America everything is brash, 'smart', tasteless, vulgar, strident, and put 'in as unpleasant a form as possible'. Politeness is considered a waste of valuable time in a society obsessed by the dollar and pervaded by 'want of reverence and respect', where everything 'must be on a vast scale or it is nothing'. American women are pushing, aggressive. 'Nothing for nothing in the U. S. of A.' is the rule, although there is an exception: 'You get nothing for your money.' (Prices he finds outrageous by comparison with London.) As for the blacks, Ashbee detests them almost as much as the Chinese. 'Decidedly these niggers are too much for me,' he

* Alfred Barber, an Ashbee Hamburg relative. Mrs Nicholson remains unidentified.

exclaims after a brush with one in an 'eating car' on the train to the Niagara Falls. 'If you don't let go my arm I'll knock you down,' he tells the waiter. 'No you won't,' the latter replies, grinning full in Ashbee's face. 'What d'yer want?' On another train Ashbee is delighted to find 'no nigger waiters but clean, respectable white girls'. In a New York bank he is distressed when confronted with a sign reading: 'Gentlemen will not smoke, others must not.' 'Surely,' he muses, '"Gentlemen are requested not to smoke" would have been equally effective and less offensive.'

Little wonder, then, that having traversed the States, all Ashbee wanted was to embark as soon as possible for England. He arrived in Liverpool on the morning of 31 July 1881. 'A feeling of delight and of thankfulness passed through me as I sat in the snug corner of a first class carriage rolling up to London,' ends his world trip journal.

Taken as a whole his account makes pretty dreary reading, particularly when buildings and monuments are being listed and described. But in America, despite his dislike of the country, there are moments when the diary suddenly springs to life. Ashbee has frequently complained about not being able to converse properly with the Indians, Chinese, Japanese and so forth because of his ignorance of their languages. In America, mercifully, this is no longer the case. Several episodes recorded in these pages have a sprightly pungency quite lacking in the previous five hundred, and suggest that Ashbee has suddenly become aware of the literary potential of dialogue. At Green River, for instance, he is accosted on the platform by a beggar who tells him he is hungry:

I said are you really in want of bread? I am. Follow me. I took him to the restaurant which I had just quitted & begged the coloured gentleman serving out provisions from behind the bar to give my begging friend a loaf. It was produced. I put down 15 cts & left the bar. From the

1 Henry Spencer Ashbee aged twenty-six.

2 The manager's house at the Hounslow gunpowder mills.
3 The Ashbee ancestral home (the Clockhouse), near Faversham, Kent.

4 Henry Spencer Ashbee in Shanghai, 1881.

5 Richard Monckton Milnes, c.1868.
6 Richard Burton by Frederick Langham, 1872.

7 Joseph Octave Delepierre.
8 James Campbell Reddie, better known as James Campbell.

9 Henry Spencer Ashbee in 1889.

10 Frontispiece and title page to an eighteenth-century edition of
Meibomius' treatise on erotic flagellation.

A
TREATISE
Of the USE of
FLOGGING
In Venereal Affairs:
ALSO
Of the OFFICE of the
LOINS and REINS.

Written to the Famous CHRISTIANUS
CASSIUS, Bishop of *Lubeck,* and Privy-
Councellor to the Duke of *Holstein.*

By JOHN HENRY MEIBOMIUS, M.D.

Made *English* from the *Latin* Original
By a PHYSICIAN.

Delicias pariunt Veneri crudelia Flagra ;
Dum nocet, illa juvat ; dum juvat, ecce nocet.

To which is Added,
A TREATISE of HERMAPHRODITES.

LONDON,

Printed for E. CURLL, in *Fleet-street,* 1718. Price 3 s.
Where may be had,
The CASES of IMPOTENCY; and EUNUCHISM
and ONANISM Display'd, in 7 Vols. Price 18 s.

Paris, 1884

Friday, March 7. Went alone to the
Eden Theatre to see the ballet – Sieba. Very
beautiful, but not so grand, or so
striking as the former one Excelsior. I met
there Uzanne, who had written me the
day before that he was going to the
country, & that he would telegraph to
me should he return before my departure.
I am grieved to find that he is a
humbug like the generality.

Saturday, March 8. Dined at Paillet's
& spent a pleasant evening; present were
Bejis, Blackley, whom I met once before at
Turner's, Paillet's son, & 4 ladies.

London. Monday March 10.

On Sunday I called on Paul Lacroix at
the Bibliothèque de l'Arsenal, & spent a
pleasant hour with him. Lunched with
Janssen, who afterwards walked with me
to Arnold's where I dined. We passed the

11 A page from Ashbee's diary.

contemptuous way in which the beggar eyed the loaf, & the want of alacrity displayed by him in possessing himself of it, I thought his hunger might not be so keen as he had given me to understand. I watched then for his exit & found that he was still loafless. I returned to the bar & found the loaf exactly where the nigger had placed it. So the man has not taken the loaf then I asked. Guess he don't want bread was the reply. You did not I hope give him any part of the money I paid you? No fear, knows them sort o chaps too well. I found my friend still loitering on the platform. Well you did not take the bread after all I said. No he replied an American gentleman can't eat dry bread, wants something to wash it down. Why did you not tell me you wanted a drink, I can hardly offer you that when you say you are hungry. Thanks one never gets in America, it is beneath anyone to be civil or polite, least of all now. I knew this bread dodge in London, but wanted to see whether it was also practised in the unsofisticated States.[44]

Even better is Ashbee's description of arriving in Chicago:

As usual on nearing the station a man came through the cars to 'check' the baggage. Brass checks were given up for luggage in the luggage van, & money paid, but everything which you have with you in the car, you must drag with you. On leaving the depot entrance, well loaded with my hand bags, etc., I was pushed into one of the numerous omnibuses there waiting, & told the man who thus unceremoniously husseled me in, that my destination was Tremont House. No answer, the door was slammed, & I found myself in a vehicle quite full. As well as I could I arranged my bags under my feet, on my lap, etc. & the omnibus drove off. The drive was a long one. Up this street, down that one. Here one person got on, there several, never a word spoken, until at last I was left alone in the omnibus. The man who had husseled me into the omnibus, & whom I took to be the conductor, did not accompany us, & there was no conductor, consequently, no one on whom I could rely, or whom I could remind of where I was going to in case of necessity. Where are you for said the driver to me, turning around on his box & looking in on me through the open window. He was a young man of 18 or 20 years, not Irish, I think. I want to go to Tremont House if you please I replied in the mildest tone possible. We've been there. I am

81

very sorry, I did not notice the house, did you stop before the door?
No, but close by in the same street. Why don't you look out? I have
been looking out, I rejoined timidly, & kept my eyes as much as poss-
ible on both sides of the street, but I assure you I did not see Tremont
House written up, otherwise I should perhaps have ventured to remind
you that I desired to get out there. Uhu! we shall have to go back then.
It seems so. I trust it is not far, for I have been riding long enough.

The horses got a little extra whip, we repassed several streets, which
I thought I recognised for the third time, & at last pulled up before
Tremont House. No conductor to the omnibus, as I before observed,
no porter at hotel, no boots, waiter, or attendant of any kind, so I again
pick up my hand bags, bundle of rugs, umbrella, etc., & march into
the lofty door of the hotel, the perspiration running down my face in
streams. Rather warm observed a gentleman standing in the portal,
whom I took to be the manager of the hotel. Yes I replied one does get
warm in this country where one has constantly to lug about one's own
baggage. Oh he responded drop it, it will get in anyway, somehow. I had
my traps, however, well in hand, so did not accept his advice, but
walked across the hall to the usual desk in front of which I again
dropped them, & made my bow before the stern gentleman presiding
there. The great book was as usual turned round to me to sign without
a word either of greeting or otherwise. I inscribed my name on the line
pointed out to me. Bath? If you please. The stern gentleman, without
any further interrogatory, added a number to my name, handed me a
key, & proceeded with the work which he had been good enough to
suspend in my favour. I took the key, again collected my things, &
looked around me. I knew well enough what I had to do, make my way
to the elevator, but as that machine was not evident, & as this was my
first visit to Tremont House, I was unacquainted with its whereabouts.
A bell sounded from the terrible desk. A coloured man got up from a
bench in the hall where he was sitting talking & laughing with some
companions, and advanced to the desk. The stern gentleman pointed
to me & told the coloured man my number. The coloured man was
good enough to relieve me of my bundle of rugs, which being my third
package & I having only two hands I was struggling with, & beckoned
me with a jerk of his head to follow him. We reached the elevator.

Number – said the dark man to the conductor, & up we went, i.e. the conductor myself & luggage. Here's your floor said the conductor, opening the door to the passage. In which direction is my room if you please? I meekly enquired. Turn to the right.

I did so, & at last managed to find my room, & to get self and baggage safely ensconced there. My portmanteau, which had been handed over in the train to the express man, had not yet arrived, so I sat down, & patiently awaited its arrival. Half an hour elapsed, & I thought I would venture to enquire for it. I went to the bell over which was a printed ticket of instructions: ring once for the Bell-Boy, twice for Ice Water, three times for Fire, four times for Boots, five times for Porter, six times for Chambermaid, seven times for Towels. Now, thought I, how many times have I to ring for luggage? It is well in the States to be careful before you ring the bell, for should you summon the wrong man you will assuredly get a sound raiting. Well, Boots or Porter seem likely men, but I am rather afraid of them, I will try the bell boy, I do not know what his office in the house may be, but he will no doubt tell me what I have to do, & besides he is a boy, & I am not afraid of him, so modestly rang once. No one came. Well there is no help for it, I must trouble boots. 4 pressures on the button, same result. Let me try five; still no one came. Well this is a much frequented house I said to myself, if I stand in the passage a short time, & I may just as well wait there as in my room, a servant will pass sooner or later. I was right in my conjecture. I had waited but a few minutes when a coloured man approached. I beg your pardon, I began, but . . . He did not wait for me to finish my sentence. Why don't you ring? I have been ringing for some time I replied but nobody comes. Well I guess the thing's out of order. What do you want? My luggage. Where do you come from? From the railway. Did you check it? Yes. Well it's all right – you wait. I did wait another half hour, & then plucked up courage to go down & apply to the stern gentleman at the desk. On giving him an exact description of my effects, it was discovered that they had been taken to another room.[45]

Ashbee's intended book on his world tour did not materialize, but his diary served as the basis for four rather pedestrian articles which he fleshed out with quotations from the relevant guide

books and other sources: 'Une Visite à la Bibliothèque de Tanjore' (1881), 'A Ride to Peking' (1881), 'A Sunday at Coney Island' (1882) and the two-part 'The Metropolis of the Manchus' (1882), an exhaustive account of his visit to Peking. While these may have been found interesting at the time, long before the era of mass tourism, they have none of the verve displayed by the diary in passages such as those just quoted.

Back in London, Ashbee resumed work on his final volume of erotic bibliography, the *Catena Librorum Tacendorum* ('String of Books Worthy of Being Silenced'), noting in his diary on 1 February 1882 that he had just sent the first batch of proofs to Gaball, his long-suffering printer. It was to take him three years to see the book through the press, longer than he had anticipated.

During this time he was constantly on the move between London and Paris, noting in his diary details of meetings, dinners, visits to the theatre and so on but, as was his custom, rarely committing anything intimate to paper or giving any indication of his curiosity about sex. One exception comes in his entry for 1 February 1882:

I saw a hermaphrodite, the first I ever saw. Rather a pretty woman, beautiful blue eyes, quite womanly, nose rather masculine, mouth rough and large, teeth bad, complexion good, hair fair, chest & breasts beautiful, form good and quite femenine, lower part of the legs rather bowed & masculine, a French woman, born in Paris, Balzac by name. Or course she is not perfect (male part very complete in appearance, yard very small but the testicles not perforated, female part through which she functions has but a very small opening, only large enough to pass water, not to insert even a quill. Never has the monthly flow, but says she feels pain, slight, periodically). Says she feels pleasure when embraced by either sex, for both she feels a desire which cannot of course be fully satisfied.

As regards his bibliophiliac cronies, there is an occasional

titbit. In March 1882 he lunches in Brussels with the erotica pub-lisher Jean-Jules Gay, son of the bibliographer, and his business partner Mlle H. Doucé, who is about to be married. 'She who hesitates not to publish and sell books of the most objectionable kind', comments Ashbee hypocritically, as if not interested him-self in such productions, 'made, played, the ingénue when the conversation turned on marriage, children, etc.' A few days later in Paris he sees Eugène Paillet, Major Ricketts and Octave Uzanne, afterwards taking the latter and Félicien Rops to visit Frederick Hankey and his erotic treasures. (Uzanne had been disappointed to discover during a visit to London the previous year that Ashbee, 'ce diable d'homme', was away on his world tour, and hence unable to show him his secret library.)[46]

It was probably the last time that Ashbee saw Hankey, who died suddenly in Paris on 8 June 1882.[47] He was buried in Père Lachaise cemetery, and there is a touching letter from his com-panion, Annie, to Monckton Milnes: 'My tears, dear Houghton are blinding me I can write no more – Do come when you pass through Paris to see me and give my love to the Burtons.'[48] Some of Hankey's papers and books now passed into Ashbee's collection.[49]

When in London Ashbee habitually goes for a ride before breakfast and frequents the theatre assiduously, often taking Elizabeth, Frances and Elsa with him. Where plays and operas are concerned, he remains very opinionated indeed (he is more hesitant about his ability as a music critic). Before seeing a new production of *Romeo and Juliet*, he re-reads the play, finding it 'full of incongruities and obscenities'. 'It would appear', he con-tinues, 'that Shakespeare, fearing that his play would not please the better class, endeavoured by means of obscene jokes to gain favour with the pit. The apothecary scene, and the tomb scene are the best – the former is carefully written, the latter really powerful.' Ashbee loathes Henry Irving, who plays Romeo, and

finds his performance abominable. Ellen Terry, though, is deemed a convincing Juliet.

The Tuesday dinners continue unabated. Among the new-comers are the novelist and biographer John Cordy Jeaffreson, who shortly afterwards holds a party to celebrate the forth-coming publication of his book *The Real Lord Byron* (he was nicknamed, as a result, 'The Real Cordy Jeaffreson').[50] 'That really terrible Lady Duffus Hardy was there with her insipid, plain and equally tedious daughter,' Ashbee noted in his diary, his flair for character portrayal coming again to the surface. 'The old rue talks loudly in a hauty patronising manner, not to, but at you about herself, her books (heaven save the mark!), the way she makes (I use the word advisedly) them, etc., always keeping her eyes "en coulisse" right and left to see whether her remarks are not having a distant as well as an immediate effect.'

Ashbee occasionally lunches with Houghton, now 'looking very old, and rather tottery', and every Saturday, as usual, with Robert Samuel Turner at Albany, where, during the holidays, his son Charles sometimes accompanies him in order to be trained in the arts and graces of bibliophilia.[51]

Cordy Jeaffreson is not the only new acquaintance: the ever complaisant Turle, of *Notes and Queries*, has introduced Ashbee to Owen, editor of the *St James's Magazine*, to which, quarrying his diary, he now contributes 'A Ride to Peking' and 'The Metropolis of the Manchus'.

In the early summer of 1882, after an Easter holiday with his family in Ventnor,[52] Ashbee embarked on a campaign of tongue-in-cheek self-promotion in French bibliographical circles (there is no reference to this activity in the diary). On 10 June the following enquiry appeared in the Parisian journal *L'Intermédiaire des chercheurs et curieux*, defined in its subtitle as 'Correspondance littéraire, NOTES and QUERIES français':

Pisanus Fraxi
Who is the English bibliographer who under this pseudonym has published in London, in 1877 and 1879, the following two bibliographical monographs:
 1. Index Librorum prohibitorum;
 2. Centuria Librorum absconditorum, reviewed in 'Le Livre' by
 M. Fernand Drujon (January, March 1880)?

The entry, signed 'A.T.', was followed by another ascribed to the same 'chercheur':

Andréa de Nerciat
What is the name of the author of the *Bibliographie anecdotique et raisonnée de tous les ouvrages d'Andréa de Nerciat*. Londres, 1876, in-12, 64 pp., 150 copies printed?

There is little doubt that 'A.T.' was Ashbee himself. In the following issue of the journal (25 June 1882), he replied to his own query concerning the 'English bibliophile', this time under the guise of 'H.R.T.' ('Athenaeum Club. London'):

Pisanus Fraxi (xv, 322)
This pseudonym stands for Henry Ashbee.

The next stage came in the 25 July 1882 issue of the journal, which provided a splendid panoply of subterfuge and shows us Ashbee at work under three pseudonyms:

Andréa de Nerciat (xv, 322)
The name of the author is hardly important. The brochure proceeds from the press of M. Sluys, otherwise known as Vital-Puissant, who was a pornographic bookseller in Brussels and in full prosperity towards 1876. At about that time there were seizures in Belgium, provoked by the complaints of foreign consuls, and Sluys collapsed. This little pamphlet exalts Puissant's reprints and denigrates those of his competitors. It is interesting only because it provides details of the private lives of the Parisian publishers exiled in Belgium, notably the marriage of M. Poulet, otherwise Malassis. And all of this apropos of Nerciat! Even

the portrait at the front of the work is merely the lithographical *contre-façon* of the etching published by the selfsame Auguste Poulet at the front of his reprint of the *Contes nouveaux*, from the pen of the author of *Felicia*.

THE BURROWER

Pisanus Fraxi (xv, 322, 378)

The person to whom H.R.F. [*sic*] applies, in error, the pseudonym in question has been dead for several years and is buried at Boughton under Blean. He was a good 'Kentish Yeoman', who occupied himself with his horses, his dogs and his farms, but not at all with bibliography.

A MAN OF KENT

– We should not place too much stock on the titles of books, particularly those 'printed for private circulation'. No matter how unfamiliar we are with private or clandestine literature, we know that the titles are often calculated to deceive, and that the town indicated is precisely that where the book has not been published. One might even imagine that the two volumes mentioned; 1. Index librorum prohibitorum; 2. Centuria librorum absconditorum, were not only not printed in the town indicated on their title pages, but that they issued from the same press as 'The Cunnusburgh Library', and indeed a comparison of the typography and the style of these two publications would tend to corroborate such a supposition. There are also sufficient internal indications to destroy the idea that these two volumes were printed other than in America. The wide knowledge of our literature, the accuracy of the details concerning our most private customs, the names of men whose notoriety has hardly gone beyond our frontiers – it all leads one to believe that the author is an American, or that he has lived for a long time among us.

This said, I desist. Since the author has chosen to disguise himself behind the veil of a pseudonym, I do not believe that anyone has a right, at the present moment, to lift that veil. Moreover it is not very opaque for those in the know, and if A.F. [*sic*] decided to visit the United States and frequent our men of letters for a while, he would not have any great difficulty, I think, in solving the problem that intrigues him.

(New-York) PENSYLVAN

– H. S. Ashbee, Esq., rich English businessman from London, with a branch in Paris, in the faubourg Montmartre. He is a member of the Société des Amis du Livre [*sic*], and moreover very affable and helpful. A true gentlemen.

THE BURROWER

The 'note' supplied by 'A MAN OF KENT' shows that Ashbee, as 'H.R.T.', had deliberately identified Pisanus Fraxi as 'Henry Ashbee', not 'Henry Spencer Ashbee', in order to prolong the joke. This Henry Ashbee, one of his uncles, described on his death certificate as 'A Farmer', had indeed shaken off the mortal coil several years earlier, on, precisely, 22 July 1874, aged sixty-six.[53] As 'A MAN OF KENT' stated, he was buried in Boughton under Blean cemetery. As for the lucubrations by 'PENSYLVAN' on the American identity of Pisanus Fraxi, they show Ashbee at his most devious. His knowledge of American erotica was, certainly, considerable, and in the *Catena Librorum Tacendorum* he was to ratify the opinion of 'PENSYLVAN' concerning the productions issued by the 'The Cunnusburgh Library':

The Cunnusburgh Library
Cunnusburgh: Published by the Officers for Members of the Bibliographical Library. 1876. Size of paper 8¼ by 6½, of letter-press 4¾ by 3¼ inches; beautifully printed in various types and colours on sumptuous paper; an erect phallus on the title-pages; printed at New York.[54]

In early August 1882, ever on the go, Ashbee sailed over from Littlehampton to Honfleur with his family, dumped the womenfolk at Houlgate and set off with Charles and one of his friends, Ned Mitchell-Innes, on a walking tour in the region of Caen. On 13 August he made a quick dash up to Paris to see how things were faring at the Rue des Jeûneurs:

Wrote letters all the morning. After lunch called on Bégis, who is now

hunting up documents concerning the Marquis de Sade; had about an hour's conversation concerning 'le joli Marquis'. Bégis is a dry old stick, out of whom little is to be got, although he likes to hear himself talk.

Called afterwards upon Paul Lacroix at the Bibliothèque de l'Arsenal; he opened the door to me himself, & was most pleased to see me. He held forth constantly about books, inventions, etc., stopping himself now and then to say 'Mais, je dois vous écouter!', & going on himself again. However he is pleased to communicate what he knows, & he knows plenty which is worth communicating.[55]

His business completed in Paris, Ashbee hurried down to Rouen to attend the Assumption of the Virgin ceremonies in the cathedral.' 'The singing was fine,' he conceded in his diary, 'but the walk round the church struck me, as do all these Roman Catholic mummeries, as debasing. What an abominable expression on the countenances of all the priests!'[56]

While waiting for Charles and his friend to join him, Ashbee champed at the bit in Rouen: 'I think I never remained so long in a place of the same size without having something to do.' Typically, given his lack of interest in contemporary fiction, there is no allusion to *Madame Bovary*, which clearly he has not read. There is one enlivening incident:

The French are not a polite people although they employ enough polite phrases. The afternoon before I left Rouen, a man, dressed like a gentleman, burst into my room, with the landlady at his heels, hat on head, to demand my room. I had already been bothered by the landlady on this score, & had been changed once already. He wanted to show me his bad leg, etc. I got up & said I would leave, but not the room only, but the hotel altogether, upon which he drew in his horns, & retired. Note. Never to return to the Hotel d'Angleterre.[57]

The tour resumed, Ashbee strode manfully through the rain with the two younger men, grimly determined not to be outdone or to catch a cold (just as he never allowed himself to be seasick);

and, as was his unrelenting custom, logged in his journal the sights, distances, prices and times. On 1 September, while the family stayed on at Houlgate, he returned with Mitchell-Innes to London. They dined at the Thatched House Club, now one of Ashbee's favourite haunts.[58]

Ashbee had apparently assumed that, on leaving Wellington, Charles would join Charles Lavy and Co. But the lad was adamant: he was not cut out for business. His mother agreed vehemently (and Elizabeth Lavy was strong-willed when she chose to take issue). Charles had once made the mistake of visiting his father's premises improperly attired – in a straw hat and flannel trousers, 'an unheard of breach of etiquette'. Henry Spencer had been much offended, and demanded an apology. 'I was made to feel a miserable worm,' recalled Charles, 'to feel as did the man in the nightmare, in Du Maurier's masterpiece, who had to sing the "Lost Chord" before the *élite* of Victorian London – naked all but for his shirt.' The experience had not increased his enthusiasm for a career in the City.[59]

Charles was not yet sure what he wanted to do, though. Publishing seemed a good idea, and his mother did the rounds with him after their holiday in France. One of their last calls was on Ashbee's friend Nicholas Trübner, where they met Charles Kegan Paul.[60] 'Kegan Paul the publisher dined with me for the first time this evening,' noted Ashbee in his diary on 24 November 1882. 'He has been kind to my son Charley, who went to him for a situation.' Instead of a situation, however, Kegan Paul suggested Cambridge. Charles jumped at the idea, and not long afterwards went up to King's College. Henry Spencer, perhaps hoping that his son would enter the business when he came down, apparently gave him £1,000 to see him through his university career. 'Such a sum, after the basic expenses of college life had been paid, would call for care and self-restraint if it were to last out the time,' Charles Ashbee's biographer, Alan

Crawford, has written. 'Perhaps H. S. Ashbee recalled his own
stern and industrious youth, before the cultured leisure of his
middle age.' Ashbee was not one for mollycoddling, certainly,
and probably felt that Charles got enough of that from his
indulgent mother. None the less the sum was not ungenerous.
For Charles, Cambridge was to prove 'the home of poetry and
divine life'.[61]

Ashbee was now back at work on the *Catena Librorum
Tacendorum* and every so often would hurry off an article or
query in French or English, usually bibliographical, to journals
at home or in Paris. Most of these contributions appeared under
his own name, but from time to time, when there was an allusion
to erotica, or he wanted to recommend his own pseudonymous
bibliographies, 'Apis' and 'Fraxinus' were detailed for the job.*

Ashbee's life continued at its habitually hectic pace. At the
beginning of November 1882 Major Ricketts, his enigmatic
Paris crony, was in London, and they spent some time together.[62]
On 24 November he accompanied Elizabeth and Frances to
St James's Hall to hear *Messiah*, recalling that as a young man he
had sung in it himself with much delight. He described 2
December as 'rather a big day'. After seeing the Queen pass
down the Strand to open the new Law Courts, Ashbee took the
1.50 p.m. tidal train for France, and reached Paris at midnight. 'A
lovely day after the fog & wet we have been having, quite queen's
weather,' he noted good-humouredly. In Paris it was the usual
pattern: deliberations, and the occasional social outing, with his
employees at the Rue des Jeûneurs office, Arnold and Janssen;

* A typical example occurred on 16 February 1884 in *Notes and Queries*, when Apis,
raising a question on a subject as harmless as King James's 'Book of Sports', slipped in
the recommendation: 'Consult *The First Century of Scandalous, Malignant Priests*,
London, 1643, *Centuria Librorum Absconditorum*, London, 1879.' What was the latter
and where could it be *consulted*? No further information was provided.

visits to the theatre; attendance at Les Amis des Livres (he found Bégis still obsessed by the Marquis de Sade); bookish chats with Paillet, Drujon and Uzanne. The latter accompanied him to a new café, the 'As de Pique', which had been got up rather too garishly for Ashbee's liking. 'The old woman who showed us around was very quaint, said she was a marquise, not desiring to employ her title, etc.,' he recorded. Afterwards they visited 'a house of a lower order, "Au Perroquet Gris" in the Rue Steinkerque, where we remained half an hour. Returned to Hotel Marguerit 12.30.' Ashbee failed to see Ricketts, but managed to pin down Isidore Liseux, the bookseller and erotica publisher, and another publisher, J. Lemonnyer, who twelve years later was to bring out the first volume of a revised edition of Jules Gay's monumental *Bibliographie des Ouvrages relatifs à l'amour, aux femmes, au mariage*, which had been so important to Ashbee when he began his incursions into the world of 'forbidden literature'. Ashbee seems to have got on well with Lemonnyer. Later he translated some La Fontaine tales for the publisher, who was bringing out a complete edition in English. They included *Imitation d'Anacréon* and *Autre Imitation d'Anacréon*.[63]

Ashbee also called on the bibliophile Paul Lacroix and, as deeply into erotica as ever, went to see Édouard Rouveyre, publisher of Drujon's *Catalogue des Ouvrages, Écrits et Dessins de toute nature Poursuivis, Supprimés ou Condamnés depuis le 21 Octobre 1814 jusqu'au 31 Juillet 1877, etc.*[64]

The Ashbee diaries do not mention any tension between father and son at this time, but we know from Charles that their wildly discrepant views on art were now causing considerable friction in the family. Not least their disagreement over the Pre-Raphaelites. Henry Spencer was adamant: Rossetti and Co. were absolute rubbish and William Morris 'a hopeless philistine'. Charles was mortified by what he considered his father's insensitivity.[65]

A confirmation of Ashbee's dislike of the Pre-Raphaelites comes in his diary on 7 January 1883:

Took Frances to see the exhibition of Old Masters at Burlington House. The collection of John Linnell particularly pleased me, but the Rossettis, the main attraction, I cannot go into raptures about, as is now generally done. It seems to me fortunate for the country that we have not many painters like Rosetti, & that our women are in no way like those which he paints. All his pictures are alike, to me at least, & when one has the opportunity of seeing on the same wall so many of his productions one can judge how limited were his powers, how absolutely a man he was of one idea only. Morbid affectation & unreality applied in one fixed & undeviating manner, skillfully if you will, seems to be the boundary of his powers.

There is little else of interest in Ashbee's diary for 1883 until 29 May, which records his first meeting with Foster Fitzgerald Arbuthnot. The introduction was effected by Edward Bellamy, who unexpectedly brought the orientalist round one afternoon to Charles Lavy and Co. in Coleman Street. As we saw, Ashbee had corresponded with Arbuthnot and and reviewed his and Burton's translation of the *Káma-Shástra; or, The Hindoo Art of Love (Ars Amoris Indica)* at length in the *Index Librorum Prohibitorum*. For years he had been wanting to know him personally. Not surprisingly, they hit it it off famously. That July Arbuthnot invited Ashbee to dine with him at the Richmond Club. Also present were Houghton, Edward Bellamy and John Payne, translator of *The Thousand Nights and a Night* (better known as *The Arabian Nights*). Soon Arbuthnot was attending the Tuesday dinners at Upper Bedford Place, and on at least one occasion Ashbee visited him at Upper House, his home near Guildford.[66]

Knowing Arbuthnot brought Ashbee several steps closer to meeting his hero (in so far as he allowed himself to have one), Richard Burton. But the great occasion would still have to wait for two years.[67]

In June 1883 Ashbee crossed over to Brussels, where he called on Henri Kistemaeckers, yet another purveyor of erotica, who invited him to lunch. Also present were Flammarion, the Paris publisher, and his wife. 'Mrs. K. is a pretty and very pleasant woman,' Ashbee noted in his diary. 'K. rather noisy, and Flammarion an intelligent, rather quiet man, Mme F a zero.' Ashbee also dropped in on Jules Gay's son, Jean-Jules, whom he deemed an 'idiot' (he was to die a few months later), and on another Belgian bookseller and publisher, Auguste Brancart. The latter, who was then thirty-three, had been operating since 1880 in Brussels, where his activities were 'open and above board, with occasional forays into clandestine erotica'.[68] Most of his books were French, but an exception was a reprint in English of *The Mysteries of Venus. A Nuptial Interlude and a Preceptor for Ladies and Gentlemen on their Wedding Eve*[69] (a 'worthless little volume' in Ashbee's view).[70] Soon, as the erotic book trade became more fraught with difficulties in Belgium, Brancart moved to Amsterdam, where Ashbee almost certainly saw him again.[71]

Ashbee had turned forty-nine, and by Victorian standards was now well into middle age. His general health was good, but his eyesight was beginning to play up. 'Bought my first spectacles, or rather eye glasses, "clearers",' he wrote in his diary on 21 September 1883. 'Time is creeping on. The "rotting age" has unfortunately set in.' At the beginning of November he was joined in Paris by an old friend, Alexander Graham, Fellow of the Royal Institute of British Architects and a frequent guest at the Tuesday dinners in Upper Bedford Place. After climbing to the top of Montmartre to see the foundations of the Sacré Coeur, and a visit to the triennial Salon in the Champs-Élysées (Ashbee did not think much of the paintings), they caught an overnight train to Marseilles, bound for Tunisia. The plan (Ashbee always had a plan): to collaborate on a book.[72]

Ashbee kept a detailed journal of their tour, which lasted until mid-December. The pair landed at Algiers, which Henry Spencer found a 'pleasant, picturesque & well ordered town', efficiently run by the French.[73] After visiting Blida, Cherchel, Tipaza and Montebello they took boat to Bejaïa, making their way thence to Kherrata, Sétif, Constantine, Batna, Biskra, Aïn-Beïda, Tebessa, Souk-Ahras and, finally, Tunis. What excited Ashbee most were the Roman ruins in which this part of north Africa abounds and, outside Tunis, the remains of Carthage. The journey over, he and Graham sailed to Leghorn via Sardinia, visited Pisa, Genoa and Milan, and, passing briefly through Switzerland, regained Paris. On 12 December they were back in London.

As was the case with the account of his travels in India, there is hardly any indication in the diary of Ashbee's interest in erotica. One exception is the brief reference to his perusal, in Algiers, of the manuscript of the Shaykh Nefzawi's *The Perfumed Garden.*[74] Another is his description of a 'stomach dance' performed by some Arab girls in a Biskra café. 'It resembles the nauch of India,' he jotted down in his diary, 'but is more gross & indecent.'[75]

Very much his own man, Ashbee had not been entirely at ease with Graham, finding him excessively set in his ways. 'With my present companion I have by dint of restraint, & giving way in all matters, managed to get through without any unpleasantness, or even a cross word,' he wrote, 'but with Alexander Graham I do not at present feel inclined to travel again, he is distant, unsociable, absent, opinionated, uncosmopolitan, wants everything as he gets it in England, is vexed when I enjoy what is not to his taste, & out of humour when anything is not to his liking.'[76]

Despite the unfavourable portrait, Ashbee was to return to Tunisia with Graham. After all, he had to produce his book.

If the *Index Librorum Prohibitorum* had been noticed in France shortly after its appearance, in England it was still all but

unknown. The situation changed marginally when, in its December 1883–May 1884 issue, the *Bibliographer* carried a tongue-in-cheek critique of the book by 'R.T.' – Ashbee's friend Ralph Thomas. The latter did not reveal, naturally, that he himself had corrected the proofs of the work under consideration:

'*Notes on Curious and Uncommon Books*'
The above is the half-title of one of the most 'curious and uncommon books' that I have ever come across, whether looked at, to use the author's own terms, from a 'Bio-, Biblio-, Icono-graphical or critical' point of view.

It is extraordinary to find a work on erotic literature – a subject that is generally tabooed – treated of by a lover of literature and written about by a gentleman in such a manner as to convince the reader that his object is the dissemination of knowledge, and not the gratifying of a prurient curiosity.

The nature of the subject compels the use of well-known and popular words, though such as are not to be found in the most voluminous dictionary of the English language; the author undoubtedly calls a spade a spade.

From the limited and privately printed impression, the work will be very little known. My object in writing about it is to let students know that there exists such a book, to certain of them indispensable, but which nevertheless is not otherwise likely to be brought to their notice.

It is the most important contribution to bibliography, and to the literature of the subject it treats of, that has yet been published; partly because we have long extracts from the books described, often forming analyses of the plots or subjects. The following is the title of it:-

Index librorum prohibitorum: being notes Bio-, Biblio-, Icono-graphical and critical, on curious and uncommon books; by Pisanus Fraxi. [Motto.] London, privately printed, 1877. 4to, pp. xxvi + 542, and contents unpaged. With illustrations. By which it will be seen that the author does not give his name; but he gives us sufficient autobiography to account for this, for he informs us he is not an author by profession, and we have the authority of the leading journal for holding the opinion

that unless a man is an author by profession, the less he avows his connection with literature the better.

The author devoted some years to the acquisition of his material and to his work. He has proceeded upon the true bibliographical but costly principle of never describing a work which he has not seen – which often necessitated visits to foreign libraries. Quite apart from his subject, he has studied bibliography bibliographically, and a most interesting introduction of seventy-six quarto pages evinces that he has given it his enthusiastic attention.

The exhaustive essay on Wilkes' 'Essay' would alone suffice to make the work important; but besides information on like works to be obtained nowhere else, there are a number of original bibliographical notices of authors, publishers, and printers.

As to languages, all seem to come alike to Mr. Fraxi; so that it would really be difficult to say whether he is English, French, German, Italian or Spanish. The book is printed in England, though the frontispiece would appear to contradict this, for it is etched by one Frenchman (M. J. A. Chauvet) and printed by another (M. Delâtre).

It concludes with a list of authorities consulted, extending to nearly forty pages, in which is included most modern biographical and bibliographical works, and an excellent alphabetical and analytical index of upwards of fifty pages in double columns, which has evidently been a labour of love to the author.[77]

Thomas's review, the only one to appear in England, was a courageous act on his part and on that of the *Bibliographer*. Perhaps it needed Ashbee's personal encouragement to persuade both to stick their necks out.

The *Bibliographer*, in fact, was walking on thin ice, for the same issue carried an article by Ashbee on Arbuthnot and Burton's edition of Vatsyayana's *Kama Sutra*, issued, as we saw, under a spoof imprint in 1883. The review was signed 'E. S. Shebsa', an anagram that had the advantage of being both suitably Indian-looking and transparent for those in the know. 'It is assuredly matter for felicitation', the notice began, 'that the

interest taken in matters connected with our Indian empire has of late years greatly increased.' The *Kama Sutra*, 'printed for private circulation, and to the extent of 250 copies only', is 'a treatise on social life and the relations of the sexes' ('Shebsa' casually lets drop that *Kama* means 'pleasure'), and of course, since Hindoo ideas on such subjects 'differ very widely from our own', it 'will not be found acceptable in its entirety to the general reader'. The long description of the sensuously decorated private quarters of a Hindoo 'Citizen' quoted by Ashbee seemed innocuous enough, but the intelligent reader could not fail to grasp that an essential detail had been minimized: the variety of women who shared the couch. Nor could the intelligent reader fail to grasp that the book's publication in English translation constituted a tacit attack on Victorian sexual mores.[78]

On 4 April 1884, almost coinciding with Henry Spencer's fiftieth birthday, the Ashbees moved house, decamping to more spacious quarters at 53 Bedford Square, on the corner of Bloomsbury Street (there is no blue plaque). 'Very uncomfortable and noisy,' Ashbee confided to his diary, 'very sorry to have left the old house at 46 Upper Bedford Place, where I have lived 19 years and enjoyed continuous good health. This house is noisy, the bed rooms specially so; my library is the only tranquil room.'[79]

Ashbee found some solace in his alternative quarters at 4 Gray's Inn Square. On 23 May 1884 he wrote from 1 Coleman Street to Richard Monckton Milnes, whom apparently he had not seen for a while:

Dear Lord Houghton

The friend you enquire about is still in existence, and spends an occasional happy hour in the nook where you once visited him, and where he will always be pleased to receive you, with a few days' notice.[80]

Foreseeing that it would take them some months to put Bedford Square in order, Ashbee decided that, for the first time in many years, the family should stay put in London during the summer and take their holidays later. They did so in November and December, first spending an intense week sightseeing and theatre-going in Paris, where Ashbee also attended to his business, dropped in on J. Lemonnyer and met the illustrator Paul Avril, who soon afterwards designed a bookplate (see p. 1) for him.[81] Then they travelled down to Bordeaux, where Ashbee found the bibliographer Gustave Brunet getting very infirm. (Agnes Ashbee and her mother told Charles that they thought him a 'dirty old bibliophile'.)[82] Brunet had not only reviewed warmly both the *Index Librorum Prohibitorum* and the *Centuria Librorum Absconditorum*, but in 1880 had sold Ashbee an important document, the manuscript of Édouard Tricotel's *Bibliographie érotique*.* No doubt Henry Spencer felt much beholden to the old man.[83]

Biarritz was the Ashbees' final destination, at least for the womenfolk. Charles, held up in Cambridge, promised to join them later. The prospect might not have enthralled him, for on 21 November 1884 his mother wrote to tell him that 'Papa as you know will not make himself sociable [. . .] ridicules every thing and every body and Frances and Elsa follow suit.'[84] A few days later, none the less, Henry Spencer deigned to join the local tennis club.[85]

It did not sound like much fun, but Charles kept his word. On Christmas Day 1884 he accompanied his father on a brief visit down to the Basque town of Fuentarrabía, just on the other side of the border.[86] Then, a few days later, the two set off on a three-week Franco-Spanish round trip that took them to Lourdes, Toulouse, Carcassone, Perpignan, Gerona, Barcelona, Tarragona,

* Now in the British Library at Add. Mss. 38827. A letter from Brunet is inserted at f. 251.

Lérida, Zaragoza, Burgos and thence back to Biarritz.[87] Ashbee's interest in Spain had been rekindled by the scholar Pascual de Gayangos, and he was glad to be back. In Barcelona Charles felt unwell, so Ashbee left him in his room, 'wandered about all day alone', and 'took, as it were, a holiday, seeing no sights, but simply enjoying the delicious sunshine on the Rambla, looking at shops, hunting for books etc.'. In the evening, always the ardent theatre-goer, he saw some *zarzuelas* (comic operettas) at the Teatro Rivas. Next day Charley was better, and together they did 'sightseeing in earnest', the highlights being the cathedral and the beautiful Gothic church of Santa María del Mar.[88] Then they travelled down the coast to Tarragona, where Ashbee conversed with the landlord and his family, 'they talking Catalonian Spanish, I Spanish of a strongly marked English character'.[89] As they travelled towards Zaragoza it became intensely cold, and father and son were glad to get back to France.

Elizabeth and the three girls stayed on self-sufficiently in Biarritz until April, leaving Ashbee to his own devices in London and Paris. 'I have been having a "good time" of it alone in London since I returned from Paris,' he wrote in his diary on 11 February 1884. He had just been to see Charles in Cambridge, and was delighted to be invited to dine at the Dons' Table with Oscar Browning, one of the most engaging Fellows of King's College. No doubt Ashbee was well able to hold his own in such company.[90] The journal shows that when Charles was in London he often accompanied his father to the theatre. It seems that for the moment they were still getting on relatively well together despite their disagreement about art and, increasingly, politics.

For three years Ashbee had been hard at work on the *Catena Librorum Tacendorum*, although the diary makes no further reference to his tribulations after the day in 1882 when he handed

the first batch of proofs to Gaball. On 10 May 1885 he recorded laconically, 'I post tonight the corrected proof of the last sheet of *Catena Librorum Tacendorum*, thank goodness the labour is over, the vol. took me a much longer time than I anticipated and I am sick of it.'

A few weeks later Ashbee at last met Richard Burton (see plate 6), to whom he was introduced by Arbuthnot at the East India Club, 14 St James's Square. Also present at the dinner were Edward Bellamy and Sir Reginald MacDonald. Burton, who was in London to publish the first volume of his carefully annotated translation of *The Book of the Thousand Nights and a Night*, did not disappoint Ashbee. The captain 'impresses one at once as a very remarkable man, whose erudition is as vast as his knowledge of the world and of humanity', he wrote in his diary that night. As for Sir Reginald, he was 'one of the most jovial men imaginable, full of anecdote, and appreciative at the same time of what others say'. After dinner Burton, MacDonald, Bellamy and Arbuthnot accompanied Ashbee to 4 Gray's Inn Square, where it can be safely assumed that Sir Richard, who must have known for some time that Ashbee was Pisanus Fraxi, was suitably astonished by the unique collection of erotica housed in those august chambers. Ashbee was never one to express strong emotion, but one imagines that this June evening must have stuck in his memory as one of the highlights of his life.[91]

On 14 July the Burtons were at Bedford Square to attend Ashbee's Tuesday evening for the first time. Four days later Ashbee's diary records that he has just been with Sir Richard to Chertsey to see Baron de Cosson, 'president of the Kernoozers Club'. Burton and Ashbee returned together to London, no doubt deep in conversation. That August they lost a mutual friend when Richard Monckton Milnes died in Vichy. Ashbee was much upset, remembering that the day before Houghton embarked for France they had dined together. He was 'very jolly

and jovial' on that occasion, although his speech was noticeably unclear. Milnes, Ashbee recalls, had sat opposite Burton, 'and they chaffed each other during the whole of the dinner'. Houghton's death probably came as a more severe blow to Burton than to Ashbee, though, for they had known each other for decades.[92] Unfortunately there seems to be no record of Milnes's impression of Ashbee – nor, for that matter, of Burton's.

Ashbee felt such admiration for Burton's first volume of *The Book of the Thousand Nights and a Night* that he wrote an appreciative and well-informed review of it for *Le Livre*, paying particular attention to Burton's 'admirable preface', from which he quoted liberally. The burden of the notice is one we are familiar with from Ashbee's special pleading in the bibliographies: customs change from country to country, and what is seen as normal in the East (that is, frankness about sex) is considered indecent in the West. It is simply a question of different mores. For Ashbee the great value of Burton's translation is that it is complete and unexpurgated; and he is convinced that, when the publication of the book is finished and readers have had the opportunity to peruse Burton's promised 'Terminal Essay', the work will be seen to mark a turning point in the literary history of the century. The review was one of Ashbee's better critical efforts, and one imagines that it must have pleased Burton. Nor could Sir Richard have been indifferent to the praise of his person:

I may be allowed, I hope, to say a word about the author, who is no doubt less known in France than in England. Captain Burton has belonged to our diplomatic service for many years. He has visited every part of the world; he speaks and writes some twenty languages. The classical literatures of Greece and Rome are as familiar to him as those of modern Europe; but his speciality, his 'dada', if I may use the word, is the literature of the East, particularly of the Arabs. It is among these people, for whom he professes a passion, that he has spent the greater part of his life, knowing how to make himself popular by reading and retelling

the wonderful stories he now brings to us in English translation. But this is not all: Captain Burton has studied the theology of the Mohammedans in Mecca and Medina, and has a doctorate; he knows the Koran better than we know the Bible. It would be difficult, I think, to find anyone more determined to carry out the task he has set himself.[93]

Charles Ashbee, who had now been at Cambridge for three years, was also impressed by Burton, with whom he sometimes coincided at his father's Tuesdays. Sir Richard and his wife made 'a strange uncanny couple', he recalled decades later (his memory apparently tricking him into thinking he was still a boy at the time). With his 'long beard and the cruel scar across his face', Burton, 'a grim splendour of a man', had all the appearance of an Arab sheikh:

Oriental stories, creepy, and if uttered so that we children could not quite hear, went up to heaven unexpurgated with the wine and the tobacco smoke. I always associated him with the drawings of my Dalziel's 'Arabian Nights', he was the Djinn who brought the hatchet and the cord, he was Agib losing his eye, the Barber extracting the bone from the hunch-back's throat, the Fire worshipper that bound Prince Assad, the Bird catcher who snared King Beder, he was Aladdin's Drug merchant, the African magician, King of the Djinns – there was no end to the possible transformations of that appalling beard of his.[94]

By this time Ashbee was deeply interested in another character with a notable beard, Don Quixote. A Cervantes *Iconografía* published at Barcelona in 1879 had fired his enthusiasm,[95] and he was now applying part of his vast energies to collecting the illustrations the novel had inspired throughout Europe. The first indication of this new passion comes in the 22 August 1885 issue of *Notes and Queries*:

Illustrations to 'Don Quixote'
I have the following, and should be pleased to know if they are complete. Twenty-four engravings designed by C. Coypel, 'sold by

G. Vander Gucht', and probably engraved by him, size of plates 12 in. square; twelve engravings and one engraved frontispiece, designed by Henry Alken, engraved by John Zeitter, London, 1831; one engraving entitled 'Don Quixote in his Study', designed by Bonnington, engraved by Sangster, Paris, Giraldon-Bovinet, and Londres, Whittaker & Co., size of engraving 4½ in. by 3¼ in.; one engraving entitled 'Don Quixote in his Study', engraved by B. Lane, no name of artist given, published by S. A. & H. Oddy, 1809, quite different from that last noted; one engraving size 13 in. by 10½ in., representing Sancho tossed in the blanket, without signatures; although the design is by Tresmolier, the engraving seems to be by Vander Gucht, and is very similar to the set first mentioned.

Before long, with the relentless determination he brought to all his activities, Ashbee would be well on the way to forming the finest collection of *Don Quixote* illustrations outside Spain, and probably the best array in the world of editions of the novel.

Meanwhile, at the end of October, and with the arrival of the first copy of the *Catena Librorum Tacendorum* imminent, he again boarded ship for Tunis with Alexander Graham, who had returned to the French protectorate that March.*

The *Catena Librorum Tacendorum* is exactly uniform with the previous two volumes in the trilogy, the only novelty being that this time Pisanus Fraxi has allowed himself the indulgence of including two verse admonitions to fellow erotica adepts and bibliographers, inserted respectively at the beginning and towards the end of the volume. They are not entirely without charm:

* *Travels in Tunisia* states: 'The present volume is the result of three distinct visits to Tunisia – in the winter of 1883 and in the early spring and winter of 1885' (p. i). One of the final chapters in the book indicates that the expedition there recorded (La Calle to El-Kef and Chemtou) took place from 7 to 16 March 1885. Ashbee's diary shows that he was in England at the time.

THE EROTOMANIAC

TO THE READER

Dear brother of the gentle craft,
Collector, student, 'bouquiniste',
Or book-worm, virtuoso daft
As oft unletter'd dolts insist,
For thee I've writ this bulky tome
(And others twain). On topmost shelf
For it I beg a secret home,
Secure from idle, meddling elf,
Who, wanting purpose, vainly pries,
Or maiden green, or artless youth,
Or him who would, Procrustes-wise,
A limit set to search of truth,
And make all letters his own size.
No book exists, however bad,
From which some good may not be had
By him who understands to read.
May this, oh brother, be my meed:
That in thy calm, impartial sight
I may be judged to read aright. P.F.

ON QUOTING AUTHORITIES

Unless you've read it with your eyes
Set nothing down, nor ought [*sic*] surmise.
Imagination leads to lies
In Bibliography. The wise
Know well this golden rule to prize.
But if a beaten path you tread,
(You surely must if much you've read)
And needs must say what has been said,
Give your Authority – be terse –
Quote Author, Title, Chapter, Verse,
That each one to the fountain head
At once and surely may be led,
And read himself what you have read. P.F.

Bibliographical accuracy in the interests of the 'search for truth': this will be the burden of the *Catena* exactly as it was of the two preceding volumes. As before, Pisanus Fraxi justifies his interest in erotica by pointing out that notions of what is decent and what is not are transient, changeable, relative. The acceptable in one place, or at one time, may be found intolerable in, or at, others. 'Modesty is a social convention, a prejudice without substance, a heresy against the religion of Nature' runs one of the epigrams quoted in support. If fiction in general provides a true view of society, it follows, Pisanus Fraxi argues in his 'Preliminary Remarks', that 'immoral and amatory fiction', too, is worthy of scrutiny 'and must unfortunately be acknowledged to contain, *cum grano salis*, a reflection of the manners and vices of the times – of vices to be avoided, guarded against, reformed, but which unquestionably exist, and of which an exact estimate is needful to enable us to cope with them'.[96] As Steven Marcus has written, 'One hardly knows where to lay hold of this sentence, it is such a mess.'[97] A mess, yes, but surely an intentional one? It is Ashbee yet again at his most deliberately devious, the crocodile tears of 'unfortunately', the grain of salt (which, as Marcus points out, delegitimizes the positive assertions that have preceded it) and the cant about avoiding, guarding against and coping with vice all being stock devices in his rhetoric of obfuscation. The *Catena* makes tedious reading, coming alive only when the author analyses the publishing history and contents of Francisco Delicado's *La lozana andaluza* (1528), scrutinizes *Fanny Hill* (in his view the major exception to the rule that British erotic fiction is of poor quality), or returns yet again to his pet subject of flagellation.

The *Catena* confirms that the latter was Ashbee's personal 'lech'. He not only revels in his synopses of flagellant books, as in the previous volumes, but quotes several times from the analyses 'kindly furnished' by a 'brother bibliophile' expert in the field, in

all probability James Campbell Reddie. A volume entitled *Curiosities of Flagellation* gets three dense pages of complaisant analysis from the said collaborator, such prolixity being justified, Pisanus Fraxi asserts unconvincingly, by the fact that the book 'is its author's maiden production'![98] The author in question is William Lazenby, a prolific London-based publisher of erotica specializing in flagellant material, whom Ashbee must surely have known personally.[99]*

But it is Pisanus Fraxi's comments on the notorious *The Mysteries of Verbena House; or, Miss Bellasis Birched for Thieving* that most give him away. The book has generally been attributed to George Augustus Sala, but, since Pisanus Fraxi asserts that it was 'concluded by the gentleman whose notes have already enriched this volume', it seems pretty clear that Campbell had a hand in it. 'After wading through so many dull, insipid, if not absolutely repulsive books on the subject,' reports Pisanus Fraxi enthusiastically, 'it is a relief to alight at last upon one which tact and clever writing render almost readable.' Then comes the following assertion:

I doubt, indeed, whether it were possible for the most talented author to make a really good and attractive book upon flagellation. Of the scant plot which runs through *Verbena House* the most has been made, and the practised writer who originated the story has, by his *savoir faire*, and light and pleasant style, been able to make acceptable, nay even entertaining, that which a lesser proficient, one with less cunning of his craft, would have rendered as flat, tedious, and revolting as are flagellation books generally.[100]

* In his copy of *Le Libertin de qualité* Ashbee wrote 'Lazenby, 1875'. Patrick Kearney comments: 'Presumably the bookseller and secret publisher supplying him this book' (no. 1,209, p. 250). In his working copy of the *Index Librorum Prohibitorum*, preserved in the British Library, Ashbee has added the indication 'D. Cameron of Southampton Buildings, Chancery Lane (formerly Lazenby)' opposite p. 224. Opposite p. 314 he notes: '*The New Epicurean* was reprinted by D. Cameron (Lazenby).'

Read at face value, this may seem reasonable enough. But in the following paragraph we are suddenly catapulted into the realm of sexual fantasy – into the realm of the kinky correspondence columns that every so often erupted in the Victorian popular press:

In *Verbena House* we have a most minute and truthful description of a fashionable Brighton seminary for young ladies, of the present day, and the tale turns upon the corporal punishments administered to the fair inmates.[101]

After providing a detailed résumé of the said punishments, Pisanus Fraxi concludes:

I have already expressed my opinion that *The Mysteries of Verbena House* (at least the first part of it) is one of the best books of its kind, and a truthful picture of what is passing around us; further, I believe the author when he writes: 'I am not narrating fiction, but fact; and throughout the entire story I shall have but very rarely to draw on my imagination.' The merit of the book, however, does not so much lie in the story, or in the descriptions of birchings, as in the digressions, consisting frequently of very judicious strictures on the occult habits of the fair sex, or of disquisitions upon some of their garments as now worn, and sometimes exposed to the gaze of the vulgar.[102]

'Minute and truthful description', 'present day', 'a truthful picture of what is passing around us' . . . It is not surprising that the French reviewers of Pisanus Fraxi's labours perceived that he was peculiarly interested in 'le vice anglais', despite claiming to find flagellant books generally 'revolting'. Challenged, Pisanus Fraxi would no doubt have argued that the extensive coverage given to the subject in his three bibliographies was justified by the fact that flagellant erotica was so prevalent in England (as later researchers such as Peter Mendes have confirmed).[103] But the fact remains that he shows again and again that he himself is far from indifferent to the subject. He knows what he is talking about. And this may prove important later.

*

Ashbee kept a detailed, day-by-day diary of his trip to Tunisia with Alexander Graham, as he had done on their first visit. The two embarked at Marseilles for Bône on 31 October and made their base at Tunis, whence they visited Carthage and other notable remains within striking distance. Then they set off on a hectic fortnight's tour. The main agenda was to visit, describe and sketch the country's principal Roman vestiges. Zaghouan, Oudena, Bou-Chater, Soussa (the ancient Hadrumetum), Msaken, El-Djem (Thysdrus), Mahedia, Sfax, Gabès, Kairouan, Sbeitla (Sufetula), Kasserine (Colonia Scillitana), Sbira, Zanfour, Ain-Hedjah, Dougga, Teboursouk – Ashbee notes with satisfaction that all these places have been seen in the two weeks allotted, thanks to the almost perfect weather conditions prevailing at this time of year. Most of the diary is occupied with the routine logging of facts, measurements, distances between places and the times taken in covering them. This sort of thing:

At 2 we passed a small kooba to the left, and in another quarter of an hour after passing over some entirely ruined Roman remains found ourselves on a desolate plain. At 2.30 we crossed a dry ouied and found Roman remains to left. At 3.30 we passed over barren rocky hills covered with stones, a wild and desolate country, a ruined Roman post on top of a hill to left and a few gourbies in the valley. It was now 4 o'clock.[104]

There is no record of any conversation with Graham, only the indication every so often that the architect has sketched such-and-such a Roman cistern or tomb. When he has a slight fall, Ashbee gives him only one line. They take on a servant–interpreter, but Henry Spencer gets no literary mileage out of him (unlike Sterne in *A Sentimental Journey*, a book he knows, where La Fleur comes wonderfully to life). Just occasionally there is a spark of genuine human interest, though, as when the

two Englishmen drop in on a 'miserable establishment' in Kairouan where four Algerian Jews, two men and two women, are entertaining the company. Ashbee has always had an eye for female dancing:

They were seated cross-legged on a platform at one end of the white-washed room, candles stuck into empty bottles formed the lighting up. Plaintive music as usual. Then one of the women got down from the platform, & danced, the company, some 20 Arabs, sticking coins on her forhead. Played Marseillaise in compliment to us as before, which we stopped. The dance was simple but lewd, putting the corners of 2 handkerchiefs in her mouth so that the ends of each hung over her shoulders, & extending her arms, she jumped up and down, advanced & retired in the small space allotted to her, then advancing to any of the company likely to have coin, she looked at him steadily & amorously & wriggled the middle of her body in a most lascivious manner.[105]

Ashbee's scorn for the Arabs pervades the diary: they are an 'effete race', filthy, 'inherently stupid', fanatical, decadent, uncivilized and, despite Mohammed's injunction, cruel to animals. ('We have suffered, why should they not suffer,' they tell him.) The fact that Tunisia is now a French protectorate, however, means that the traveller is able to go about his business relatively unmolested by the natives (although he and Graham carry revolvers just in case). Ashbee, predictably, is appalled that Britain has currently no stake in Tunisia. The Liberals, of course, are to blame (he is becoming increasingly Tory):

British influence is entirely lost in this country since the Gladstone–Granville rule, even the Italians have managed to preserve those rights which our late rulers threw away. One never meets an Englishman and English beer is not to be procured.[106]

On 6 December 1885, their hectic tour over, Ashbee and Graham embarked at Bône for Marseilles, and were in Paris four

days later. Ashbee saw a play at the Comédie Française, another at the Gymnase, dropped in on Eugène Paillet and was back in London on 12 December. 'Weather cold after Tunis,' he noted laconically, before dropping his journal for a month.

The Last Years (1886–1900)

———

Ashbee was now busily transforming his Tunisian diaries into a book. He painstakingly marshalled relevant material from other sources as he went, obtained the help of his friend Gayangos in compiling a glossary of Arabic terms, and gradually put together a comprehensive bibliography. An entry in *Notes and Queries* on 2 January 1886 shows that his reading on the subject was already considerable, and there were to be appeals to the same journal for more information. Meanwhile his social and professional round maintained its course unabated: frequent cross-Channel trips to see to the Paris house at Rue des Jeûneurs and visit his bibliophile cronies, the Tuesday dinner parties at Bedford Square, concerts and plays in both capitals. With so much competition, *Travels in Tunisia* was to be two years in the making.

Ashbee continued to collect erotica. 'Received of Cameron/ Jany 5, '86,' he pencilled on the inner front pastedown of his copy of *Memoirs of the Life, Public and Private Adventures, of Madame Vestris*.[1] 'Cameron', as we saw, was William Lazenby, a London erotica publisher specializing in flagellation.

The diary was becoming increasingly sporadic. On 10 March 1886 Ashbee records that he has been with Elizabeth and Frances to the inaugural meeting of the Shelley Society, held in the Botany Theatre of University College. For the following month there is only one entry:

On Friday evening April 9, I left London via Harwich for The Hague. Thence I proceeded to Amsterdam where I remained one day. Returned to The Hague where I spent Thursday. Left in the evening and remained Friday in Rotterdam. Returned to London Friday evening via Harwich reaching home Saturday morning April 17.

Why this unexplained trip? Perhaps because the centre of erotica publishing in Europe was now shifting from Brussels to Amsterdam, where, given the more benevolent attitude of the law in Holland, many of the Belgians, both publishers and printers, were setting up shop.[2] Rotterdam was also acquiring importance in the same field.[3] There is no reference in Ashbee's diary to any commercial interests there, so that visit, too, may have had more to do with erotica than business. This is further suggested by the fact that the Private Case at the British Library contains 'a group of three or four Dutch translations of erotic "classics" in the mid-1880s' proceeding from Ashbee's collection and probably printed in that city.[4]

It is almost certain that during his quick dash to Holland Ashbee renewed his acquaintance with the erotica publisher Auguste Brancart, who had moved there in 1884. Brancart had just published a French translation of *An Experimental Lecture on Flagellation*. The inscription in Ashbee's copy,* probably acquired during the visit, reads: 'Published in March, 1886 by Auguste Brancart, Amsterdam. Price 10 fl.'[5] From 1886 Brancart was to issue from Amsterdam 'a stream of clandestine pornographic reprints, first in French and later in English'.[6] Ashbee acquired some twelve of these volumes, another indication of a close relationship with Brancart.[7] Since the latter almost certainly organized the printing of *My Secret Life* (between approximately 1888 and 1894) it may be surmised that, if Ashbee did not write the book, he may well have known from Brancart who did.

* Now in the British Library, P.C. 31.d.29.

Perhaps the visit to Amsterdam was made in order to set up the operation.

In May 1886 Ashbee's diary records another London social event, the inauguration of the Goethe Society, which he attends with Elizabeth and Agnes (Frances is down with chickenpox). Max Müller (first Professor of Comparative Philology at Oxford) reads 'an excellent address'. Oscar Browning is one of the speakers. Music follows the speeches.

Ashbee did not approve much of women's rights, and there were increasing conflicts at home. On 19 June he attended a private view at the Royal Holloway College. 'The College is very beautiful, too beautiful,' he complains, 'for it will tend rather to make the girls who frequent it dissatisfied when they leave it.' A further sign of decadence is that the Society of Antiquaries, of which Ashbee had been elected Compounder in 1877, has decided to admit women to its proceedings. He deigns to take Elizabeth along to a 'conversazione' at the society's premises in Burlington House on 23 June.

The following day he's in Plymouth to see the new 'sailing yacht' belonging to a friend, Coward. On 4 July he dines with Edward Bellamy and Sir Roland Blennerhasset at the Richmond Club. Blennerhasset, like Ashbee, hates and despises Gladstone, and amuses the company with some disparaging anecdotes. Bismarck, according to Blennerhasset, once commented: 'Gladstone stands in the congress of nations hat in hand apologizing for England having been a great nation.' A few days later Ashbee votes for 'Duncan, the conservative candidate' before crossing to Paris where, on 6 July, he has 'rather a slow dinner' with Les Amis des Livres. Back in London he enjoys an altogether more lively evening in Greenwich with Arbuthnot, Richard Burton (now ailing) and Sir Charles Wingfield. They go down by boat, return by train and, still talking animatedly, spend an hour at the Arundel Club. On 20 July Burton, Arbuthnot and Robert

Samuel Turner are among the guests at Bedford Square. For the summer, Ashbee takes the house of his yachting friend Coward at Hurst Wood, near Hastings. They visit all the local places of interest, and stay put until mid-September.

The tension between Ashbee and Charles is building up. On 27 December 1885 the disgruntled son had written in his diary, 'I here enter a solemn protest against paternal indifference and warn myself against *future* intolerance which papas of certain sorts and certain *creeds* tend to fall into.' Now, on 6 September 1886, he notes, 'It is the paternal element that is difficult to deal with.'[8]

Charles had just come down from Cambridge (where he obtained a second class in the historical tripos) and, supported by his adoring mother, had confirmed his decision not to enter the family business. He was now certain that he wanted to be an architect. During the summer he had explored some possibilities in London, staying at Toynbee Hall, the university settlement in the East End devoted to bringing new graduates into contact with the realities of working-class Whitechapel. 'All the idealism of his university days led there,' writes Alan Crawford.[9]

At Cambridge, Charles had lost faith in the 'economic rightness' of the way of life in which he had been reared. 'Liberalism, as I knew it, was a negation,' he wrote later. 'It had no bowels.'

All it wanted to do was to destroy, and it more or less succeeded in destroying the country gentry. It had no constructive policy because it hated labour; such policy as it had it borrowed from the Socialists. Let anything be done, but don't touch the profits of my business, and any increase of wages is nobody's business but the employer's. It is for the employer to regulate wages. You mustn't interfere, and I'll be d...d if I let you. My father, in the 70s and 80s before he veered towards Conservatism, was a very good Liberal, and that was more or less how he stated the Liberal position. He combined this, a sort of d...d if I do attitude, with his hatred of Gladstone.[10]

Ashbee was now well enough known in the French capital to merit an entry in the Larousse *Grand dictionnaire universel du XIXe siècle*.[11] Most if not all of the information was probably supplied by himself. There is no reference to his pseudonymous activities:

ASHBEE (HENRY SPENCER)
English traveller and bibliophile, born at London on 21 April 1834. Like many of his compatriots leading an active life and involved in important business undertakings, M. Ashbee devotes his spare time to literature and collaborates in London on the *Bibliographer*, *Book-lore* and *Notes and Queries*; in France on *L'Intermédiaire des chercheurs et curieux* and *Le Livre*, where he has interesting bibliographical articles as sober in style as they are accurate and well informed. A fervent traveller, M. Ashbee, after having visited almost all the countries of Europe, embarked on a world trip, and his impressions, rapid notes jotted down hurriedly at the time, have appeared in various English 'magazines'. We may mention particularly: *A Ride in* [*sic*] *Peking* (London, 1881); *The Metropolis of the Manchus* (1882); *A Sunday at Coney Island* (1882). He is a member of several literary societies, among them The Society of Antiquaries, The Royal Geographical Society, of London, and Les Amis des Livres, in Paris.

The French were impressed by Ashbee's fluency in their language and by his respect for their culture. In 1882 he had begun to publish erudite notes, in French, on Englishmen who had written in that language, commencing with William Beckford (whose famous novel *Vathek* first appeared in French) and moving on, in 1886, to consider the French compositions of some contemporary English poets. These included Lord Houghton and 'notre grand poète' Algernon Charles Swinburne. Later in the series came such little-known figures as Quintin Crauford, Sir Charles Hanbury Williams and Charles Kensall ('Mela Britannicus'). Naturally, having demonstrated the prowess of the English in French, it occurred to Ashbee to review the efforts of

Frenchmen in English. Jean-Paul Marat (the revolutionary), Voltaire, Octave Delepierre and Pierre Motteux (who also produced a fine English translation of *Don Quixote*) were to receive his learned attentions in the early 1890s. They were hardly exciting, these Anglo-French pieces: solid, bibliographical, packed with detail and notes and only occasionally affording an anecdote or a flash of humour.

An exception is the article on Pierre Motteux, where the Ashbee fascinated by sexual oddities comes closer to the surface. 'Of Motteux's morality the less said the better,' he tells us. 'It seems to have been the reverse of pure.' Motteux's death, characteristically, was 'at once peculiar and mysterious'. On 18 February 1718, it transpires, he went to celebrate his birthday with a 'doxy' in a brothel near St Dane's Church, where he was later found strangled. The investigation seemed to suggest that the death was due 'possibly to negligence rather than premeditation or intended murder'. Negligence? Ashbee proceeds: 'It has been suggested, indeed, by some who have devoted attention to such subjects, that Motteux's death was of a nature impossible to explain here, even were such explanation desirable or profitable.' The allusion to temporary strangulation, or auto-asphyxiation, as a means to erection is obvious. It is a subject Pisanus Fraxi glosses in the *Catena Librorum Tacendorum*.[12]

Ashbee's diary is silent between 6 October 1886 and the end of January 1887, when we find him shuttling once more between London and Paris.[13] On Saturday 26 February 1887 there is an interesting entry:

Returned this afternoon from Brussels, where I went hurriedly last Monday night, both ways via Ostende. Lunched one day with Kistemaeckers, or rather he with me, and heard him talk *much* about himself; his imprisonment, his literary projects, etc., especially his forthcoming journal of scraps of 18th century.

Why did Ashbee go 'hurriedly' to Brussels? The couching of the entry makes it clear that lunching with the erotica publisher Kistemaeckers was incidental. Could the main reason have been to see Auguste Brancart (the latter was Belgian although now resident in Holland, and may have been in Brussels)? Might the visit have had to do with the printing of *My Secret Life*?

Between 9 March and 18 May 1887 Ashbee again allowed his diary to lapse. When he resumes, we learn that he has been in Paris for ten days ('nothing of importance') and that, in London, he has been elected a member of yet another society, the Cocked Hat Club. Then, at the beginning of June, there is bad news:

My dear friend Robert Samuel Turner committed suicide on the 5 Inst. by throwing himself down the ventilating shaft of the Grand Hotel, Brighton. His nephew Benjamin wrote it me the day after, and in today's *Times* there appears a brief account of the Inquest. He was a good friend and a most worthy man, his loss is to be deeply regretted. I saw him several times lately – indeed the very morning of the day he left for Brighton. He told me that he felt as if a mill-stone were on his head and that he should not live long. Such a melancholy termination however of what ought to have been, to all appearances, a happy existence, could not have been foreseen.[14]

Turner's Saturday mornings at the Albany, effervescent with book talk, had become almost a way of life for Ashbee, and are mentioned frequently in his diary. As he pondered on the suicide, he may have recalled that it was in Turner's chambers, almost ten years previously, that he had first met Richard Monckton Milnes (in the presence of Fred Hankey and his mistress). He must have felt the loss of Turner keenly – although the diary entry is characteristically unemotive.

The journal now falls silent again for a month. On 10 July 1887 a stark entry reveals that something is going seriously wrong on the domestic front:

Since my last entry many things of personal interest and of general interest have taken place: The Jubilee Procession I saw with my niece, Mary Barber, from the stage erected by the Thatched House Club – a grander display of the kind I never saw. My Silver Wedding, one of the most unhappy days I ever spent, let me forget it. A visit to Paris of a week immediately afterwards.

What had happened on 27 June to make Ashbee's Silver Wedding one of the most unhappy days in his life? It is impossible to be sure, although, in the light of what took place later, it seems that a bitter argument might have arisen about Charles's refusal to follow in his father's professional footsteps. Ashbee's grandson Guy Langham has written in an unpublished memoir:

In 1887 my Uncle Charley was 24 and had come down from Cambridge; it was just the moment to start him off on a money-spinning career in the City. But Charley was a man whose tastes and abilities were diametrically opposed to such a life. Besides possessing much talent in the fields of Art, and Literature, he was obsessed by what Germans call 'Weltverbesserungswahn' – the Urge to Set the World Aright. He was a follower in the ideas of William Morris and his outlook was socialistic, although I doubt if he was politically minded in any practical way. According to family hearsay, the quarrel between father and son caused a serious division between the parents, as his mother sided with her only son against her husband's plans.[15]

The diary now cuts off until 31 December 1887. 'It requires an effort of resolution to enter up regularly the day's doings,' we read on the last day of the year. 'When one is active all day long one does not care to sit down at night – thoroughly weary – to record those doings. No entry for over 5 months. And yet those five months have been as pregnant as my time generally is.'

The Ashbees, we learn from the diary, spent the summer at Worthing, where some of the Hamburg side of the family, the Robertsons and Scheyers, descended on them to celebrate the

Silver Wedding.* That the atmosphere must have been pretty tense is confirmed by a letter written fifty years later to Guy Langham by Janet Forbes, the wife of Charles Ashbee. She had read Henry Spencer's diary, and commented: '[Your] Uncle Ch. gave me a most ghastly acct. of the Clan Gathering, Scheyers, etc. I believe they all went to the Mikado – and a turquoise bracelet was presented! But things were evidently patched up after that.'[16]

Ashbee goes on to record that at Worthing he laboured over the index and bibliography for *Travels in Tunisia*, which was published in early November. We discover that he has just written an obituary of Robert Samuel Turner for the *Annuaire des Amis des Livres*; that he has made his 'faithful assistant' Arthur Ludewig Petersen a partner in his thriving London house; and that he has been forced to take to spectacles – a sign of age, he has to admit, 'but my general health continues excellent. Indeed I have not known a day's illness since I started in life to my recollection, certainly not since I have been married.'

Travels in Tunisia, illustrated by some fifty phototypes, heliogravures and woodcuts prepared by Alexander Graham, follows Ashbee's journal day by day (with the addition of Graham's account of his March 1885 visit to La Calle, El-Kef and Chemtou). Ashbee had improved the prose of his diary, inserted the necessary erudite references, and ensured that his bad spelling was corrected. The bibliography, Ashbee being Ashbee, was exhaustive – and was later published separately as a monograph (with supplementary material and corrections).

There are some tiny clues in *Travels in Tunisia* to Ashbee's current interests. He refers a few times to the Great Mosque at Córdoba, for example, which he does not do in the diary: further

* William Robertson, an Englishman, was married to Jenny Lavy, one of Elizabeth Lavy's sisters, and Julius Scheyer to another, Caroline (information included in letter from Esther Craseman, one of the Hamburg relatives, to Guy Langham, February 1960; GLA).

proof of his growing interest in Spain (prompted by Pascual de Gayangos and probably also by Graham, who had been there on a sketching tour in 1877).* He indicates that, in his opinion, British women are now receiving 'excessive education' – perhaps he has in mind his own daughters, who were attending the North London Collegiate School, run by the earnestly progressive Frances Mary Buss, a family friend.[17] And, in lamenting the illiteracy of contemporary Tunisia, he slips in an allusion to Burton and Arbuthnot's translation of *The Perfumed Garden*, the manuscript of which he had perused at Algiers in 1883:

The history of literature in Tunis may be recorded as blank. It is true that the Sheik Nefzaoui, who flourished in the sixth century, made it his home, and probably wrote within its walls the very remarkable work on the social and domestic manners of his countrymen, which has lately been introduced to the curious of both Paris and London.[18]

Little could the reader of *Travels in Tunisia* have suspected that the volume in question was a detailed treatise on sex. Nor that, behind the scenes, Henry Spencer Ashbee was now Britain's major authority on erotica.

Ashbee continued to annotate his acquisitions. In his copy of *Rondeaux et Sonnets Galants*, by 'E.D.', he wrote: 'Received from A. Brancart of Amsterdam Dec. 1887. 10 francs. Author Edmond Dumoulin, St. Seurin de Cadourne, Medoc, Gironde, France.'[19] Another recent addition was *The Whippingham Papers*, which included two flagellant poems by Swinburne. The volume was probably produced by his own printer, James Henry Gaball. A pencilled note on the fly-leaf reads: '1½ guineas/250 copies/E. Avery, publisher/Dec. 1887.'[20]

*

* The Drawings Collection of the Royal Institute of British Architects includes a view of Córdoba by Graham (dated 1877) and another of the Giralda at Seville.

On Christmas Day 1887 Ashbee wrote to Richard Burton, who had just returned a book to him and had expressed interest in *Travels in Tunisia*. A further volume of Burton's *Supplementary Nights* had recently gone on sale:

Dear Sir Richard,

The book is back quite safe and sound, I am glad you found it of some little service, I feared you would not be able to pick anything out of it.

You are good enough to ask about my *Travels in Tunisia*. It has passed out of the binder's hands a few days ago and Dulau has instructions to send you a copy, which pray do me the favour to accept. Should you find it worthy of a few lines in any of the journals to which you contribute pray do it that honour.

We are all well and spending our Xmas day quietly at the fireside. In spite of heavy food and comfort (?) we envy you who are free from fogs and no doubt see the sun occasionally.

The last issued vol. of the Supplementary Nights was a fat one, really too much for the money. I suppose you are now nearly at the end of your monster undertaking.

My wife and daughters send their affectionate regards to Lady Burton and yourself (especially Elsa does).

Believe me yours very truly

H. S. Ashbee[21]

It seems that a letter from Burton to Ashbee was already in the post, offering to review *Travels in Tunisia*. On 6 January 1888 Ashbee replied:

My dear Sir Richard

Nothing would please me more than that you should notice the 'Travels in Tunisia', of which I sent a copy at the time to 'The Academy'. If *you* think well of it what more can I desire! What part of it should be brought forward I leave entirely to you. This is what we endeavoured to produce: A truthful, not a funny, book, containing reliable information for future travellers, distances from place to place, accommodation, &c. We described nothing which we did not see,

avoided padding and generalizations. The illustrations are quite truth-ful, and were all taken on the spot, no palm trees where none grow, etc., were added (as in some of Bruce's drawings) to give effect. The photo-graphs, unpublished I believe, are of interiors which we would not have been allowed to sketch, especially of the mosques, or had no time to sketch, and of female costumes. The bibliography is not the first of Tunisia, but is certainly the most complete, and I hope the best arranged, an ordinary traveller need not trouble himself to wade through it, as the *necessary* books are grouped for him in the introduc-tory note. Finally in the Index are given alphabetically the names of every town, ruin, lake, river, mountain etc. mentioned in the book – names both ancient and modern. The colours of the binding – green and red – are those of the prophet.

Next week I go to Berlin for a few days, and on the 26th Inst. I am off for a voyage round South America. Here is my route: Royal Mail to Panama, Quiaquil, Lima, Tacna, Valparaiso, then across the Andes (if I am in time before the passes are closed) to Buenos-Ayres, Monte Video, Rio Grande, Rio de Janeiro, Bahia, etc. Any letters of intro-duction will be welcome.[22]

Burton kept his word and reviewed the book. '*Tunisia* is exactly what it should be [. . .],' he wrote in the *Academy*. 'The two friends distinctly perceived the requirements of the age.' He thought the exhaustive bibliography 'truly valuable'.[23] *The Times* judged *Travels in Tunisia* 'one of the very best books on Tunis' (hardly surprising in view of the lack of competition).[24] There were at least eleven other reviews. The general feeling was that Ashbee and Graham had done a sound job, and that the illustrations were excellent.

Ashbee crossed to Berlin on 14 January 1888. His purpose was to set up a branch of his business in partnership with his rep-resentative there, Janssen, before setting off for South America. They found a suitable place at 7 Werder Strasse. The weather was very cold, and Ashbee noted that all the girls were carrying skates. He saw *Carmen* at the Schauspiele, and was disappointed

along with the rest of the audience when the Emperor failed to turn up as expected. 'It is many years since I was in Berlin,' the diary records. 'I do not remember to have been there since the entrance of the troops after the Franco-German War, the city is much enlarged.' In fact, though, he had spent a few days in Berlin in 1874, and had also passed through in 1880 on the way back from Oberammagau.[25]

Back in London, Ashbee records that Elizabeth and Frances have got up a concert for the English Goethe Society, and that on 22 January he dined with Arbuthnot, Bellamy and another acquaintance at the East India Club, 14 St James's Square. The closing entry in the diary comes on 23 January 1888:

Went down to Faversham, thence to Westwood Court, to see my aunts Kite and Fanny Ashbee, the latter seems to be on her last legs, the former as lively and well as ever. Elizabeth and the three girls accompanied me. Spent a pleasant day. Lovely weather, the dear old aunts both delighted to see me. It was a parting visit before my departure for South America, for which journey I have engaged a berth on board the Orinoco which sails on 26th. Inst.

We know next to nothing about Ashbee's visit to South America: no diary has been discovered, no letters have come to light. Did he make the trip out of mere curiosity? For business reasons? To follow in the footsteps of his father, who had allegedly spent some time in those parts, bringing back, according to Charles Ashbee, a handful of exotic watercolours executed during his visit?[26] Guy Langham, pondering on his grandfather's possible motives for the expedition, recalled that there were family links with South America on the Lavy side. Perhaps this was one of the motivations:

Elizabeth Ashbee's eldest sister, Anne Catherine Lavy, married an English husband, Alfred Barber. They had five sons and two daughters. Two of these sons, named Alfred and Stanley, went to Bolivia where

they had an estate of some kind, in the province of Cochabamba. I remember, when Stanley Barber's wife Juanita, who was a great friend of my mother's, came on a visit to England, hearing with awe that the journey from the coast to their home in Bolivia took three weeks on mule back. This, to a small boy brought up in civilized England, had the authentic ring of Adventure and Exploration, and I found it difficult to picture Juanita Barber, an extremely handsome and soignée young lady, bumping about through the wilds of South America on the back of a mule.[27]

Did Ashbee push inland from Tacna, in southern Peru, to cross into Bolivia and visit the Barbers? It seems likely. But there are no records. What we do know is that, obsessed as he now was with *Don Quixote*, he kept a sharp eye out during his trip for possible South American editions of the novel. With no luck. Three years later he recalled:

When travelling in South America, I sought, in vain, native editions of *Don Quixote*, either of Buenos Ayres, Lima, or Valparaíso. The people of those countries are little given to reading, much less to publishing, and I scarcely met with a copy of the great book, even in an edition of the mother country.[28]

Three days before leaving for South America, Ashbee informed Eugène Paillet that he intended to be away for six months.[29] When he returned to London is not clear. He resurfaced in *Notes and Queries* on 19 January 1889, almost exactly a year later, which suggests that by then he had been in London for some time. He had put on weight (see plate 9).

Ashbee's interest in erotica remained unflagging. A note pencilled in his copy of a volume entitled *La Maison à plaisirs ou La Passion de Gilberte* states that he was sent the book by Kistemaeckers in August 1889.[30] A few months later it was the turn of *Callipyges, ou Les Délices de la verge par E.D., auteur de Jupes troussées*. This time Ashbee's pencilled note reads:

'Received from Amsterdam, Oct. 28 '89'. It seems that the publisher may have been, once again, Auguste Brancart.[31]

On 9 July 1890 Ashbee's daughter Frances was married to a Hastings lawyer, Frederick George Langham, at St George's Church, Bloomsbury.[32] Since Charles, immersed in the activities of the Guild of Handicraft, was no longer living at home, the household was now considerably reduced. At the same time death was continuing to take its toll of Ashbee's circle of erotophiles and bibliomaniacs. John Davenport (1877), James Campbell Reddie (1878), John Doran (1878) Octave Delepierre (1879), William Simpson Potter (1879), Frederick Hankey (1882), Richard Monckton Milnes (1885), Robert Samuel Turner (1887), Jules Gay (1887), Edward Bellamy (1889) and General Studholme Hodgson (1890) were all gone.[33] The latest was Richard Burton, who died in Trieste on 20 October 1890. Ashbee must have been deeply upset by the loss of such an extraordinary friend.[34]

The fame of Ashbee's collection of erotica was growing, as was the knowledge that he and Pisanus Fraxi were one and the same person. In 1890 Octave Uzanne's *Le Livre moderne* published a brief description of the library at Bedford Square, joking that it would refer only to the books Ashbee showed to those who had *not* been introduced to 'his intimate friend and *alter ego* Pisanus Fraxi'. The visitor barred from entrance to Ashbee's 'Enfer', a place that many bibliophiles 'would happily make their Paradise', could gain, the note said, but 'a very incomplete notion' of the treasures contained in his library.[35]

'I'm delighted to think your home troubles are pretty nearly over,' Goldsworthy Lowes Dickinson, one of Charles Ashbee's best friends at Cambridge, wrote to him on 21 May 1891. It seems that Charles may have informed him that his mother was about

to take the astonishing step of moving out of Bedford Square, taking Elsa and Agnes with her.[36]

Charles Ashbee's journals offer no explanation for the traumatic break. Indeed, it is hardly mentioned. He never told his wife Janet and his four daughters what had really happened, and always shied away from talking about his father.[37] In 1939, three years before his own death and twenty after his mother's, he produced a privately printed memoir, *'Grannie': A Victorian Cameo*. It was addressed to his daughters and contained a watered-down version of the separation:

It is at this point in Victorian development that we of the younger generation first became aware of a cleavage, a parting of the ways. The picture I am drawing for you begins to change. My mother moved on, my father stood still. Or shall we say their thought went different ways. With the man was the conventional and superficial machinery of life, with the woman the fundamentals, an instinctive search for realities. She held by them; and a part of her tenacity was to win a wider scope and freedom in thought for herself and her children. The eighties saw a weakening of the 'patria potestas' in the home [. . .] To my father the pre-Raphaelites brought no message; Swinburne was a flood of empty words; Browning a jaw-cracking conundrum; Wagner mere noise, 'the music of the future'; the women of Rossetti and Burne-Jones were likened by him and his crony James Orrock, the painter–dentist, to 'squint-eyed Byzantine saints' [. . .] For my mother it was different. She felt the new influences whenever she touched them, and though she cared little to possess, she loved to feel, whether by way of music, architecture, poetry, painting – but principally music; and when any of her children, as do the young, caught the meaning of a new message, she sprang to it and made it her own [. . .] And so it came that one day she just passed as moving sunlight out of the house, and all her children, believing her to be right, went with her. There was no capriciousness in this action of hers, it was taken from a stern sense of duty and after long thought. She kept clearly fixed in her mind the distinction between the material and the sacramental bond in marriage; the one you might

sever, the other not ... To act after long and careful thought, and, once having decided, never to go back; that was her way [...] She had been a great prize for, apart from her beauty, her dowry had been the partnership in a great house of business. Even after the law of England had been altered* men still could not believe that the change had come in their own homes. They could not believe that a woman might have a life and soul of her own.[38]

Elizabeth Lavy never recanted, and it seems that she destroyed every trace that she could of her relationship with her husband, including all the letters she had received from him over the years. He too appears to have carried out a similarly brutal purge. They were both proud people.

Ever afterwards the family was to speculate on what had been the real reasons for Elizabeth Lavy's decampment. If it was generally accepted that Ashbee's profound disagreements with Charles, in which Elizabeth invariably took her son's part, were the main cause of the rift, Henry Spencer's handling of her marriage portion (as Charles Ashbee intimates) was probably also crucial. Guy Langham has commented:

A hundred years ago, a husband often acquired a complete control over his wife's property by the terms of a marriage settlement, and this seems to have been the case with the Ashbees. Henry Ashbee is said to have used his wife's marriage portion to help in setting up his business in London, which was a branch of his father-in-law's Hamburg Merchant House of Charles Lavy & Co. In return for this investment his wife was paid a fixed rate of interest, perhaps only a modest four per cent or so. This continued through the years while the business grew and prospered and eventually was earning a far higher return on the invested capital than this original fixed rate. The discovery by his wife, presumably communicated by some third party, that she had been underpaid, so to speak, for many years, is said to have been a powerful reason for

* The Married Womens' Property Act, 1870.

the approaching parting of the ways. It is not suggested that she regarded this as an injustice to herself personally, but rather as a deprivation of the opportunity to help her beloved only son in his struggle for independence and the right to live his life in the way he wished, and for which he knew himself to be fitted.[39]

Guy Langham considered that two further factors might have contributed to the separation. First, the alleged discovery by Elizabeth Lavy that her husband had a second, clandestine ménage, a rumour 'very persistent in the family' but never substantiated.[40] Although there was some talk of a widow in Paris, the gossip centred around an English family, the Montaubans, much favoured in Ashbee's will, where Edward Henry Montauban, of 16 Queen Elizabeth Walk, Stoke Newington, is appointed executor and trustee (with Ashbee's partner Arthur Petersen) and apportioned one-fifth of the substantial residuary trust funds. The will provided, moreover, that Edward's sister, Irene Montauban, was to receive £1,000 and that, if she was not of age at Ashbee's decease, the money was to go on trust to her mother, Ellen Mary Jane Montauban.* Was Irene Montauban perhaps Ashbee's illegitimate daughter? It is just possible.

Edward Henry Montauban's birth certificate states that he was born on 3 September 1869 at 44 Milner Square, Islington. His father, Marco Wilhelm Montauban van Swyndregt, was a 'Provision Broker'. His mother was one Ellen Donnelly.[41] Where he went to school is not known, but since he had an MA it can be assumed that he attended Oxford or Cambridge. In the view of Ashbee's descendants, it was Henry Spencer's will that made him a man of substance. Janet Forbes, Charles Ashebee's wife, who was never allowed to meet Henry Spencer, vaguely heard about 'young Montauban, thro' Agnes and Elsa [Charles's

* Ashbee's will is reproduced as an appendix, pp. 235–42.

sisters], as being "in the firm", and with only a very sous-entendre suggestion of anything else'.[42] Mountauban set up a preparatory school, The Hall, in Hampstead, which became 'highly prosperous', and he was a founder of Stowe School. He died on 29 June 1954, and so far as is known never elucidated his relationship with Ashbee.[43]

Another possibility for the separation proposed by Guy Langham is that Elizabeth Lavy discovered about her husband's collection of erotica. 'This, if kept secret for many years, as is supposed,' comments Langham, 'could well have been a very nasty shock to a strictly brought up Victorian lady, on suddenly discovering that her husband had indulged himself in this way.'[44]

It is hard to believe, though, that Elizabeth Lavy had failed to become aware over the years of her husband's obsession with erotica. Another matter would have been her discovery that he had himself compiled three bibliographies of erotic books under such a scatological pseudonym as Pisanus Fraxi. If she ever dipped into them one can imagine that she would have been profoundly upset, particularly by the flagellant material (in the *Index*, as we saw, Ashbee actually makes the point that flagellomania has caused the separation of man and wife).[45] The fact that Elizabeth collaborated with him in preparing the index to his many-volumed, extra-illustrated copy of Nichols's *Literary Anecdotes* means that she must have had pretty free access to the library at Bedford Square (although not, almost certainly, to that housed at 4 Gray's Inn Square).[46] It is not impossible that she might have come across some dubious tome, or papers, inadvertently left lying around by her husband.

As for Charles Ashbee, he must have known by this time that his father was Pisanus Fraxi and the author, in *Notes and Queries*, of the many entries ascribed to 'Apis' and 'Fraxinus'. The fact that Charles himself had published a (witty) item in *Notes and Queries* as early as 1884, when he was nineteen, is relevant.[47] He

had no doubt been encouraged to do so by his father, and presumably often dipped into the journal. Moreover he must have met Henry Frederick Turle, the editor of *Notes and Queries*, at his father's Tuesday dinners, and his successor, Joseph Knight. By 1890 Charles was a luminary of the Arts and Crafts movement, a committed reformer, an idealistic Socialist. He was involved in the intellectual life of London. He was homosexual at a time when the Criminal Law Amendment Act (1885) had made all homosexual acts, and not just sodomy, illegal. He and his homosexual friends, who included Edward Carpenter, must have talked endlessly about the problems involved in trying to lead satisfactory lives. Taking all these circumstances together, how could Charles have failed to discover that his father was Pisanus Fraxi?

Elizabeth Lavy and her only son had a relationship of almost incestuous intensity. It might even be, then, that it was Charles who opened her eyes to the true nature of her husband's secret activities. It is also possible that, when Ashbee discovered that his son was homosexual, he told his wife that he wanted nothing further to do with him, which would have strengthened her determination to leave.

Janet Forbes was fascinated by the unexplained rift, and maintained a correspondence on the subject with Guy Langham in the 1940s and early 1950s. She considered that Elizabeth Lavy's 'growing dislike' of Lord Houghton, allied to her rejection of Henry Spencer's paternalistic views, 'may have thrown her into the camp of Womens' Rights, Ibsen, anti-man, and all the stuff your mother [Frances Ashbee] wisely complains of! [. . .] I am still searching in my mind for a sufficient *reason* for the estrangement and crash, apart from jealousy of his son (which latter may have sent *him* out seeking more amiable ladies).'[48]

Like their mother, Agnes and Elsa held strongly feminist attitudes at the time of the separation. Guy Langham received the following confidence from Janet Forbes:

The legend told *to me* by Agnes or Elsa was in their best *anti-man* style, viz. that H.S.A. had begotten an infant on the eve of his trip round the world (par mégrade, or an 'afterthought'?), and this (boy) had died or was born dead; and the special *vitriolic* remark was that of the cruelty of husbands, even when their wives were on the verge of 'Change of Life', etc., to cohabit!!! All, all TOO, TOO silly, but they evidently believed this (nonsense as I see it!). I consider it was just one of those bad lucks.[49]

Janet Forbes had no illusions about the mother-in-law she acquired as a result of marrying Charles Ashbee. Elizabeth Lavy's 'inordinate adoration' of her only son, she recognized years later, must have been 'quite maddening' to Henry Spencer, and probably made him 'intensely jealous'. Had the second son survived, she surmised, things might have been easier in the household: 'A great pity for [your] Uncle Ch. that he did not live, as it might have drawn off a lot of the terrible mother-clutch and also been something *male* for [your] Uncle Ch. to be FOND OF.'[50]

The only daughter of Charles Ashbee and Janet Forbes to show much interest later in her paternal grandfather was Felicity Jane. In 1960 she read Henry Spencer's three erotic bibliographies when these were reprinted in London by Charles Skilton. Her reaction was enthusiastic, as she reported, with characteristic verve, to Guy Langham:

I don't believe from the way he writes of these things that he was himself much of a pervert, tho' from what I have picked up from Mummie's fairly awful descriptions of Grannie Ashbee, and from Daddy's as near as dammit homosexuality and mother complex, he might well have been drawn to such things by frigidity in his wife. I must confess I am beginning to have a very warm feeling for the old boy, and wouldn't be surprised if his sex 'values' weren't a great deal more normal (and more in tune with the world of today incidentally) than the other members of his family.[51]

*

It seems that on abandoning Bedford Square Elizabeth, Elsa and Agnes first stayed with Charles at Essex House, the Guild of Handicraft's headquarters in the Mile End Road.[52]

The Deed of Separation legalizing the estrangement of Ashbee and his wife was dated 30 January 1893.[53] Unfortunately it has not come to light.[54] Ashbee's will, however, tells us something about it, and shows that it contained a covenant whereby Elizabeth Lavy was to receive an annuity of £500.

Shortly after abandoning Bedford Square, Elizabeth bought a freehold building plot at 37 Cheyne Walk, Chelsea, on her son's advice. On it stood the remains of an old public house, the Magpie and Stump, which had burnt down seven years before. The house that Charles Ashbee built here for his mother (and for his own architectural office, with bedroom attached) appears to have been finished in 1894, and was featured in the May 1895 issue of the *Studio*. If Henry Spencer saw the article, one can imagine that it irritated him greatly to discover that his family was managing to survive without him. The Modernist style of the building would not have been at all to his taste.[55] Agnes, who was now twenty-five, had taken to painting and bookbinding and, perhaps influenced by her surroundings, looked like a Pre-Raphaelite 'stunner' straight out of the Rossettis her father so detested. Elsa, four years her junior, had taken a maths degree at Girton, 'and was now reacting in favour of sports and frivolity'. The house was not without its tensions.[56]

Elizabeth Lavy was to battle on in Cheyne Walk until her death in 1919, at the age of seventy-eight. In her latter years she became, characteristically, an ardent suffragette.[57]

Henry Spencer Ashbee remained in Bedford Square until 1895, when he moved down to Hawkhurst, in Kent. There is no evidence that he ever saw Elizabeth, Charles, Elsa or Agnes again. Only Frances, who had left home in 1890 when she married Frederick George Langham, was allowed access.[58]

Ashbee never forgave his family, and when the time came to make his will he wreaked fearful revenge.

Don Quixote was now Ashbee's principal passion, although he continued to collect erotica.[59] In 'Quelques Illustrateurs de Don Quichotte', published in the *Annales littéraires des bibliophiles contemporains pour 1890*, he had announced that he was compiling an iconography of *Don Quixote*. Similar declarations of intent had followed in *Notes and Queries* in 1892, with requests for information.

On 20 March 1893, two months after the Deed of Separation was drawn up, Ashbee lectured to the Bibliographical Society of London on 'The Iconography of *Don Quixote*'. In the chair was Pascual de Gayangos, who, as Ashbee later acknowledged, had afforded him 'great assistance', some fifteen years earlier, at the outset of his study of Spanish literature.[60] The paper demonstrated that Ashbee was now applying to the iconography of the *Quixote* all the energies formerly devoted to erotica. He had brought with him, for the inspection of his fellow bibliographers, a selection of his treasures.

The lecture suggests that Ashbee had made an unrecorded trip to Spain not long before ('During my last visit to Madrid I had the good fortune to meet with a set of twenty-four copper plates . . .'), and is also interesting for its comments on the possible influence of the *Quixote* on *The Pickwick Papers*, a theme he was to develop in a short paper published in 1899.

In July 1895 Ashbee brought out his *An Iconography of Don Quixote, 1605–1895*, exquisitely produced for the author by the University Press, Aberdeen, and issued by the Bibliographical Society of London. Here again was Ashbee the meticulous, obsessive bibliographer, determined not to let a single item slip through his grasp. He openly acknowledged his debt to the *Iconografía* of the *Quixote* published at Barcelona in 1879 (with

101 plates taken from 60 editions), but insisted that his own work was on 'an entirely different plan'. Which indeed it was. As one would expect from the author of the *Index Librorum Prohibitorum* and the two sequels, the accompanying critical apparatus was of the most punctilious. 'I have endeavoured to render the Table of Editions Noticed and the Index as thorough, complete and exhaustive as possible,' he explains, 'so that by their aid the reader, if he knows but the name of the publisher or place of publication, may find the edition he seeks, or with a knowledge of the artist, engraver, or even the printer, he may be able to identify an engraving be it one only of a set.'[61]

An Iconography of Don Quixote was noticed in the *Revue Hispanique* by a newcomer in Ashbee's life, destined to be a distinguished Hispanist. James Fitzmaurice-Kelly was a Glaswegian of 1857 vintage. 'Catholic and three-parts Irish, he inherited sociability, wit, and sympathy with a profoundly Catholic civilization like that of Spain,' wrote another Spanish scholar, William J. Entwistle.[62] Fitzmaurice-Kelly had learnt French from his maternal grandmother. At school in Kensington a Spanish friend had taught him enough of the language to enable him to work his way through the *Quixote*. 'Love of Cervantes gave him to Spain,' observes Entwistle. In 1885 Fitzmaurice-Kelly was in Andalusia. When he returned to London the following year he began to make a name for himself as an authority on the country, reviewing for the *Spectator*, *Athenaeum* and *Pall Mall Gazette*. In 1892 he published a well-received *Life of Miguel de Cervantes Saavedra*. Presumably it was at this time that he and Ashbee met, their common love of Cervantes laying the basis for what seems to have developed into a friendly relationship.[63]

Fitzmaurice-Kelly's review of Ashbee's *Iconography* was slightly condescending. He felt that the book was overly ambitious and not altogether happily organized. Ashbee had not

discovered much of importance. On the other hand he had 're-arranged and co-ordinated with skilful patience information that lay scattered in obscure corners'. Basically, Fitzmaurice-Kelly said, the work was extremely sound. Ashbee's reaction to the review, which did not appear until 1897, is not known.[64] In 1898 Fitzmaurice-Kelly brought out his remarkable *History of Spanish Literature*, which, perhaps to Ashbee's chagrin, contained no reference to his work on Cervantes. Despite this, the two seem to have remained on good terms, for in his will Ashbee appointed Fitzmaurice-Kelly his literary executor. After Ashbee's death the Hispanist went on to become Gilmour Professor of Spanish at Liverpool University (1909) and Cervantes Professor of Spanish Language and Literature at King's College, London (1916). No documentation has come to light concerning his association with Ashbee. He died in 1923.[65]

The house Ashbee took in Hawkhurst, a village four miles south of Cranbrook, in 1895, was called Fowler's Park. Guy Langham takes up the story:

This house was one he had for some time had his eye on, as the one he would like to live in. He wanted to buy it, but it was not for sale and he had to be content with renting it, and it was not vacant till after the death of a previous tenant in 1894. The name 'Fowler's' evolved from the fact that the place had originally been a Falconry and at its first appearance in the Hundred Rolls of Kent in 1273 it was called 'Fogglere' and later 'Foghler'. It was the home of the Kilburne family in the 17th century. The house, to which Henry Ashbee took such a fancy, was of a size sufficient to qualify it in house agents' language as a Mansion. It had been built, or rebuilt, in about 1814 and was 'improved' in 1869. At the time we are concerned with, the house had 5 or 6 large rooms on the ground floor and 23 bedrooms on two further storeys. There were only 2 bathrooms, but this shortage was compensated for by a 'Baronial Hall' 61 feet by 23 feet, in which the inmates could keep far enough apart to offset the effects of bathroom shortage. The gardens

and park of 25 acres contained a noteworthy collection of beeches, sycamores, and wellingtonias and was screened from the road by a laurel hedge 25 feet thick. All this must have seemed to Henry Ashbee as a highly appropriate setting in which a man of his wealth and culture could spend his last years.[66]

Ashbee installed his first cousin Louisa Maud Ashbee, daughter of his uncle Edward (a papermaker who had died in 1883) to look after him. She was fifteen, and it seems that her presence in the house made some local tongues wag.[67]

Henry Spencer's closest neighbour at Hawkhurst was Major Henry Fothergill, a manic tennis player and keep-fit enthusiast who had put together a collection of exotic birds (emus, rheas, peacocks, unusual ducks) which he took great pride in showing to his visitors. Fothergill kept a diary, and between 1896 and 1898 there are frequent references to Ashbee, who often dropped in to see the birds or play billiards. He was no match for the major ('Ashbee to billiards, can give him half the game'; 'giving Ashbee 40, he made 80 to my 100'; 'Ashbee to billiards, gave him 150 in 300 and beat him'). Ashbee was fond of the major's son, Gerald (later a Catholic priest), and once took him to a steeplechase at Catsfield, near Battle, about ten miles from Hawkhurst. The boy never forgot the outing.[68] On 29 April 1896 Fothergill found Ashbee playing billiards with Edward Montauban, who was down at Fowler's with his sister. It seems that in Henry Spencer's affections he had taken the place of Charles.[69]

On 22 July following Ashbee gave a tea party for some thirty-five guests. Fothergill does not tell us who was in the company, although he makes it clear that Ashbee was at his convivial best. Four days later he was visited by his daughter Frances Mary and her husband, Frederick George Langham, accompanied by their two children, Cecil and Guy. The latter retained only a vague memory of a bearded man. Throughout 1897 Ashbee continued to visit Fothergill assiduously, often bringing friends,

among them, on 8 August, 'Graham' – presumably Alexander Graham, with whom he had collaborated on *Travels in Tunisia*.[70]

One of Ashbee's visitors in 1897 was his nephew Oswald Barber, over from Hamburg, who in 1949 recalled in a letter to Guy Langham (written in German):

I don't know if I ever told you that I was invited by H.S.A. to Hawkhurst for a weekend in the spring of 1897, while I was staying for four weeks with Aunt Elizabeth after my law examination in London. This weekend visit led to my being further invited for a month's stay in August 1897. He and I then became great friends. He was a good forty-five years older than the erstwhile law student, Oswald Barber, but I found that he was a many-sided, well-informed and much-travelled man from whom a twenty-year-old student could hear and learn a great deal. He lived at Hawkhurst like a little king ['wie ein kleiner König'], with carriages, horses, and servants, and, above all, the fabulous library with the famous *Don Quixote* collection which was his chief hobby. Naturally we never talked about Aunt Elizabeth, from whom he had been separated about five years, nor about the antagonism which had existed for years between him and Charley. I knew little enough about it and was not inquisitive. My mother had told me that Aunt Elizabeth and Uncle Harry had lived apart for some years, that there was absolutely no contact between Charley and his father and that Agnes and Elsa lived with their mother.[71]

Ashbee's will shows that he did not abandon London entirely when he removed to Hawkhurst, but kept on his chambers at 4 Gray's Inn Square. He probably went up to town quite often. By this time his business had removed from 1 Coleman Street to 119 and 120 London Wall, and presumably most of the running was done by his partner, Arthur Petersen.

Ashbee was now a highly respected man in the City, a patriarch almost. In 1895 he had been elected Renter Warden of the Curriers Company, in 1896 he became its Upper Warden and for a year from 15 October 1897 he was its Master.[72]

In June 1896, on the strength of his *An Iconography of Don Quixote*, Ashbee was elected a Corresponding Member of the Spanish Royal Academy.[73] On 7 July he wrote (in very competent Castilian) to the Secretary of the Academy, the playwright Manuel Tamayo y Baus, to express his profuse gratitude:

I am profoundly moved and I appreciate extremely the great honour which the Spanish Royal Academy has done me by electing me to corresponding membership of its learned corporation – an honour which will be my pride as long as I live.

From my youth I have diligently studied the noble Castilian language; and Spanish literature, above all the works of the 'Prince of Spanish Intelligences' [Cervantes], has been for me a delight and a distraction from my other occupations. The favour bestowed by the Royal Academy, so benevolent although so little deserved, will stimulate me to continue my studies.

Should the Royal Academy ever need my cooperation in any of its investigations relating to the cultivation of Spanish literature in England, the corporation may make use of me as it will.[74]

On 20 April 1897, the day before Ashbee's sixty-sixth birthday, printing was completed in Paris of the second volume of his friend J. Lemonnyer's monumental reworking of Jules Gay's *Bibliographie des Ouvrages relatifs à l'amour, aux femmes et au mariage*. Gershon Legman has written that Lemonnyer's *magnum opus* remains today 'the principal bibliography of French and Italian erotica. No equivalent work has ever been published wholly devoted to the erotic literature of the English language – the only major language of which this is true.'[75] In Lemonnyer's first volume, published in 1894, he had been lavish in his praise of the *Centuria Librorum Absconditorum*:

It is impossible to be more scrupulous or conscientious than is our author in the description of the works he notices, his rule being to discuss only those volumes he has seen and handled; he is not frightened to give long quotations from the most striking passages of the works

under review, always in the original language of the author. But where Pisanus Fraxi becomes a marvellous bibliographer is in the innumerable footnotes that occur throughout the book, full of curious information drawn from collections, newspapers, catalogues, etc.[76]

Turning to the *Index Librorum Prohibitorum*, Lemonnyer now terms Pisanus Fraxi 'one of England's most distinguished bibliographers'. The book, by its very nature, cannot easily be openly circulated in France, he tells his readers; it is a 'catalogue raisonné' of works that have fallen foul of the law – or may well do so soon. Lemonnyer has been struck by the 'remarkable introduction' in which the author, reviewing the dominant erotic tastes of each European country, concludes that 'the element of pleasure most appreciated by the English' is flagellation. Pisanus Fraxi has furnished, with a plate in support, 'the most detailed explanations possible on the subject'.[77] This comment sounds familiar: as Ashbee must have realized, Lemonnyer is drawing almost word for word, without acknowledgement, on Fernand Drujon's review of the *Index* and the *Centuria* published seven years earlier in *Le Livre*.[78]

At some point in the 1890s the young German sexologist Iwan Bloch (1872-1922), perhaps alerted by Lemonnyer's comments on Pisanus Fraxi, got in touch with Ashbee. Bloch was working on his *Das Geschlechtsleben in England. Mit besonderer Beziehung auf London* ('Sexual Life in England. With Special Reference to London'), which was published under the pseudonym of Eugen Dühren in 1901-3 and drew heavily on Pisanus Fraxi's three bibliographies. He apprised Ashbee of the project, promising not to reveal his true identity. 'That you have no intention of associating my name with P.F., I am thankful,' Ashbee wrote to him. '*That must never be done.*'[79] It is not clear if Bloch met Ashbee, and his description of the bibliographer, 'ein auffallend schöner Mann mit einem sehr sympathischen Gesicht' ('a very handsome man with a most friendly appearance'), may derive

from one of his bookplates.[80] According to Legman, Bloch was so impressed by Ashbee's injunction not to indentify him as Pisanus Fraxi that he continued to keep the secret a dozen years after Ashbee's death, still referring to him only as 'Fraxi' in the second edition of his work, now entitled *Englische Sitten-geschichte* (Berlin, 1912).[81]

No doubt stimulated by his election to the Spanish Royal Academy, Ashbee visited Spain during the winter of 1897–98. We know very little about the trip except that it included a visit to Cadiz in February 1898. There he had 'the honour of an interview' with one Adolfo de Castro, who in 1848 had perpetrated a magnificent literary hoax by bringing out an allegedly unknown text by Cervantes, *El buscapié*, in defence of the first part of *Don Quixote*. As a considerable hoaxer himself, meeting Adolfo de Castro, 'now full of years and literary honour', was a source of great enjoyment to Ashbee, who was delighted to find that the old man 'willingly permitted a chat and a laugh over his innocent imposture'. Back in England, Ashbee tried to discover who had been responsible for translating the Spaniards's little deception into English.[82]

Ashbee had himself indulged in a recent bit of 'innocent imposture'. On 10 March 1898, in *L'Intermédiaire des chercheurs et curieux,* 'X' replied to a request for information about Henry Spencer Ashbee:[83]

This remarkable man is gifted, as a writer, with a precision and a tact fairly unusual; author of *A Ride to Peking* (not *in* Peking) as well as of the very interesting book on the Manchus (not *Manchers*). To the works mentioned he has recently added other contributions to geographical and historical literature. *Travels in Tunisia*, published in 1887. Lond: Dulau & Co., 8° in collaboration with Alexander Graham, author of the engravings. This very carefully produced book was followed by *A Biblio-graphy of Tunisia from the earliest times to the end of 1888*: same publishers 8° 1889. This work took him an infinite amount of labour and is of

positive value to the amateurs of the history of this ancient part of Africa.

His most recent publication is *An Iconography of Don Quixote*, London: specially printed for The Bibliographical Society, July 1885, 4° illustrated, not sold commercially. The readers of Cervantes will find therein all they need, and everything that has been published up to now, from the first edition onwards, in Spanish, French or English. He is a learned, practical and patient man; he is not frightened of involving himself in the most arduous undertakings, and owes his success to his talent and his perseverence.[84]

Can there be any doubt that 'X' is Ashbee? 'He owes his success to his talent and to his perserverance': Ashbee had not been to university, but, thanks to his business acumen and to his tenacity in the field of bibliography, both conventional and profane, he had been accepted by figures of the status of Houghton and Richard Burton, and was equally welcome in Paris and in London. He was a corresponding member of the Spanish Royal Academy. He was rich. Why not blow his own trumpet a little? Perhaps it helped to offset the breakdown of his marriage, and the loss of three of his children, particularly his son.

That September Charles married Janet Forbes, the daughter of a businessman. The wedding was celebrated at Seal Church, near Sevenoaks. Guy Langham, then four, was a page boy. It had been a long-drawn-out, tortuous and tormented courtship, with constant doubts on both sides. 'Ever since she had decided to marry him she had been wondering whether it was the right decision. The whole thing was so definitely *not* overwhelming. She became quite ill with worry,' writes Alan Crawford, Charles Ashbee's biographer. The wedding night, spent at Essex House, was not a success. Janet tossed and turned in her bed, wondering what was going to happen. Nothing did. Charles undressed in the next room. 'In his flannel night clothes he looked unfamiliar somehow. He got into his own bed, smiled at her reassuringly, and blew out the light.'[85]

Two months later Ashbee *père* was back in London to give a lecture to the Bibliographical Society, entitled 'Some Books about Cervantes'. He was as enthusiastic about Cervantes as ever, but no longer just about the illustrations to *Don Quixote*: the novel itself had been engaging his close attention, as well as Cervantes's other literary productions. No critic (Ashbee is by instinct a classifier, a tabulator), he had none the less grasped that *Don Quixote* signalled a revolution in the art of fiction. And it is clear, too, that he has carefully read all the English translations of Cervantes's masterpiece, as well as those of the *Exemplary Novels*.[86]

Ashbee had not relinquished his search for Cervantes illustrations. On 21 January 1899 he announced in *Notes and Queries* that he was preparing a continuation of *An Iconography of Don Quixote* 'in which the other works of Cervantes are to be similarly treated'. One quails at the thought of the labours this would have involved. During the year the *Revue Hispanique* published his article 'Don Quixote and Pickwick'. Developing an idea first sketched out in 1893, Ashbee now feels sure that Dickens's novel owes an unacknowledged debt to *Don Quixote*. The reasoning is weak enough: both books 'were written with a purpose, both inaugurate a new departure in the field of fiction'; and both include interpolated stories. It is not brilliant literary criticism, but it confirms that Ashbee has been thinking for some years about novel-writing.

Ashbee was also planning a dictionary of all the books in which *Don Quixote* had been mentioned[87] and, not content with his Cervantes projects, had conceived the idea of compiling a work on everything ever written in French by Englishmen.[88] An obsession with tabulation, allied to a compulsive need for thoroughness and accuracy, was clearly a major driving force in his character.

*

In the winter of 1899–1900 Ashbee set off for Spain. With no diary and no correspondence to go on, we know hardly anything about what he did there, or where he went. According to his friend Eugène Paillet, he also intended visiting Morocco, but it seems he never got there. 'He left us brimful of life and health,' wrote Paillet. 'It was to be his last trip. In Burgos he was afflicted with a heart disease that nothing could have allowed us to foresee, and he had to return to England as quickly as possible.'[89]

Ashbee recovered sufficiently to prepare and deliver a paper, 'Don Quixote and British Art', in London on 28 April 1900. It was his last public appearance. Ralph Thomas was shocked by his decline:

Little, indeed, did the friends who gathered round him at the Royal Society of British Artists to hear his lecture on 'Don Quixote', on 28 April, imagine it would be for the last time. He was fearfully changed, and told me he had received 'his first serious warning', to which, by-the-by, he would not pay attention, but continued to go out and about when totally unfit.[90]

The lecture was Ashbee's final tribute to Cervantes. On a table were displayed some of his treasures, 'copies of most of the editions of *Don Quixote* and of other books containing engravings'. The main point made in the lecture was that England had been 'first and foremost among nations, not even excepting Spain, in promoting the cult of Cervantes'. Ashbee had borrowed the adjective 'Cervantick' from *Tristram Shandy* (one of his favourite books) and had invented 'Cervantophile'. Hamlet and Don Quixote, he felt, were 'the two most remarkable monomaniacs of fiction', and *Don Quixote* 'perhaps the greatest satirical romance ever penned'. He noted how 'the qualities of the Knight unfold themselves as the narrative proceeds, and the Quixote of the second part becomes a philosopher rather than a monomaniac'; and made the point that, if Avellaneda had not

brought out his imitation of the novel, Cervantes might never have finished his own Part Two. *Don Quixote* he proclaimed a 'work of profound philosophy'.[91]

Ashbee died at Fowler's Park on 29 July 1900 in the presence of his cousin Louisa Maud Ashbee.[92] Only a week before he had written to a fellow member of the Ex Libris Society (of which he had been Vice President), asking for help in the location of Cervantes plates, and enclosing a copy of his lecture 'Don Quixote and British Art'.[93] A signed copy of the lecture, dated 'July 1900', went to a Spanish scholar, Ramón León Mainez, author of a book on Saint Theresa of Avila, and is now in the Biblioteca Nacional at Madrid.[94] There is further evidence that Cervantes was with Ashbee until the very end: shortly after his death, the Honorary Secretary of the Bibliographical Society (of which he was a founder member) revealed that Ashbee had told him of his plans to extend his iconographical studies to the other works of Cervantes.[95]

Ashbee's death certificate states that the cause of decease was 'myocarditis and cirrhosis of the liver, 7 or more months, syncope minutes only'. One of his obituaries put it slightly differently: 'He was attacked by congestion of the lungs, then came heart trouble, liver and kidney complaints, and finally dropsy.'[96] He was cremated at Woking Cemetery, according to his wishes, on 1 August.[97] And on 2 August, perhaps contrary to them, his ashes were placed in the family tomb at Kensal Green.[98] 'Carefully, however, as he seems to have considered everything, here he made an omission,' wrote Ralph Thomas in December 1900, 'for he did not provide that the ashes should not be kept; probably he did not know that it was necessary.'[99]

A scattering of obituaries appeared in the London newspapers. It fell to the lot of *The Times* to let the cat out of the bag. Ashbee, 'a well known City merchant', had achieved a considerable reputation as a book collector and bibliographer:

His most important, though perhaps least known, compilation was an exhaustive account of curious and out-of-the-way books, entitled 'Index Librorum', etc., and was privately printed in three volumes between 1877 and 1885 under the pseudonym of 'Pisanus Fraxi'.[100]

So much for Ashbee's injunction to Iwan Bloch. The revelation may have come as something of a shock to Ashbee's family and to some of his associates. The *Athenaeum*, whose editor, McColl, Ashbee had met socially, made no mention of the latter's authorship of the erotic bibliographies, and put the emphasis on his contribution to Cervantes studies. His death, it said, removed 'one more name from the short list of our Spanish scholars'.[101] A fortnight later, in an appreciative obituary in *Notes and Queries*, Ralph Thomas also avoided the subject of the bibliographies, although there was a teasing allusion to Ashbee's collection of 'top-shelf' literature: he had 'left his books (including those which will never appear in the catalogue) and prints to the British Museum'. An editorial note to the obituary, appended between square brackets, was more forthright, and quotes Lemonnyer in support:

Under the name Pisanus Fraxi he wrote, we have always understood, some bibliographies of literary *kruptadia*,* which are now scarce and highly priced. These comprise the 'Centuria Librorum Absconditorum', the 'Index Librorum Prohibitorum' and the 'Catena Librorum Tacendorum', privately printed. Of these works the 'Bibliographie des Ouvrages relatifs à l'Amour, etc.,' quatrième édition, says: 'Il est impossible d'être plus minutieux et plus consciencieux, etc.'[102]

A reader soon took issue with the editor's attribution of the bibliographies to Ashbee. 'This appears hardly consistent with Mr. Ashbee's statement in a note on an "Essay on Women" (5th S. vii.409),' he wrote.[103] In the said 'statement', Ashbee, writing

* *Kruptadia*: neologism from the Greek for 'hidden'.

as 'H.S.A.', had quoted from the *Index Librorum Prohibitorum* immediately after its publication in 1877, without any indication that he was the author.[104] In December Ralph Thomas wrote to the journal to put the record straight:

The note on the 'Essay on Woman' is a little bit of literary deception; the fact of his leaving out the name of the author of the 'Index Librorum' seems to show me it was written by him, as it undoubtedly was. Any one else would have given it, namely, Pisanus Fraxi – some play upon his own name?[105]

Some play upon his own name indeed!

Ashbee's estate was valued at almost £63,000, some £1.22m. in today's terms.

The principal beneficiaries were Ashbee's business partner, Arthur Petersen, and his cousin Louisa Maud Ashbee, who had looked after him at Fowler's Park. His wife and children were passed over completely in favour of his grandchildren (with the exception of his daughter Frances, who got a consolation prize in the Ashbee Folio Bible, which contained the family pedigree). There were substantial legacies to persons of whom Ashbee's immediate relatives knew little or nothing, particularly the Montaubans, the rumoured 'second family'.

Arthur Petersen and Edward Henry Montauban were appointed Executors and Trustees of Ashbee's estate. His cousin Edith Blaxland and Irene Montauban, Edward's sister, got £1,000 each. Louisa Maud Ashbee received £1,000 plus all Ashbee's 'carriages carts garden implements horses dogs cats poultry furniture and wine spirits household goods ornaments and curios not otherwise disposed of' in the will, as well as the use of the family tomb in Kensal Green that had formerly belonged to Henry Spencer's father Robert. All Ashbee's engravings went to the Trustees of the British Museum. His

employees Reick, Maskell and MacGregor Rogers got £1,000 each. Another employee, Atkins, £500 if still working for Ashbee at the time of the latter's death. His servants were to receive £100 each if they had been in his employment for more than two years at the time of his death.

All Ashbee's antiquities and curiosities in glass, earthenware, metal and other materials from Cyprus, Egypt, Peru and other countries, or such of them as they might consider useful, were to be proposed to the Trustees of the British Museum. In the event of their rejecting them, or any of them, they were to be offered to the Trustees of the South Kensington Museum upon similar terms. Any of the antiquities and curiosities rejected both by the Trustees of the British Museum and by those of the South Kensington Museum were to sink into the residuary estate. Ashbee's oil paintings and watercolour drawings were left to the English Nation, the Trustees being enjoined to select some London location for them, preferably the National Gallery or the Victoria and Albert Museum; those refused were to fall into his residuary estate.

Ashbee's watch and chain, personal jewellery, ivory-headed walking stick and writing desk he left to his 'dear friend' Charles Cordery Graham. To the Bibliographical Society of London he bequeathed all copies, whether in their possession or his, of *An Iconography of Don Quixote*, 'together with all engraved copper plates electros printers ornaments and all other things used to illustrate the said Iconography'. (This was an indication of how proud Ashbee was of this book, which had led to his election as Corresponding Member of the Spanish Royal Academy.) To the Hispanist James Fitzmaurice-Kelly he left all his manuscripts or unpublished writings, with the petition to publish them should they prove to be of sufficient interest (they did not). Fitzmaurice-Kelly was to receive £1,000 for his trouble. Alexander Graham got 100 books or single volumes of books from Ashbee's library.

All the other works were left to the British Museum and were to be known as the 'Ashbee Collection', a small label bearing the two words to be placed in each volume. The Museum was empowered to distribute at its discretion among the public libraries of the United Kingdom any books of which it already had a copy. The authorities were further authorized 'to destroy any book of which they already possess a copy and which they do not deem it expedient to send out of the Museum' (an obvious allusion to the erotica). The testator desired that in addition to the 'Ashbee Collection' label, one of his bookplates should be placed in each volume, except in those which the Museum considered should be 'withheld from the General Public'. To this end he also bequeathed to the Museum the original plates.

The Arundel Club (one of Ashbee's favourite haunts in London, as the diaries show) was to get any engravings left by the testator on the premises. Then came the nasty, humiliating clauses:

I DIRECT my Trustees to pay the sum of £500 per annum (provided for in manner hereinafter appearing) to the Trustees for the time being of the Deed of Separation dated the 30th day of January 1893 in the manner provided by such Deed in satisfaction of the covenant therein contained and from and after the decease or second marriage of my Wife whichever shall first happen. I DIRECT that my Trustees shall set apart out of my residuary Trust funds such a sum as will when invested in securities authorised by Law for trust funds produce the yearly income of £312 and shall stand possessed of such yearly income IN TRUST to make to all or any of my daughters a weekly allowance of 40/- in case they or any one or more of them shall personally apply to my Trustees for the same such weekly allowance to commence from the date of such application or respective applications but my Trustees shall not pay to any of my said Daughters the sum of 40/- per week unless such personal application be made and they or she shall to the satisfaction of my Trustees prove that through accident sickness or other reasonable cause they or she are or is in indigent circumstances and unable to obtain a livelihood and that they or she are or is not living

with my Son Charles Robert Ashbee and from and after the decease of
one of my said daughters one third of the capital producing such yearly
income of £312 shall fall into my residuary estate and from and after the
decease of another of my said daughters another third part of the said
capital shall fall into my residuary estate and from and after the decease
of all my daughters the whole of the said capital shall fall into my resid-
uary estate I DECLARE that the granting or withholding to all or any one
or more of my said daughters of the said weekly allowance shall be in
the absolute discretion of my Trustees and they shall if they think fit
discontinue the said weekly allowances without being called upon to
justify such discontinuance . . .

Having disposed of Ashbee's daughters, with the repellent
proviso concerning Charles, the will then apportions £5,000
each to the Worshipful Company of Curriers (of which Ashbee
has recently been Master) and to the Worshipful Company of
Armourers and Brasiers, with indications as to the use to be
made thereof. The Curriers also get some silver articles –
Ashbee's kettle and stand, coffee pot, milk jug, cream jug and
teapot (all of them 'large').

As regards his partnership, the Trustees were instructed to
settle all Ashbee's accounts and to quantify his capital and prof-
its at the day of his death. His share and interest in the business
was bequeathed to Arthur Petersen, along with any of his books
and engravings found on the firm's premises.

The Trustees were enjoined to call in the residue, convert it into
money and invest it in trust funds. Two-fifths of the resultant
income was to go to Petersen during his life and, on his death, to the
children of Ashbee's daughter Frances Ashbee and Frederick George
Langham. Another two-fifths was to go to Louisa Maud Ashbee
on the same terms as those laid down for Arthur Petersen. The
remaining fifth portion of the income was to go to Edward Henry
Montauban on the same terms. Some further provisions followed
concerning Ashbee's business and the payments covenanted

under the Deed of Separation. Then came Ashbee's final request: 'I desire to be cremated in as inexpensive manner as possible I do not wish any mourning worn for me or other demonstration made nor do I desire that any monument whatever be erected to my memory'.

The reaction of Ashbee's immediate family must have been one of stupor and indignation. Janet Forbes later gave Guy Langham a fascinating snippet of information:

Strangely, and I can't think why, H.S.A. went to my father's lawyer, Dr H. Owen, to make said will. Possibly he was ashamed to employ his own lawyer? But Dr O (who told my father this) *refused* to draw up such a document, and said to H.S.A., 'I am afraid you will have to get someone else to draw up your will for you.'[106]

The press gave considerable coverage to the will. The account that appeared in the *Daily News*, under the heading 'A Remarkable Testament', was the most sensational:

By his will, of the 28th June last, Mr. Henry Spencer Ashbee, of Fowler's Park, Hawkhurst, and of 119 and 120, London Wall, F.S.A., a great traveller, and a book collector and bibliographer, who died on 29th July last, aged 66 years, leaving personal estate valued at £62,989 15s. 2d., bequeathed to his executors £312 a year to allow to each of his daughters 40s. a week on her application for it, if she shall not be then living with a relation whom he named, and if the executors shall be satisfied that such daughter, owing to illness, infirmity, or other circumstances, is unable to earn her own livelihood . . .[107]*

The British Museum, informed of the bequest on 6 August 1900 by Ashbee's solicitors, Kennedy, Hughes, and Ponsonby,[108] found itself in something of a quandary. The Trustees pointed out that the will made it clear the Museum must take all or

* The account given by the *Daily Telegraph* (26 September 1900, p. 6) is almost identical but omits all reference to Ashbee's wife.

nothing. So rich was the Cervantes collection, which included 384 editions of *Don Quixote* alone,[109] so unique were some of the other items, that there could be no question of rejecting the bequest out of hand despite the presence of the erotica. But what to do about the latter?

The first step was a preliminary report to the Trustees drawn up G. K. Fortescue of the Museum's Department of Printed Books. After describing the conventional elements in the collection it continued:

There are also about 1000 books in 1600 vols. (exclusive of duplicates) of an erotic or obscene character. These include numbers of early editions of the works of Sade, Andréa de Nerciat, together with [. . .] the 'Elegantiae Latinae Sermonis' published with the name of Johann Meursius, works by, or attributed to, Mirabeau and other books of a detestable character of some historical or bibliographical interest and of much pecuniary value. Mr. Fortescue begs to recommend that the books of this class be placed in the 'private cases' where their inspection by the readers may be subject to the same rigorous restrictions as the other books thus treated [. . .] With regard to the duplicates of obscene books, Mr. Fortescue has been through the whole collection and has placed in six boxes the duplicate copies together with a quantity of offensive matter which is of no value or interest and which could not possibly be distributed. He asks permission of the Trustees to destroy the contents of these boxes, in acceding to the terms of Mr. Ashbee's will, which can be done on the premises.[110]

Peter Mendes has pointed out that, in the last sentence, the phrase 'in acceding to the terms of Mr. Ashbee's will' has been crossed out.[111] The reason, almost certainly, is that Fortescue, on consulting the will again, discovered that, while it explicitly authorizes the Trustees 'to destroy any book of which they already possess a copy and which they do not deem it expedient to send out of the Museum', it certainly does not give them the right to destroy any 'offensive matter which is of no value and

could not possibly be distributed'. In the definitive version of the report, dated 27 October 1900, the entire passage from 'With regard to the duplicates of obscene books' down to 'which can be done on the premises' was suppressed and the following one substituted:

With regard to the collection of obscene books Mr. Fortescue has gone through the whole of them and has packed in six boxes the duplicate copies. He asks the permission of the Trustees to destroy them.[112]

On 10 November 1900 the Trustees approved the Fortescue report and recommended 'acceptance of the literary works; also of certain books of an erotic character to be kept especially locked up, and destruction of certain duplicates as sanctioned by Mr. Ashbee's will'.[113] Peter Mendes has come to the conclusion that, along with the 'duplicates', the British Museum authorities destroyed the greater part of Ashbee's collection of 'poorly produced, illustrated pornographic fiction (particularly in English) of the nineteenth century', perhaps some hundred items. Many of these books, he points out, had belonged to Ashbee's friend James Campbell Reddie. The loss to research is definitive because often no other copies of the works are known to have been preserved.[114] If they indeed carried out such destruction (which conjures up the purging by fire of Don Quixote's library) the British Museum authorities might have felt themselves morally upheld by Ashbee's estranged son. When Charles was invited to the Museum's vaults in December 1901 to choose books for Essex House, he wrote in his diary:

Going through the library the other day at the Museum where it had been collected for cataloguing before distribution, was like reviewing an army of ghosts – 'Si, parva licet' – like the ghosts in the witch's cave that never ended. Here were all the books that my father had collected with a refined bibliomania and my grandfather before him over a period of some 70 years. They contained too all one's own childhood, and

every link in the past that had made an impression. The British Museum, Mr. Fortescue told me, had kept some 8,000 volumes of which it had no duplicates, and let us hope will destroy a certain number which can be of no service to anyone on this earth.[115]

It can be added, finally, that the British Museum Trustees declined 'the classical portion' of the antiquities included in the bequest; selected several ancient Peruvian vases and other objects collected by Ashbee from that country; accepted some engravings; and, as regards the Egyptian antiquities, regretted that they 'did not include any object desirable for the Museum'.[116]

On 2 October 1900 a detailed report on the Ashbee British Museum bequest, clearly based on inside information, appeared in the *Daily Chronicle*. It did not do full justice to the erotica, but it followed the lead given by *The Times* in establishing that Ashbee and Pisanus Fraxi were one and the same person:

The bequest of the late Henry Spencer Ashbee of his beautiful library to the British Museum is one of the choicest 'windfalls' which our great national collection of books has received in modern times. Mr. Ashbee, who died at Hawkhurst, Kent, on July 29, was an ideal book-collector, an accomplished antiquary, and a linguist of considerable attainments – three things which are rarely found in the circle of City magnates. For many years Mr. Ashbee was senior partner in the firm of Charles Lavy and Co., of Coleman-street; he was a member of several City companies, and had been Master of at least one; he had travelled extensively in India, China, Japan, Tunis, Algeria, Egypt,* North and South America, whilst nearly every part of Europe was as familiar to him as England. He was a rich man, and nearly all his life he had been an inveterate book-collector, and the associate of book-collectors, in Paris as well as in London.

Mr. Ashbee's library comprises many thousands of volumes, nearly

* A trip by Ashbee to Egypt has not been substantiated. Perhaps one took place during the silent years of his diary (1858–73).

every one of which is handsomely bound by one or other eminent binder, for a shabbily-coated volume was to him an abomination. He was in the rare circumstance of being able to purchase almost whatever he wanted. Perhaps his most valuable collection, from a literary and artistic point of view, is that [of] the editions of 'Don Quixote', of which he compiled an 'Iconography', 1895, which was the result of many years' labour and enterprise in various parts of the Old and New Worlds. But another very interesting book in the collection is the extra-illustrated copy of Nichols's 'Literary Anecdotes', which is extended from nine to thirty-four volumes by the addition of upwards of 5,000 portraits, views, etc. A very large number of Mr. Ashbee's books will never be found entered in the General Catalogue, for of what is generally known as 'top-shelf' literature he had a unique collection, and of this he privately printed an exhaustive bibliography between 1877 and 1885, under the pseudonym of 'Pisanus Fraxi', a compilation which is itself very rare.

So far as the British Museum is concerned, the great value of the Ashbee library will lie in the section of French books, printed chiefly in small numbers for the members of several short-lived 'bibliophile' clubs. These books rarely appear in the market, and the funds of the British Museum do not allow the authorities to indulge in 'luxuries'. Now, however, Mr. Ashbee's bequest renders the Museum not only complete in this respect, but far ahead of any other public library. Not only this, but Mr. Ashbee had several of these exquisitely-produced books specially illustrated, commissioning eminent French book-illustrators to execute a given number of drawings in water-colours, etc., and having these original designs bound up with the book which they illustrate. For instance, the copy of 'Les Contes Rémois' (1885), by the Comte de Chevigné, the best work of its kind since La Fontaine, is in this way extra-illustrated by a number of pen-and-ink drawings by M. Chauvet, each poem having a charming little illustration. One of Mr. Ashbee's most enviable rarities is a copy of Sainte-Beuve's 'Livre d'Amour', bound up with the same author's 'Portraits des Femmes'; the former volume was suppressed by the author almost as soon as it was printed; the Ashbee copy contains the author's own corrections, and

thus a rare book is rendered unique. In Marat, the revolutionist, Mr. Ashbee took a keen interest, and wrote, in French, a most interesting pamphlet on his career in England, and collected some rare literature by and relating to him.

Chodowiecki, the Cruikshank of Germany, was an especial favourite of Mr. Ashbee, who probably possessed, in books or otherwise, nearly everything done by this prolific artist, including a translation of 'Clarissa Harlowe', translated by Le Tourneur, in 1785, and one of 'Tristram Shandy', 1769. Only a catalogue could do justice to the richness of the Ashbee bequest, for the 'unique' and very rare books may in this collection be numbered by hundreds. Many, of course, are already in the British Museum, and having regard to the congested condition of our national library it seems a pity that the bequest should be tantamount to accepting all or none. But there can be no manner of doubt about the decision of the trustees.[117]

On 9 November the nature of Ashbee's bequest to the Victoria and Albert Museum became known. It confirmed that Henry Spencer had no time for the Pre-Raphaelites:

The paintings bequeathed by the late Henry Spencer Ashbee, F.S.A., are now exhibited in the Picture Galleries of the Museum at South Kensington. The collection, which comprises two hundred and four works, mainly consists of water-colour paintings, including early works by such men as J. R. Cozens, William Payne, Thomas Hearne, J. M. W. Turner, R.A., H. Edridge, A.R.A., T. Rowlandson, John Varley, R. P. Bonington, George Chambers, David Cox, Samuel Prout, William Hunt, P. De Wint, W. Clarkson Stanfield, R.A., and George Cattermole. Among the more modern works are drawings by Sir John Gilbert, R.A., H. G. Hine, Carl Haag, E. M. Wimperis, T. Sidney Cooper, R.A., Charles Green, J. Pulleylove, and Sir James Linton. There are also fifty water-colour drawings by L. P. Cassas for 'Voyage Pittoresque et Historique de l'Istrie et Dalmatie', published at Paris in 1802. The oil paintings include works by Sir A. W. Callcott, R.A., G. S. Newton, R.A., A. V. Copley Fielding, John Linnell, Sir. John Gilbert, R.A., and T. Sidney Cooper, R.A.[118]

Ralph Thomas, Ashbee's old friend, was outraged by the contents of the will. At the beginning of November 1900 a certain F. Marcham had expressed the view in *Notes and Queries* that the Ashbee bequest was 'an example of public spirit too little followed'.[119] Thomas did not agree:

I am sorry that what Mr. Marcham looks upon as public spirit was the result of lamentable family disagreements. I refrained from making any allusion to them, but the comments in the press seem to render it desirable. The fullest extract from his will was in the *Daily News*, 26 September. I think I never saw a will that seemed to me to do every-thing it ought not to such an extent as this one. It seems to me that there are no circumstances whatever which should allow parents entirely to disinherit their children. However, it is not forbidden in England, though it is in other countries. I do not think a man ought even to be allowed to pass over his children in favour of his grandchildren. By the trusts in Ashbee's will the dead hands will (or may) rule the land for seventy years to come.[120]

The subject of the will was rarely brought up by the family afterwards. Guy Langham was not told about his forthcoming share, and discovered with amazement and delight, on reaching his majority in January 1915, that wicked old Henry Spencer had actually left him some funds.[121] Mary Elizabeth, Charles Ashbee's daughter, once commented ruefully how 'disgusting' it was to think that her grandfather's lovely watercolours, instead of gracing the Victoria and Albert, could have been hanging on all their walls. No doubt because, their inherent merits aside, they were worth a lot of money.[122]

There was a tiny, if poignant, postscript to the stir caused by Ashbee's will. Charles Ashbee refers in *'Grannie'* to a portrait of the family done by Sir James Linton, one of Henry Spencer's favourite artists. This watercolour, entitled *A Gentleman Seated in his Library*, was sold at Christie's on 30 March 1901 (Lot 26) to an unidentified 'Mr. Atkins'. Today its whereabouts are

unknown. Who put it up for sale so soon after Ashbee's demise? Christie's cannot help, but it seems reasonable to conclude that it was Henry Spencer's own immediate family. Perhaps, having been cut out of the will, they could not bear to retain this token of past happiness. It went for five guineas.[123]

That same year, 1901, the *Dictionary of National Biography*, following the forthright lead given by *The Times* a few days after Ashbee's death, stated that the latter 'formed an unrivalled assortment of Kruptadia' and was the author, under the pseudonym of Pisanus Fraxi, of *Index Librorum Prohibitorum*, *Centuria Librorum Absconditorum* and *Catena Librorum Tacendorum*. 'Not only is the work the first of its kind in England,' wrote T.S. (Thomas Seccombe), 'but as a guide to the arcana of the subject it far excels the better known "Bibliographie des principaux ouvrages relatifs à l'amour" (Brussels, 1864, 6 vols.) of Jules Gay.' Coming in such an authoritative publication, there could henceforth be no doubt about Ashbee's authorship of the three bibliographies signed by Pisanus Fraxi.[124]

None the less, some of the English learned journals, noticing Ashbee's death, preferred to ignore his activities in the field of erotica. The *Ex Libris Journal*, for example, breathed not a word, informing its readers that their deceased colleague possessed not only a fine general library but 'also some remarkable special collections, the chief of which was probably his Cervantes collection'.[125] The Society of Antiquaries (to which Ashbee had been elected in 1877) was no more forthcoming: Ashbee's collection of 'works relating to *Don Quixote* in every language' had been bequeathed 'along with many others' to the British Museum.[126] The Bibliographical Society made no allusion whatsoever to the matter.[127] In 1908, in *Modern English Biography*, Frederick Boase accepted that Ashbee was Pisanus Fraxi and

adduced the titles of his three volumes of erotic bibiography. He added that Ashbee 'collected a splendid library of facetious works' and 'bequeathed his books (including his facetiae)' to the British Museum. Only those in the know were aware that 'facetiae' was a booksellers' euphemism for erotic, and not funny, books.[128]

Despite such reticences, it was now widely known that Ashbee was Pisanus Fraxi and that he had led a double life of considerable deviousness.

That life spanned almost exactly the reign of Queen Victoria, who had come to the throne in 1837, three years after Ashbee's birth, and who survived him by six months. He seems to have felt some admiration for 'la dame bien-aimée qui occupe notre trône', as he once termed her, not least for her ability as diarist and amateur author (*Leaves from a Journal of Our Life in the Highlands*).[129] And he was immensely proud of the Empire that knew its finest hour under her rule. Nevertheless, he came to abhor British 'ultra-squeamishness and hyper-prudery',[130] sexual cant and the inability to call a spade a spade. The conviction that the denial of the sexual urge leads to atrophy pervades his bibliographies. As does his admiration for the more sensible attitude to love-making professed by the French, whose freedom in this respect was a permanent object of obloquy in England. Pondering on Ashbee's efforts in his chosen field, it is impossible not to conclude with Peter Fryer that he 'soberly and deliberately violated his society's most cherished taboos'.[131]

We are left with the fascinating question of *My Secret Life*. Among his other achievements, did Ashbee write the Victorian era's greatest erotic *tour de force*, the authorship of which has now been a major literary enigma for a hundred years? If he did, we are dealing not just with an outstanding bibliographer of banned books but with a novelist of considerable talent. It seems well worth while to pursue the matter further.

PART II

H.S. Ashbee
1894

Previous page: C. W. Sherborne's 1894 bookplate shows an Ashbee younger than his years.

Ashbee and My Secret Life

How on earth this highly sophisticated connoisseur of erotic literature [Ashbee] can seriously be regarded as likely to have been the author of *My Secret Life* we find it difficult to imagine.

EBERHARD AND PHYLLIS KRONHAUSEN[1]

There is no possibility whatsoever that Ashbee could have been the author of this book.

CHARLES FARRELL[2]

The evidence against the author being Ashbee seems overwhelming.

J. H. PLUMB[3]

As far as the attribution of authorship to Henry Spencer Ashbee is concerned, *si non è vero, è ben trovato*. A more likely candidate will not easily be found.

GERSHON LEGMAN[4]

The story of the authorship of *My Secret Life* begins with Paul Harry Ferdinando, alias Charles Carrington, who was born in 1867 at Bethnal Green, London, of Portuguese parents. Carrington began as 'an errand boy, vanboy, and then lavatory assistant', and at sixteen was running a book barrow in Farringdon Market.[5] He moved to Paris in 1885, set up as a publisher, and, between 1894 and 1914 'dominated' the European erotica market in the English language.[6] This most shifty of characters became Oscar Wilde's

publisher when the writer was in Reading Gaol. 'I saw Carrington the other night,' Wilde wrote from Paris to Leonard Smithers on his release. 'He tells me of a wonderful book of poems you have published, and has promised to let me see it. Carrington looks twisted and hysterical. What a curious type he is!' Oscar knew his man.[7] He also had the measure of Smithers, considering him 'the most learned erotomaniac in Europe'.[8]

At the turn of the century Carrington obtained some copies of *My Secret Life*. 'It is evident, from Carrington's way of puffing it,' writes Gershon Legman, 'that he had come into the possession of the remainder of the edition, and was trying to sell it off at 60 pounds sterling per set, an astronomical sum at that time.'[9] In 1901 Carrington printed the first six chapters of *My Secret Life* under the title of *The Dawn of Sensuality*. They take the adventures of 'Walter', the book's narrator, up to the age of seventeen.[10] Then, in 1902, he offered copies of the complete set of eleven volumes for sale. A catalogue of his forthcoming publications included a lurid description of the book – and provided a few hints as to its printing and authorship:

<div align="center">

MY SECRET LIFE

or

The modern Casanova

</div>

Curious, sensational, phenomenal! . . .

No adjectives known are eloquent enough to qualify this exceptional work, no words can paint its peculiarities, because it is simply and honestly true.

The hero of this story has written his own life, with the exactness and scrupulous order of the English nation. His erotic existence, or *private confessions* and autobiography is here set down day by day, from boyhood onwards.

The celebrated Don Juan is outdone, our hero having revelled in the charms of over two thousand women. He has travelled all over the world and everywhere, except in Lapland, he enjoys many females, and

narrates in the most painstaking manner their habits, customs, and modes of sexual pleasure, not forgetting to describe the physical idiosyncrasies of every different typical race. These interesting details form a faithful panorama of celebrated and ordinary styles of beauty and comeliness, as well as of male and female prodigies and monsters, such as double-sexed beings and hermaphrodites of various kinds, giants and dwarfs of the tender sex, and when he meets with men of abnormal proportions, he does not forget to give every astounding incongruity.

See everything, know everything and above all try to feel everything, such seems to have been the line of conduct of our hero, who wished to taste every known vice, such as tribadism, sodomy, etc.; and after having essayed certain strange delights, he continued to practise such lusts as pleased him most, and discourses of them boldly and knowingly in real philosophical vein.

All public or private places where he procures the partners of his lubricity are also studied with the minutest precision, such as theatres; churches; hotels; ships; railways; omnibuses; carriages; baths; by the sea; *tables-d'hôtes* [*sic*]; public parks; the streets of London by night, etc.

The different sort of brothels are naturally fully analysed, from the stews of the lower classes and sailors' houses up to the sumptuous seraglio frequented by the rich voluptuary, where every system of special lechery is practised.

To sum up, we have the unvarnished tale of his stupration and carnal delights, where sometimes love predominates, but with him licentious passion always reigns supreme in his marvellous adventures in every social category, reaching from the gutter to the most aristocratic drawing-room and in all countries, composing a varied succession of scenes of the most unique interest.

He even omits nothing concerning the medical side of free love and the mechanical instruments appertaining thereto.

What makes this masterpiece of eleven volumes, on fine Dutch paper, of 380 pages each, a true literary curiosity, is that only six copies were printed, of which four only are to be sold at the net price of £100-0-0.

(Three copies only remain to be disposed of.) This expensive

whim, the printing of an Englishman's double life, cost the author the trifle of £1100–0–0, and it took seven years to complete.

We persuaded the writer to allow four copies to be sold, as he desired to destroy the limited edition by fire before his death, but luckily he yielded to our arguments, as we endeavoured to show him that such conduct would be well-nigh criminal.[11]

The experts agree that *My Secret Life*, all 4,200 pages of it, was almost certainly printed in Amsterdam between approximately 1888 and 1894.[12] 'At least four paper stocks were used, all good quality laid writing papers,' the British Library informed me in 1978, after carrying out a conscientious test on their set. 'At least two, and probably all, were made by the well-known Dutch paper manufacturer Van Gelder.'[13] There is also general agreement that Auguste Brancart, the Belgian publisher, arranged the printing. It is not possible to establish how many copies of *My Secret Life* were issued, although certainly more than the six claimed (in italics) in the 'Preface' to the book's index: 'It is in print *in eleven volumes, of which six copies only have been struck off and the type then broken up.*'[14] Today only four complete sets of the book are known to exist apart from that in the British Library: one at the Kinsey Institute for Research in Sex, Gender and Reproduction (Indiana University, Bloomington), and three in the hands of private collectors in London, Hamburg and Switzerland respectively.[15]

In 1902 Carrington issued a volume entitled *Forbidden Books. Notes and Gossip on Tabooed Literature* (attributed to 'An Old Bibliophile') which not only provided another description of *My Secret Life* but added a few more 'details' about the author:

My Secret Life. Amsterdam, (N.D.) Not for publication.
11 vols., crown 8vo., of 378, 373, 379, 380, 388, 384, 369, 387, 376,* and

* Here the printer has omitted by mistake the tenth volume, of 396 pp.

394 pp. (The first volume contains an introduction, a preface, and a second preface. The last volume has only 255 pp. of text, and the rest to page 394 is made up of an exhaustive alphabetical index.)

About the year 1888, a well-known bookseller and publisher of Amsterdam, whose specialty was literature of an incandescent kind, was summoned to London by one of his customers, a rich old Englishman, who desired to have privately printed for his own enjoyment an enormous MSS.; containing in the fullest detail all the secret venereal thoughts of his existence. He defrayed all costs of printing, on condition that no more than six copies should be struck off. A few years afterwards, this eccentric amateur shuffled off the mortal coil; and a few copies of the extraordinary work made a timid appearance on the market, being quoted at the high figure of £100! It is evident that many more than the half-dozen copies stipulated must have been printed – let us say about twenty-five or so – as I have [?not] unfrequently seen a complete series, and I should say that at the time I am writing the book may be obtained by carefully searching for about £60 to £75 according to the condition.

In July, 1894, the publisher issued a volume without any title, save the words: 'My Secret Life, Contents', on the half-title and this was simply the index to the chapters; the introduction and prefaces, and the alphabetical index from the eleventh volume.

This was evidently to whet the curiosity of collectors and serve as a kind of prospectus.

Opinions may and must differ as to the peculiar perversity which induced the author to take notes all his life about his sexual pleasures, and finally have them all printed, but nevertheless nothing can be more astonishing than the extraordinary variety of the adventures narrated, ranging through all sorts and conditions of women, from a street-walker to a princess. No doubt the writer was a strong and hearty Englishman, who travelled a little, and whose only pleasure was in hunting for all kinds of diversions with any women he might come across, no matter or how. To his credit be it stated that he never initiates us into the secrets of his married life, and certain of his mistresses he refuses to speak about so that really we are only told about those women he did

not feel any love for, but only lust. And that is what the work really is – a book of pure, unmitigated lust.

It is written carelessly, and there are many printers' errors. It reads like an ordinary rapid correspondence, and makes me think that it must all be true, as there is not the slightest attempt to cultivate a literary style.[16]

Carrington now proceeds to reprint the prolific entry entitled 'Copulation' from the index to *My Secret Life*. In order to allow the reader 'to form some idea of this peculiar work', the notice ends by reproducing the racy episode in which 'Walter' seduces the attractive wife of a retired French Army officer in Paris.[17]

According to a little-known literary hack called St George Best, who acted as American agent for Carrington, the latter told him that the author of *My Secret Life* was Henry Spencer Ashbee. St George Best later transmitted the confidence to Gershon Legman, who, after much consideration, came to the conclusion that Ashbee was indeed the most likely candidate for the distinction.[18]

But how, first, to reconcile Ashbee's authorship with Carrington's assertion that in 1888 the man who wrote *My Secret Life* was 'old'? Ashbee was then fifty-four. By Victorian standards it meant that he was getting on. In Britain the average age of death at the time was forty, and seventeen in the industrial areas of the North-West. Obviously, the more favoured did better and 'a country gentleman in Somerset might expect to live to fifty-eight'.[19] The matter is touched on in *My Secret Life* itself: 'He was fifty-five, she twenty-six, her relatives thought it a good match so she married him, tho he was so old,' 'Walter' tells us about two acquaintances.[20] At another moment he spies through a peep-hole on the performance of 'a man full fifty years old'.[21] If we take into account that Carrington may have been exaggerating somewhat, his remark concerning the author's age cannot be taken to preclude Ashbee.

It seems impossible, too, that Ashbee was not known personally to Carrington. There is evidence that the latter might have acted as agent for Edward Avery, the distributor of Ashbee's three bibliographies, and that he liaised between London, Paris and Brussels dealers at a time when erotica publishing had become suicidal in England after the legal clamp-down on its purveyors effected in November 1886.[22] Carrington was no more trustworthy a source than any other publisher in the field, agreed. None the less his assurance to St George Best that Ashbee was the author of *My Secret Life*, allied to his evident knowledge of the circumstances surrounding the printing of the work, cannot be dismissed lightly.

The 'well-known bookseller and publisher of Amsterdam' summoned to London, according to Carrington's account above, by the author of *My Secret Life*, was almost certainly Auguste Brancart. In 1886 Brancart had issued in Amsterdam a volume entitled *Mémoires d'un Vieillard de 25 ans*, which shares many typographical ornaments and tailpieces with the later volumes of *My Secret Life*. Peter Mendes, to whom we owe this valuable information, concludes that Brancart was probably the 'original publisher' of the book, which could well have been printed for him by the Dutch Binger Brothers.[23]

We know from Ashbee's diary that he visited Brancart in Brussels on 24 June 1883, before the latter decamped to Amsterdam, and it is likely that he saw him later in Holland. Ashbee's collection of erotica included several of Brancart's publications, as we have seen.[24] There is as yet no book on the shady Belgian, but it would not be surprising if information were to come to light some day about his relationship with Ashbee.

Peter Mendes believes that, between 1888 and about 1892, Carrington may have acted as courier during the printing of *My Secret Life*, ferrying batches of manuscript from the author in London to the publisher in Amsterdam (or Brussels), and

smuggling printed sheets into England for proof-reading and then out again.[25] When Brancart left Amsterdam for Antwerp in July 1894, it seems likely that Carrington purchased the extra sheets from him before himself switching his headquarters from London to Paris.[26]

But enough of the preliminaries. Let us now consider the book itself, which according to Carrington's puff is no fiction but an authentic erotic autobiography.

The author of the 'Introduction' to *My Secret Life* has recourse to a well-tried narrative convention when he claims that he is not the begetter of the work, but merely the transmitter of a text written by his 'oldest friend', now dead. 'This device is transparent and is meant to convince no one – not even the author, since he makes absolutely no further use of it,' comments Steven Marcus in *The Other Victorians*, adding that it is reminiscent 'in a sad and feeble little way of the Introduction to *Waverley* and of the frame of *Sartor Resartus*'.[27]

The 'Introduction' reads:

In 18— my oldest friend died. We had been at school and college together, and our intimacy had never been broken. I was trustee for his wife and executor at his death. He died of a lingering illness, during which his hopes of living were alternately raised, and depressed. Two years before he died, he gave me a huge parcel carefully tied up and sealed. 'Take care of but don't open this,' he said; 'if I get better, return it to me, if I die, let no mortal eye but yours see it, and burn it.'

His widow died a year after him.* I had well nigh forgotten this packet, which I had had full three years, when, looking for some title deeds, I came across it, and opened it, as it was my duty to do. Its contents astonished me. The more I read it, the more marvellous it seemed.

* The narrator's first wife dies when he is approaching forty. There is no reference to a second marriage in *My Secret Life*. Presumably we are being asked to deduce that in the interval between completing his manuscript and dying he married again.

I pondered long on the meaning of his instructions when he gave it to me, and kept the manuscript some years, hesitating what to do with it.

At length I came to the conclusion, knowing his idiosyncrasy well, that his fear was only lest any one should know who the writer was; and feeling that it would be sinful to destroy such a history, I copied the manuscript and destroyed the original. He died relationless. No one can now trace the author; no names are mentioned in the book, though they were given freely in the margin of his manuscript, and I alone know to whom the initials refer. If I have done harm in printing it, I have done none to him, have indeed only carried out his evident intention, and given to a few a secret history, which bears the impress of truth on every page, a contribution to psychology.[28]

An anonymous introduction, then, to an anonymous 'secret history', the manuscript of which no longer exists. The 'editor' forgets to tell us whether his fair copy of the original has also been destroyed in order to mask *his* identity. Why go to the immense trouble of making such a copy, one might ask (it would have taken many, many months of appalling labour) when he could simply have crossed out the marginal annotations made by 'Walter' and sent the vast manuscript as it was to the printer? We cannot be expected to swallow such a tall story. Moreover, the 'editor' forgets that, towards the end of volume ii, 'Walter' informs us that he is currently correcting the proofs of his book.[29] He also forgets that 'Walter' makes remarks such as the following:

But I must add something [i.e. to the proof] which was omitted when I abbreviated the manuscript for printing.

I have read the two volumes in print. There are typographical errors . . .

It is too late. The manuscript is burnt, that printed in its stead must be taken as truth or not, as scepticism or faith prevails in the reader, if ever there be one but myself.

I add this now before it goes to press.[30]

'Walter' claims consistently to be drawing on a 'diary of his erotic enjoyment'[31] begun when he was about twenty-five,[32] a year before the 'fatal error' of his marriage (for money).[33] This diary is habitually referred to as 'the manuscript' (the terms 'amatory diaries', 'memoranda' or 'memorandum', 'notes' and 'fragmentary papers' are also used at times to indicate the original manuscript).[34] The diary, 'Walter' assures us, was written exclusively for his 'secret pleasure': 'I revelled in the detail as I wrote it, for in so doing I almost had my sexual treats over again.'[35] Having decided in middle age to publish his manuscript, however, he is now 'revising' and 'abbreviating' it for the press and suppressing the dates as he goes – in order, he says, to reduce the clues to his identity.[36]

At the beginning of volume iii 'Walter' even asks us to accept that the abbreviations (necessary to reduce printing costs) have been pernicious to the quality of the book. His original, he claims, was better than the printed version now offered to the reader. It is a good joke:

In the manuscript, items of conversation, and numerous details of the behaviour of myself and female partners in my amours, were written down just as they occurred, and showed how the climax was reached, how little by little man and woman inclined to each other, how one pressed, and the other yielded, how from modest talk and chaste kisses our chastity gradually was lost, how by touch and sighs and yielding to the swooning lust which coursed stronger and stronger through our veins, our genitals inflamed, swollen, and sweating, drove us to contact with each other, till the carnal coupling ensued, and prick and cunt revelling and wallowing in each other's juices, downed [sic] both wants and senses in voluptuous oblivion.

These details also gave studies of character, and specially of my own character, and as I now read the narratives in print after the lapse of so many years they seem to me to be needed to explain myself, even to myself. It is too late. The manuscript is burnt [...] The narratives were written in the present tense, but in print have been altered to the past,

which gives them the air of a studied composition, written as a man might write a novel; but the writing extended over well nigh forty years, and barely a word has been altered, excepting those due to omissions.[37]

To effect such radical modifications to a manuscript of this size (the book as it stands has approximately a million and a quarter words) would have been a Herculean task. Can we doubt, again, that 'Walter' is joking?

Every so often 'Walter' forgets all about his erotic diary, and forgoing his normal editorial practice of using square brackets when commenting, during revision, on the original manuscript, writes as if he were recalling past events in the here and now with no journal to jog his memory (when this happens he habitually uses the word 'recollect'):

As I write and look back years, I don't recollect one woman to whom I gave such cunnilingual attention as I did to Lucy.

I can recollect all I write and lots more.

I thrill with delight at the recollection as I write of it now.

The whole evening's spectacle is photographed on my brain. – I recollect almost every word that was said.[38]

Moreover, 'Walter' has total recall for the period of his erotic life not covered by the diary, that is from the age of sixteen to twenty-five or so, and reproduces without batting an eyelid long conversations that could not possibly be remembered in such detail. What we are dealing with is a humorous literary *supercherie* of the type detected with glee by Ashbee in many of the books noticed in his three bibliographies. The more 'Walter' insists that he is writing his true history and underlines that he is reporting facts and only facts, the more we realize that *My Secret Life* is fiction. That this is so will become increasingly clear as we proceed.

The 'Introduction' is followed by a 'Preface', this time

ascribed to the author, not the 'editor'. The opening paragraph is of the greatest interest:

I began these memoirs when about twenty-five years old, having from youth kept a diary of some sort, which perhaps from habit made me think of recording my inner and secret life.[39]

This immediately makes one think of Ashbee, the last entry in whose first diary comes in December 1858, *when he was twenty-four*, that is, almost exactly the same age at which, according to himself, 'Walter' began the diary of his 'inner and secret life'. Ashbee did not take up his conventional diary again for fifteen years. During the gap he became one of the leading authorities in the world on erotic literature. It is perfectly conceivable, *prima facie*, that, bored with the daily routine of jotting down the external features of his life, he opted during these 'missing' years for something much more exciting: a diary of his fantasies and, if he had them, of any erotic adventures that came his way.

The next two paragraphs of the author's 'Preface' concern his attitude to erotic books and, in particular, his opinion of *Fanny Hill*:

When I began it [his secret diary], [I] had scarcely read a baudy* book, none of which, excepting *Fanny Hill*, appeared to me to be truthful: that did, and it does so still; the others telling of recherché eroticisms or of inordinate copulative powers, of the strange twists, tricks, and fancies of matured voluptuousness and philosophical lewedness,[†] seemed to my comparative ignorance as baudy imaginings or lying inventions, not worthy of belief; although I now know, by experience, that they may be true enough, however eccentric and improbable they may appear to the uninitiated.

Fanny Hill's was a woman's experience. Written perhaps by a woman, where was a man's written with equal truth? That book has no

* 'Walter' uses this form of 'bawdy' throughout.
† Throughout *My Secret Life*, 'lewd' is spelt 'lewed', 'lewdness' as 'lewedness'.

baudy word in it; but baudy acts need the baudy ejaculations; the erotic, full-flavored expressions, which even the chastest indulge in when lust, or love, is in its full tide of performance. So I determined to write my private life freely as to fact, and in the spirit of the lustful acts done by me, or witnessed; it is written therefore with absolute truth and without any regard whatever for what the world calls decency. Decency and voluptuousness in its fullest acceptance cannot exist together, one would kill the other; the poetry of copulation I have only experienced with a few women, which however neither prevented them nor me from calling a spade a spade.[40]

The American scholar Gordon Stein has argued that Ashbee could not have penned this paragraph, since he knew perfectly well that *Fanny Hill* was not 'perhaps' written by a woman but by John Cleland (numerous editions of the book are noticed at length in the *Catena Librorum Tacendorum*).[41] But such reasoning is naïve. If we accept that *My Secret Life* is fiction, it would be perfectly in keeping for Ashbee to have 'Walter' swallow the possibility of female authorship. The appreciation shown by 'Walter' for *Fanny Hill*, reiterated throughout *My Secret Life*, closely parallels that of Ashbee, for whom the book 'undoubtedly is, and will probably long remain, the best erotic novel in the English language'.[42] Ashbee, like 'Walter', is impressed by the fact that the language of *Fanny Hill* avoids all vulgarity. 'Every detail is given,' he tells us, 'but in such clear and well chosen language that one is not disgusted, as is almost invariably the case in English works of this class.'[43] It would seem that the circumstantial evidence for Ashbee's authorship of *My Secret Life* is boosted, rather than diminished, by the comments 'Walter' makes about *Fanny Hill*.[44]

As regards the identity of the characters who play a part in his narrative, 'Walter' would have us believe that 'the Christian name[s] of the servants mentioned are generally the true ones, the other names mostly false, tho phonetically resembling the

true ones'. Initials are 'almost always' the real ones, 'although in most cases the women they represent are dead or lost to me' (in fact initials are hardly used). Street and house names are 'nearly always correct'. The description of roads, houses, rooms or gardens is 'exactly true', right down to 'the situation of a tree, chair, bed, sofa, pisspot'. 'The district is sometimes given wrongly; but it matters little whether Brompton be substituted for Hackney, or Camden Town for Walworth' (little, indeed, given the drab sameness of the endless episodes). Whenever needful, however, 'the places of amusement are given correctly' (the notorious Argyle Rooms, for example). The justification for such a procedure? 'All this is done to prevent giving pain to some, perhaps still living, for I have no malice to gratify.' But it is done, principally, to make the narrative appear more truthful, more convincing, more *real*.

Labouring the point, 'Walter' explains how he has disguised the identity of his family and relatives:

I have mystified family affairs, but if I say I had ten cousins when I had but six, or that one aunt's house was in Surrey instead of Kent, or in Lancashire, it breaks the clue and cannot matter to the reader. But my doings with man and woman are as true as gospel. If I say that I saw, or did, that with a cousin, male or female, it was with a cousin and no mere acquaintance; if with a servant, it was with a servant; if with a casual acquaintance, it is equally true. Nor if I say I had that woman, and did this or that with her, or felt or did aught else with a man, is there a word of untruth, excepting as to the place at which the incidents occurred. But even those are mostly correctly given; this is intended to be a true history, and not a lie.[45]

If, as is alleged, the names figuring in *My Secret Life* phonetically resemble those of their real-life counterparts, it ought to follow that the Christian name of the secret author should resemble 'Walter'. In this connection it may be worth pointing out that Harry (as Ashbee was called by his wife) assonates with 'Wattie'

(the name by which 'Walter' is known familiarly as a child).[46]

As regards street and place names, sometimes these are given in full, sometimes fully in one place but with a combination of letters and asterisks, or occasionally dots, in another; sometimes just with asterisks or dots. Usually the missing letters can be replaced instantaneously. There is humour here, of course:

O***d*n Street	Oxendon Street
N*v**s	Nevers
G**n*b*e	Grenoble
F*r***n office	Foreign Office
H…f..dshire	Herefordshire
R.g..t Street	Regent Street
K**s***t*n	Kensington
F**r***e	Florence
R**e	Rome
R.m.n	Roman
C…s.a	Chelsea
B**l***t*n Arcade	Burlington Arcade
S..o S….e	Soho Square
O*f**d Street	Oxford Street
D**d*e	Dundee
B**l*n	Berlin

One adventure begins 'In the month of *** four years after' – hardly a test of the reader's intelligence.[47] Nor is 'a polyglot of English, German and ******'[48] On the other hand 'H…dfs…e…', the country seat of the narrator's aunt, is clearly a deception.[49] My own favourite is the brothel in 'B*w Street', which 'Walter' helpfully tells us was 'nearly opposite to the Opera House since built' (Covent Garden).[50] Like the accommodation house in propinquitous J***s Street (James Street), the Bow Street location will be one of the narrator's principal 'knocking shops'.[51] 'Walter' clearly enjoys this little game of hide-and-seek – an obvious clue here, a dead alley there.

'Walter' now adds a 'Second Preface'. 'Some years' have passed since he wrote the first one. During them he has gone through 'abnormal phases of amatory life', with tastes and 'letches' that previously he would have considered 'the dreams of erotic mad-men'. He has re-read his voluminous manuscript and decided that it would be 'a sin' to destroy it. (In the 'Introduction', the 'editor' has already told us that it would be 'sinful to destroy such a history'.) 'Whatever society may say,' 'Walter' argues, his book 'is but a narrative of human life, perhaps the every day life of thousands, if the confession could be had.' Moreover it could be useful to society (or, as the 'Introduction' states, 'a contribution to psychology'):

What strikes me as curious in reading it is the monotony of the course I have pursued towards women who were not of the gay class; it has been as similar and repetitive as fucking itself; do all men act so, does every man kiss, coax, hint smuttily, then talk baudily, snatch a feel, smell his fingers, assault, and win, exactly as I have done? Is every woman offended, say 'no', then 'oh!', blush, be angry, refuse, close her thighs, after a struggle open them, and yield to her lust as mine have done? A conclave of whores telling the truth, and of Romish Priests, could alone settle the point. Have all men had the strange letches which late in life have enraptured me, though in early days the idea of them revolted me? I can never know this; my experience, if printed, may enable others to compare as I cannot.

Shall it be burnt or printed? How many years have passed in this indecision? why fear? it is for others' good and not my own if preserved.[52]

Two thousand pages later (in the Grove Press edition), as the book draws to its close, the 'editor' informs us of the author's death:

Here abruptly terminates the narrative. Some years after the writer died and the manuscript came as already told into the possession of him who arranged and abbreviated it. A wonderful narrative of something like fifty years of secret life.[53]

Into the possession of '*him who arranged and abbreviated it*'? There has been no previous mention of any editorial intervention by the alleged best friend of 'Walter', other than the suppression of proper names. On the contrary, 'Walter' has attributed to himself all the rewriting and abbreviation of the original. Now we are being asked to accept that, as well as the alleged authorial emendations, the editor has introduced his own. This is too much insistence, surely. Moreover the exhaustive index has evidently been made by the author himself, not by the 'editor', for it contains hundreds of first-person references which it is difficult to conceive were devised by someone else ('Flesh. Smoothness of mine', 'Frigging myself', 'Linen wrapped round my prick', 'My sexual habits', 'Keyholes, my prick shewn to a lady', and so on). Indexes are made from page proofs, and that to *My Secret Life* can have been made only by the author.

My Secret Life asks us to believe that it is the carefully revised version of a huge erotic diary stretching over some four or five decades, abbreviated and rewritten by the author in the past tense and pruned of dates and all references that could identify the characters, beginning with himself. On top of this we are required to accept that the entire, revised version has been laboriously copied out by a close friend of the defunct author, who in so doing has further abbreviated and edited it. Given such a framework, how can we possibly accept that *My Secret Life* is a 'true history'?

I am convinced that it is fiction, not only because of the narrative framework, a manifest and not very witty confidence trick, but, among other things, because of the intrinsic improbability of the episodes themselves. It is inconceivable that anybody who had really lived as 'Walter' did would have had the time, or felt the need, or been so narcissistic, as to keep a diary of his innumerable copulations, the vast majority of them with prostitutes. But had he done so, the results would have been very different

from this account. They would have evidenced some growth in the author's understanding of himself and others. But there is no such growth. The sexual behaviour described throughout the book's thousands of pages shows that the author of *My Secret Life* had little real experience of what he is talking about. Where female sexuality is concerned he is, in fact, an ignoramus.

In middle age 'Walter' tells us: 'I have probably fucked now – and I have tried carefully to ascertain it – something like twelve hundred women, and have felt the cunts of certainly three hundred others of whom I have seen a hundred and fifty naked.'[54] Later he ratifies this approximate computation.[55] *My Secret Life* chronicles relationships with female genitals rather than with women. The vast majority belong to prostitutes, with those of servant girls coming second on the list. 'Walter' may think himself sexually attractive (he says repeatedly that women adore his smooth, white skin), but without his money he would be powerless. 'Shiners [sovereigns] ain't got at barrows are they,' a coster girl mutters before succumbing,[56] and throughout his narrative we find 'Walter' glorying in the persuasive power of coin:

Gold, omnipotent gold!

I am an old stager – money will open every female's legs.

Many a girl has had her first bit of gold from me, has found out the ready money-value of her cunt.

Gold offered to women when their cunts tingle will get most of them.[57]

 'Walter' is a voyeur. He not only wants to copulate as often as possible but to subject each new vagina to a minute examination:

There is nothing like novelty in cunt. – A fresh one almost always seems to have a charm, however plain the owner of it may be.

She was a cunt of superlative voluptuousness, a magnificent bit of fucking flesh, but nothing more.[58]

'Cock and cunt will come together, check them as you may': the theme of *My Secret Life* is epitomized in these lines from a 'smutty chorus' that 'Walter' claims to have chanted with his friends at school, and which reverberate throughout the book.[59] 'What vigilance can keep a willing cunt from an aggressive prick?' the narrator asks. 'All history, all experience, tells me that they WILL come together.'[60] Human beings are always 'dying' for copulation, even though such yearning may at times be 'unconscious': of one girl he tells us that 'unconsciously she wanted fucking';[61] another was 'almost unconscious of yielding to her lust whilst refusing'.[62] In order that they shall be up to the task, Nature has provided men and women with an apparently inexhaustible reservoir of libido, and, given half a chance, they will 'fuck as much as they can'[63] – until, as the narrator likes to put it, they are completely 'fucked out'.[64] 'My darling,' a now middle-aged 'Walter' assures one of his women, 'fucking is all in life worth living for.'[65]

In the narrator's conception, the sexual organs are practically autonomous machines, with wills of their own. 'Burning hot and demanding their lewed pleasure',[66] no law, no convention, no modesty, no restriction can stop the genitals, once initiated, from searching out fresh opportunities to abandon themselves to 'unrestrained lust'.[67] Tingling, boiling, smouldering, swelling, melting, bubbling, lathering, seething, wallowing, flaming, stewing, quivering, flooding, shuddering, throbbing, pulsating, stinging, churning – sexual organs in such a state of permanent ebullience are not to be controlled by considerations of morality. 'I could not dally with my prick, but let it satisfy itself as soon as it liked,' 'Walter' reports on one occasion.[68] On another: 'This was a hot June, and cunts were sweating with lust.'[69] 'A standing prick stifles all conscience,' the narrator insists several times.[70] At another moment he notes, 'The irritation of her cunt killed all moral consciousness.'[71] 'By that time my pego was stiff enough to

be driven through a post,' he recalls, 'for I had been some days sleeping alone, and it had hinted to me that morning that at its roots lay a cunt-lubricating essence which it wished to get rid of.'[72] 'No cunt can refuse a prick when once it has had it,'[73] he assures us confidently. 'What a fascinator a prick is when once tasted,' we read elsewhere.[74] And again: 'Once done, you may always do it to a woman. That is my experience. The hint of a stiff prick after once fucking it, is "open sesame" to a cunt.'[75]

'Walter' wants to convince us, then, that, once modesty is broken down, everyone, male and female alike, will devote themselves as often as possible to the 'mingling of spermatic juices', or, as he puts it habitually, to 'spending'. He is prepared to use almost any means to demolish the modesty barrier: money, first and foremost, gifts (a cheap but suitably flamboyant dress, for example), alcohol, blackmail, posing as a doctor,[76] bribery, near rape, threats (in the case of servants, that he will have them sacked without a character).[77] It's all the same to him provided he gets what he wants.

To overcome a woman's futile resistances, moreover, Nature has put at men's disposal a fabulous additional ally: the clitoris. All that is necessary is to get at this 'little button of flesh',[78] this 'button made for frigging',[79] strategically placed 'so that it cannot escape man's fingers' even when the girl closes her thighs. It is this magic organ that enables the male 'to incite and incline the woman to submit to his will in copulation':[80]

I rubbed gently over the little bit of her clitoris that her tightly-closed little thighs let me feel, until she began to feel lewed.

Nature helped me. She could bear no longer the friction on her clitoris, her voice fell to a whining tone, she breathed short.

Ah! The effect that the male fingers produce on the woman, when they twiddle that sensitive little red protuberance at the upper end of her cunt, a part so easily reached by the finger, so impossible to get it out of

its reach, and so placed that man can always incite the woman to his will, and the great plan of propagation be unchecked.

Ah, those male fingers, how few women can say nay when they have rubbed the clitoris for a minute.

So soon as I'd found her clitoris and had frigged it a little she was quiet – they all are.[81]

So potent is the action of the male finger, that even in church a girl cannot resist:

Then during the sermon I got my finger on to her cunt tip, and frigged her till she spent. – As she did so, she gave such a loud sob of pleasure that people must have heard it, tho perhaps they may not have noticed it – and she gave such a violent start of her bum forward that it came quite to the edge of the seat.[82]

There is a parallel assumption that, once a woman has had a man's erect penis unexpectedly thrust into her hand, or 'that supreme article of feminine worship'[83] has been suddenly exposed for her contemplation ('Walter' is a confirmed flasher), she cannot but be turned on. 'Show her your prick, my boy, as soon as you can,' an old army rake advises 'Walter' early in his amatory career.[84] 'Walter' takes the injunction to heart:

Nothing persuades a woman like a stiff-stander. Many a woman will say, 'no, no,' till she sees the red-tipped cunt-stopper ready, and then she can say it no longer.

I pulled out my prick and that quieted her, and she got lewed I suppose.

Then I wanted to piddle, and taking up a pot, emptied my bladder in very open fashion before her, and exposed my prick as much as I could – (It is a thing I always do as soon as I can before a woman whom I want to get over).

I never spoke, but laying hold of her hand put it to my prick, knowing the quiet persuasive eloquence of a stiff one.

The feel of the prick makes every woman yield.

A stiff red capped prick has a fascination, and a knowing cunt heats, tingles and sweats its lubrication at the sight of one.[85]

Obsessed as he is with his erections and his performance, the narrator's not infrequent moments of temporary impotence cause him intense anguish and shame. What price now, 'cunt plugger', 'cunt prober', 'cunt prodder', 'cunt rammer', 'cunt stopper', 'cunt stretcher', 'cunt whacker'? How now, 'comforter', 'flesh stick', 'generator', 'love staff', 'life giver', 'procreant tool', 'truncheon', 'tube'?

I have been subject to this sudden revolt and prostration, sometimes even when the woman was most beautiful. Nervousness, fear, some sudden dislike, and even most ridiculous reasons have caused it.[86]

'Walter' is convinced that his penis is not big enough, that he will be laughed at in brothel and boudoir. Is it this anxiety that causes his sporadic failures? A doctor diagnoses 'nervousness', which is hardly helpful. Nor is the advice proffered by a young whore: 'Don't be nervous, if you are you won't do it.'[87]

The knowledge that I had once been so affected, affected me often afterwards when I went indoors with girls. 'Shall I be able to fuck?' I used to think, I who had already fucked two hundred women. But so it was, a fear of inability brought on the inability.

All was useless, a nervous feeling that I could not fuck her came over me and out my prick came as big only as a walnut. It is always so directly I have such a fear.[88]

On one occasion a prostitute desperate to copulate gives a 'little, quiet laugh' when she contemplates his shrunken penis. This, 'Walter' records, 'finished my discomfiture'.[89] Not surprisingly. Behind it all lies the memory of an incident in his youth with a maid who said to him contemptuously, 'Oh – *you're*

not *man* enough.' 'Forty long years perhaps have elapsed since
that was said,' he muses in middle age, 'but even now the recol-
lection of it annoys me.'[90]

It is hard to think of any Victorian book in which the misery
of impotence is transmitted so convincingly. That the author of
My Secret Life knows what he is talking about when on this sub-
ject there would seem to be little doubt. He cannot allow 'Walter'
to be too troubled about failing in bed, otherwise there would be
no erotic chronicle. But he has put in just enough of himself to
give these episodes a ring of authenticity.

If *My Secret Life* is an impassioned paean to copulation, a
veritable 'anti-Acton', Victorian England's great taboo words are
its true protagonists, spreading themselves profusely on every
page. We have been prepared for this in the 'Preface', where
'Walter' tells us that 'baudy acts need the baudy ejaculations; the
erotic, full-flavoured expressions which even the chastest indulge
in when lust, or love, is in its full tide of performance'.[91] Even the
chastest? It is ludicrous. For 'Walter' the mere articulation of
such words is an aphrodisiac. 'I whispered in conversation,
"prick", – "cunt", – "fuck", – that magical triad,' he tells us as he
recalls pressing home his attack on yet another servant girl.[92]
'What sane person is there,' we are asked to accept, 'but feels
pleasure in hearing the exciting triad?'[93] 'I thought of Lydia,'
'Walter' muses, 'and in voluptuous words, and for the first time,
said "cunt, prick, fuck," that trinity of words which conveys all,
expresses all.'[94] When about to have an emission, 'Walter'
habitually has recourse to what on one occasion he terms his
'fucking slogan':[95]

I threw one arm round her neck and kissed and coaxed, in frank,
strong, concupiscent phrases, no longer mincing words. Prick, cunt,
fuck, spunk, and the choicest of the vocabulary of love, in undisguised
carnal strength I uttered.[96]

'Walter' believes, in fact, that sexual liberation consists to no small extent in freeing the 'plain language of love' from the strictures imposed on it by a sexually repressive society,[97] and he gets a tremendous kick from initiating girls into the use of the 'magical triad' and other bawdy words:

It is to me one of the great charms of liaisons with women who are not gay, to make them speak in the coarsest language of their organs, wants and sensations, whilst I look them in the face. Two or three days afterwards in the middle of a fuck, I raised myself up and leaning with both hands on the bed, whilst my belly pressed hers, and my prober was to its full length up her cunt: 'Where is my prick now?' said I. No answer; her cunt tightened and moved my prick in it, but she replied not. 'Where is my prick? say, dear, say in my cunt,' and I gave a thrust. 'Say in my cunt,' another thrust. Her eyes closed, she was coming in spite of my prick being motionless. The grip of her cunt was on me. 'Say in my cunt, or I'll pull it out. Say cunt, love.' I moved spite of myself. 'Say cunt.' 'Oh –a –har,' she sobbed. – 'Cunt dear.' 'In my cunt a – ha,' – burst from her. 'Oh,' and dropping on to her and thrusting my tongue into her sweet mouth, in a transport of all-pervading voluptuousness we lay speechless in each other's arms, whilst the juices of our mouth mingled, and the thick hot sperm filled her cunt to overflowing.[98]

The passage just quoted shows that sadism is an important component in the narrator's sexuality. 'Walter' becomes 'savage' when he doesn't get what he wants, and particularly enjoys deflowering virgins, for whom he is prepared to pay a lot of money (according to him, the girls never fail to enjoy the experience). In July 1885 the *Pall Mall Gazette* published a sensational, four-part investigation into child prostitution in London entitled 'The Maiden Tribute of Modern Babylon'. Its author was W. T. Stead, the magazine's combative editor, who was sentenced to three months' hard labour for having procured children in order to establish the validity of his research. Two sections of the report in particular brought home the reality of what was

happening in the metropolis: 'Why the cries of the victims were not heard' and 'Strapping girls down'.[99] The articles appeared while the latter part of *My Secret Life* was being compiled. While the author does not refer directly to Stead's revelations, there is a dismissive allusion. It comes when, after deflowering 'Phoebe', 'Walter' informs us, 'She'd felt my stiff prick, I'd fucked her again, she had given down her maiden tribute to mix with her ravisher's, and our spendings had mingled in our pleasure.'[100] The remark cannot be fortuitous, nor the twisting of the sense given by Stead to 'maiden tribute'.

Not long before, 'Walter' has lashed out against 'the senti-mental bosh about young girls being bought and sold', which looks like another reference to Stead.[101] One is reminded of a comment earlier in the book, when, referring to a recent round-ing up of prostitutes in the Haymarket, 'Walter' observes that 'the London public had a fit of virtue to which it is subject periodically'[102] – a remark that in turn recalls an earlier diatribe by Macaulay:

We know of no spectacle so ridiculous as the British public in one of its periodical fits of morality. In general, elopements, divorces, and family quarrels, pass with little notice. We read the scandal, talk about it for a day, and forget it. But once in six or seven years our virtue becomes out-rageous. We cannot suffer the laws of religion and decency to be violated. We must make a stand against vice. We must teach libertines that the English people appreciate the importance of domestic ties. Accord-ingly some unfortunate man, in no respect more depraved than hundreds whose offences have been treated with levity, is singled out as an expiatory sacrifice. If he has a profession, he is to be driven from it. He is cut by the higher orders, and hissed by the lower. He is, in truth, a sort of whipping-boy, by whose vicarious agonies all the other transgressors of the same class are, it is supposed, sufficiently chastised. We reflect very complacently on our own severity, and compare with great pride the high standard of morals established in England with

the Parisian laxity. At length our anger is satiated. Our victim is ruined and heart-broken. And our virtue goes quietly to sleep for seven years more.[103]

According to the erotic 'philosophy' of the narrator of *My Secret Life*, reiterated throughout the book, 'what men and women choose to do together they have a right to do'.[104] Since sooner or later girls are going to get fucked, why not sooner – and by a gentleman? Moreover, to initiate them young is to do them a signal favour, since they will enjoy copulating once they start, and thereby get more fun out of life:

Fucking is the greatest pleasure of life, and the woman who delays getting it for years, loses much.

A gentleman whose prick had moistened many a cunt, a connoisseur in female beauty, should have ruptured her virginity, and not a man servant. – It was pearls to swine.

Verily a gentleman had better fuck them for money, than a butcher boy for nothing. It is the fate of such girls to be fucked young, neither laws social or legal can prevent it [. . .] A man need have no 'compunctions of conscience' – as it is termed – about having such girls first, for assuredly he will have done no harm, and has only been an agent in the inevitable.

And she also was fucked when sixteen, all her class are, they *will* be fucked. – Ladies must only frig themselves till they are married, – until five and twenty often. What a loss of pleasure.[105]

'Walter' has no more time for Christianity than Ashbee, Burton or Swinburne, and holds it responsible for 'the absurd finical notions about nudity and the necessities of nature, which my own countrymen have'.[106] He also blames it for the persecution of prostitutes, against whom he won't hear a bad word:

They are much what society has made them, and society uses them, enjoys them, even loves them; yet denies them, spurns, damns, and crushes them whilst frequenting them and enjoying them. In short, it

shamefully ill treats them in most Christian countries and more so in protestant England than in any others that I know.[107]

At times 'Walter' cannot resist the urge to parody the Anglican liturgy. 'As in the beginning, now and ever it will be – Fucking,' he intones wickedly. In the subject index to one of his chapters he includes the item 'Unto us a child is born'.[108] Like the author of an oriental love manual, he is also capable of giving thanks to the Deity for having created the generative organs and for expecting his children to enjoy them to the full:

How grateful I am to my Creator that he has thus far made me better and wiser than the beasts of the field, to whom the heavenly delights of gamahuching and minetting* are unknown [. . .] To lick such a lovely cunt and give delight to its possessor is a sign of the divinity which lives, whilst I live, within me. It justifies my hope of a heaven, when I have such a taste of paradise on earth as gamahuching and fucking gives me.

In a minute cock and cunt were one, and the Divine function of fucking went on. – 'Increase and multiply' is the law, the Divine command, and that means fucking, therefore is fucking Divine.[109]

Desirous that children should be properly instructed in the pleasures and procedures of sex, instead of kept in total ignorance, 'Walter' breaks off from his narrative of phallic feats to provide a detailed treatise on the physicalities of copulation. Having concluded his exposition, he makes a novel proposal. His treatise, he suggests,

may be read usefully after evening family prayers also, by older members of the family as well, to whom at times it may serve as an aphrodisiac, and it will spare many young, but full grown people, trouble and loss of time in searching for knowledge which ought to be known to all, but which owing to a false morality, is a subject put aside as improper.[110]

* From the French for cunnilingus and fellatio respectively.

It cannot be denied that the author of *My Secret Life*, whatever his other failings, has an original sense of humour. Sometimes the wit comes through in a deft turn of phrase: 'I did not care what I spent, so that I could spend up Louise';[111] 'When I had cooled her cunt, she was cool to me';[112] 'I could resist no longer, my spout went up her, and spouted.'[113]

The narrator's line of argument in this treatise on the subject of sexual freedom is very close to that of John Davenport, whose *Aphrodisiacs and Anti-aphrodisiacs* (with its chapter on 'Ancient Phallic Worship') is noticed at length in Ashbee's *Index Librorum Prohibitorum*.[114] So close, indeed, that one feels sure the author of *My Secret Life* has it in mind as he writes, as well as Davenport's posthumous *Curiositates Eroticae Physiologia; or, Tabooed Subjects Freely Treated* (1875). The latter work, as we saw earlier, was financed by Ashbee. In it Davenport launches an impassioned attack on Victorian prudery:

Let it not be supposed from these remarks that the author's intention has been that of writing an *obscene* book, or even to employ obscene words. He holds that the grand subject – the Reproduction of the Human Race – which runs more or less through all the Essays in this volume, is, in itself, most pure, and that the words which are necessary, adequately and correctly to describe it in its various phases and ramifications, have acquired the stigma of obscene only in modern times, and, through an ultra-fastidiousness.[115]

Davenport's 'ultra-fastidiousness' reminds us of Ashbee's 'ultra-squeamishness and hyper-prudery',[116] while the latter phrase can be related to the use of the word 'squeamishness' in *My Secret Life*, applied twice by 'Walter' to some erotic hesitations contrary to his 'philosophy', and once to what he sees as Englishwomen's silliness after the onset of late-Victorian extreme puritanism.[117]

*

The accounts given by 'Walter' of his sensations when copulating are so shot through with fantasy, and so repetitive, that it is impossible to believe that he has much idea of what he is talking about. He tells us, for example, that his penis changes to crimson 'as the lustful want gets fiercer and it stands erect',[118] and that once he has penetrated the woman he can feel his 'machine' banging or pressing against her 'womb neck' or 'womb portals': 'The hammer of my prick against the womb neck stuns the cunt for a moment';[119] 'My prick tip's found the nook of nooks close to her womb, it's lodged, it's buried there alive and keeps there nestling';[120] 'Its tip found its nook, and nestled against her womb portals.'[121] Since 'Walter' is a considerable sadist, this ability to knock forcibly at the gateway to the womb is a source of intense pleasure:

The letch for the hairless cunt was on me, I rammed as violently as I could, longing to hit her womb portals – my prick seemed far stiffer than before. – 'Ho! you hurts,' cried she. Harder than ever then I thrust, and felt my prick at each push banging hard against the bottom of her womb, I was delighted at hurting her.[122]

If all of this is grossly exaggerated, the strongest proof that 'Walter' is floundering in a morass of fantasy comes in his portrayal of what we might term the 'phantom female ejaculation', repeated hundreds of times throughout the book with scarcely any variation. 'Walter' believes that when a woman has an orgasm she discharges a liquid akin to sperm (not to be confused with genital moistening prior to copulation). Fecundation of the womb cannot, he believes, take place without the fusion of male sperm and this female emission.[123] The female ejaculation, not attested by science (but akin to the 'Love-seed' alluded to in the *Káma-Shástra*) can take the form of a veritable deluge:

I felt her bum and belly wagging, and a perfect torrent of cunt-liquor ran down on to my balls.

Thick and copiously it gushed out, whilst in loving unison with my precious flood came Lizzie's vaginal juices, issuing from every pore, from every duct of her lovely sheath.

A gentle oscillation and quivering of her backside told of her discharge.

My prick gushed out its sperm, her cunt tightened, gripped, and liquefied, in the blissful spasms of spending, and mingling of our sexual juices.

My bursting prick shoots forth hot spunk with pulsating throbs into her cunt, which tightens, grinds, and sucks it with combined sensations of pleasure, intense, inseparable, indescribable, as the mucilaginous injection floods it, and the soft spendings come out from every pore of its lovely surface to mix with mine.

Our power of talk left us, and we could only ejaculate baudy words, as our seminal juices squirted and oozed and mingled.

Such moments must be bliss only excelled by the ecstatic crisis, when they are joined in one and the sperm gushes up her cunt, and cunt grips, sucks, receives, absorbs it, shedding its own to blend with his in the warm avenue to her womb.[124]

The fluid ejaculated by women as they reach their climax is salty to the taste, 'opalescent' in colour and in texture 'mucilaginous', 'pearly', 'milky', 'glairy' or akin to a 'thinnish gruel':[125]

Her cunt at the same time tightening round his prick and grinding it, and distilling over it on all sides its thin, salty, milky juices.

A flush of salt moisture met my tongue. The sweet little lass had spent.

I fucked her four times, and always she poured out her salt pearly juices, to mix with my glutinous libation in her pretty cunt.

Opalescent moisture issuing from the furrow between the lips shewed she'd enjoyed the lingual that I'd given her.

So soon as she felt the warm mucilage, her cunt discharged its glairy juices to mix with mine.[126]

12 The scopophobic Englishman as seen by the French (1897).

13a Frontispiece to Pisanus Fraxi's *Index Librorum Prohibitorum* (1877), by Jules Adolphe Chauvet.

INDEX

LIBRORUM PROHIBITORUM:

BEING

𝕹𝖔𝖙𝖊𝖘

𝕭𝖎𝖔= 𝕭𝖎𝖇𝖑𝖎𝖔= 𝕴𝖈𝖔𝖓𝖔= graphical and Critical,

ON

𝕮𝖚𝖗𝖎𝖔𝖚𝖘 𝖆𝖓𝖉 𝖀𝖓𝖈𝖔𝖒𝖒𝖔𝖓 𝕭𝖔𝖔𝖐𝖘.

BY

PISANUS FRAXI.

. Quis enim non vicus abundat
Tristibus obscœnis ? Juv., Sat. 2.

LONDON:
𝕻𝖗𝖎𝖛𝖆𝖙𝖊𝖑𝖞 𝕻𝖗𝖎𝖓𝖙𝖊𝖉:
MDCCCLXXVII.

13b Title page to the *Index Librorum Prohibitorum*.

14 Frontispiece to Pisanus Fraxi's *Centuria Librorum Absconditorum* (1879), by John Lewis Brown.

15 Frontispiece to Pisanus Fraxi's *Catena Librorum Tacendorum*.

16 Spring Grove, Isleworth, in 1856, where the loop line had just arrived. Arguably the station is evoked in *My Secret Life*.

17 A page from the index of *My Secret Life*.

There are many other references in the book to the female ejaculation, carefully observed by 'Walter' – but by no one else.[127]

'Walter' believes, as some of the quotations we have seen demonstrate, that when women are about to 'spend' their vaginas tighten involuntarily, 'clipping' the penis. The fallacy is repeated hundreds of times:

The warm, smooth, juicy clip of her cunt was round my prick.

Her tightening cunt fetched me.

A throbbing grip of her cunt hurried me into action.

Then I told her of the pleasures of fucking, of the stiff penis spending its essence in the cunt, of the tightening of the cunt round the prick while the pleasure came on.

Her cunt constricted and held my prick with that peculiar, grinding grip which a cunt gives when spending.

As she spent, I felt as if the gland was being nipped by a hand.[128]

After the 'tightening' that heralds the phantom female ejaculation, there is an inevitable post-coital 'loosening':

Bella's tight cunt grew tighter and tighter, then seemed all at once to get loose, and my prick felt as if it would push up into her womb, and then was wallowing softly up her, in our joint effusions, in a flaccid cunt.

A deluge of her own seemed to have filled her cunt, which loosened round my tool as cunts do after their spend, while I was still ramming with steam engine energy. Her quietness and relaxed vagina annoyed me. I don't like a woman to spend so quickly, nor to lose that exquisite cuntal grip that dies away with her spend.

Her little cunt loosened as all cunts do after a spend.[129]

'Walter' also asks us to believe that by groping in a vagina he can both assess the quantity of sperm he has emitted and tell whether the woman has 'spent' – two further impossibilities:

I put my finger up her cunt to feel if I had spent much, and was pleased with the investigation.

Then again I put my hand on her cunt, and after a broad handed fingering under the prick receiver, I satisfied myself that she had ['spent'].

Not being too ready, I withdrew my prick from her, and felt that her cunt was well wetted with her own spending.[130]

The description of the multiple rape of two girls at the battle of Solferino in 1859, as allegedly recounted by one of the victims, shows that 'Walter' even believes that a woman raped by a dozen soliders cannot avoid having an orgasm:

Then lewed wants came which she tried to stop, but couldn't [. . .] the larger prick did not hurt her, and again she spent [. . .] Then with endearing terms he went on shoving, saying he'd not had a woman for weeks, and finally so stirred up her senses that she spent with him [. . .] The very night of the affair, tho half dead with fright and fatigue, the excitement and irritation of her cunt and brain was such that she frigged herself.[131]

It is difficult to imagine that the author of *My Secret Life* has made 'Walter' subject to sexual misinformation of which he himself is not the victim (it would be a narrative feat beyond his capabilities). The telling of the Solferino episode makes it clear once again that we are reading fiction, not the true history of a man with an intimate knowledge of female sexuality.

Credit must go to Gershon Legman for having been the first in the field to argue, in 1962, that Ashbee was almost certainly the author of *My Secret Life*. An amplified version of his groundbreaking essay served as the introduction to the complete Grove Press edition of the book issued four years later (a symptom of the newly gained sexual freedom of the 1960s). According to

Legman, 'three elements in particular' make Ashbee 'the abso-
lutely right choice as probable author' of the work: his 'total and
lifelong immersion in the field of erotic literature'; his wealth,
which enabled him to pay for the private printing of the eleven
volumes; and his 'lifetime óf travel in all parts of the world,
exactly as with the author of *My Secret Life*'. While none of these
elements is 'perhaps conclusive in itself', Legman believes that
taken together 'there is really no one else who offers all three of
these particularities at once':

Their necessary combination – that is the essential point: their
necessary combination in the author of *My Secret Life* is too closely
paralleled by their known combination, uniquely, in Henry Spencer
Ashbee, for there to be any mistake here.[132]

Just in case, Legman tests the qualifications of the person he
considers the 'only other possible candidate'. This is Edward
Sellon, author of *Annotations on the Secret Writings of the
Hindus* (1865) and the posthumous *The Ups and Downs of Life*
(1867), which purports to be a true autobiography and manifestly
is not (despite the fact that Ashbee makes this claim for it in the
Index Librorum Prohibitorum).[133] Like Ashbee, Sellon had
travelled widely. He committed suicide in 1866, however, twenty
years before the printing of *My Secret Life* began, which rules
him out. (So, too, do the many allusions in the book to events
occurring after his death.)[134]

Having disposed of Sellon, Legman points out how alike are
the indexes of Ashbee's three bibliographies and the 56-page
tour de force appended to *My Secret Life* (see plate 17). He finds
that they have 'a striking stylistic similarity', particularly the respec-
tive entries on 'Copulation', a selection from which he tabulates:

Index Librorum Prohibitorum
Copulation:
 The two most natural modes are the best.

A woman may be enjoyed by two men at the same time.
The woman should not be quite naked.
The woman has more pleasure than the man . . .
Pleasures of rape.
Time when a virgin should be enjoyed . . .
Preliminaries described.
Various postures enumerated.
Monotony condemned.

My Secret Life
Copulating and Copulative organs:
 Essay on the nature of
 – described fully.
 – aesthetic aspects of.
 – is not obscene or filthy.
 – is obedience to the Divine command 'Increase and Multiply.'
 [*ending*:]
 – Eccentric postures:
 – against gates.
 – against railings.
 – against trees.
 – against windows.
 – against a bed.
 – against a kitchen dresser.

In fact the similarity between the two indexes is more struc-
tural than 'stylistic', and it is in the obsessive subdivisions of that
of *My Secret Life*, rather than its terminology, that we may suspect
the presence of Ashbee. One distinguished student of erotica,
E. J. Dingwall of the British Museum, refused to accept the poss-
ibility that Ashbee wrote the book: he could not have done the
things recounted and, if *My Secret Life* is fiction, he lacked the
imagination. Dingwall was prepared to concede, however, that he
might have had a part in the index.[135] In the present writer's
opinion it is unthinkable that Ashbee would have spent months
of his valuable time compiling an index to *My Secret Life* had this

been the work of some other person. Can he really be imagined occupying himself with such a thankless task down in his Hawkhurst retreat? He was not that sort of altruist. If he had a hand in the index, we can be sure that he was the author.

Legman, despite his hunch, is not able to produce any solid proof that Ashbee wrote *My Secret Life*, and he never gets to grips with the internal evidence in favour of or against such authorship. Indeed, he cannot even make up his mind if *My Secret Life* is true history or what he terms 'fantasy autobiography'.[136] Had he had access to Ashbee's diaries, he would, one imagines, have opted for the latter, for it is impossible that Ashbee, with his hectic life, his business commitments and his complicated social round in London and Paris could have had the fifteen-hundred-odd sexual experiences recounted in the book, some of them stretching over months and even years. On the face of it, Ashbee had all the qualifications for authorship of a 'fantasy autobiography', but very few, if any, for that of a true erotic memoir.

Legman's thesis was combatted aggressively by an American academic, Gordon Stein. In a letter to me of June 1978, Stein insisted that *My Secret Life* was a true autobiography, not fiction, and that, since internal evidence suggests that 'Walter' was born in 1820–21, Ashbee could not have written it (as we shall see in a moment, though, other internal evidence suggests a later date for the narrator's birth).

Stein told me that he had almost discovered who was the author of *My Secret Life*:

I have identified the family name of the man who most probably did write *MSL*. I have only to find out which male member of the family was the actual author. This involves a bit of genealogical research in England, now being undertaken for me by a fellow scholar [Peter Mendes]. I have a profile of the man (from *MSL*), complete with a

number of solid factual requirements. I also know the full names of some of his close relatives. A little more investigation, and I will be able to fill in the first name. Let me assure you that 'Ashbee' is *not* his last name.[37]

Stein died without publishing the results of his researches. A draft of his article shows that his confidence in his findings was less than justified.[38]

In the first place, Stein provides no evidence that *My Secret Life* is not fantasy, or largely so. Indeed it never even seems to occur to him that it might be. His entire case rests on the naïve assumption that 'Walter' is telling his true story (although scrupulously changing names and places in order to mask his identity). This being so, it is a question of finding a suitable candidate born in 1820–21 whose biography is consistent with the 'information' contained in *My Secret Life* (number of brothers and sisters, indications concerning relatives, places of residence, countries visited, etc.). Having rejected Ashbee's candidacy, Stein proceeds to rule out convincingly all the other people 'who have ever been proposed in print as the possible author of *My Secret Life*': Edward Sellon, George Augustus Sala, John Walter (editor of *The Times*), Richard Monckton Milnes, William S. Potter, John Stephen Farmer and Augustus John Cuthbert Hare.[39] He then homes in on one particular episode narrated as follows by 'Walter':

Just at that time a case filled the public journals. It was a charge of rape on a married woman, against a man lodging in the same house. She was the wife of a printer on the staff of a daily paper, who came home extremely late; she always went to bed leaving her door unlocked, so that her husband might get in directly he came home. The lodger was a friend of her husband's, and knew the custom of leaving the door unlocked, – in fact he was a fellow-printer.

She awakened in the night with the man between her thighs, had opened them readily, thinking it was her husband. It appears to have

been her habit, and such her husband's custom on returning home, or so she said. The lodger had actually all but finished his fuck, before she awakened sufficiently to find out that it was not the legitimate prick which was probing her. Then she alarmed the house, and gave the man in charge for committing a rape. The papers delicately hinted that the operation was complete before the woman discovered the mistake, – but of course it left much to the reader's imagination.

Fred read this aloud. I knew more, for the counsel of the prisoner was my intimate friend. He had told me that the prisoner had had her twice before, that she had spent with him; that he had often said he meant to go in, and have her, that she had dared him to do it, and that she only made a row when she thought she heard her husband at the door on the landing, although it was two hours before his usual time of return. His prick was in her when she began her outcry.[140]

Stein discovered that the case was almost certainly *Regina v. Richard Clarke*, tried at York Assizes on 16 July 1854, and that the 'counsel of the prisoner' was a Sheffield man, William Overend (1809–1894), who in 1855 became an MP and Queen's Counsel.[141]

If *My Secret Life* is true history, it has to be said that it was extremely unwise of the author to put on record that he was an 'intimate friend' of the defendant's counsel in the rape trial. Given his constant concern to mask his identity, indeed, it is unlikely that he would ever have left such an obvious clue lying around. But if *My Secret Life* is fiction, then this is just the sort of invention one might expect, enabling the narrator to add a few salacious 'details' about the incident, gleaned, as it were, almost from the horse's mouth. In July 1854, it may be worth pointing out, Ashbee was twenty and, as we have seen, was getting ready for a trip to the Continent. It is not inconceivable that he and his fellow apprentices at Bow Church Yard read and discussed the reports of the trial appearing in *The Times* and elsewhere. The inclusion of the incident in *My Secret Life*, that is, does not necessarily invalidate the possibility of Ashbee's authorship.

Peter Mendes has drawn my attention to the fact that the narrator's account of the rape trial enables us to date his birth around 1830, not, as Stein insists, in 1820–21. This is because 'Walter' inserts his account of the trial into that of a protracted orgy which he says was among the first described in his diary.[142] Since he explains in his 'Preface' that he began his erotic journal at about the age of twenty-five, 1854 minus 25 gives a date of approximately 1830. Ashbee, we recall, was born in 1834. Probably none of this should be taken too seriously, however, since the author goes out of his way to blur the chronology of his narrative.[143]

Stein's next task is to discover who were William Overend's 'intimate' friends, and, having done so, to decide which of these was 'Walter'. He can turn up only two candidates. The first is a certain Charles Stanley who, like Overend, was born in Sheffield in 1809. Stanley founded the firm of Charles Stanley & Co., registered London stockbrokers, and may also have been a barrister. He and Overend were involved together in some property transactions. They must have been good friends, for Overend left Stanley a large portion of his estate when he died in 1884.[144]

The other candidate is Overend's nephew, Thomas James Overend (1822–1895). 'The attractive thing about Thomas James Overend are his dates, which couldn't be closer than those suggested for the author of *MSL*,' writes Stein. But nothing else about him is 'attractive': he was a humble silk weaver and did not live in London 'for the extended period required'. There are other marks against him, too. So Stein eliminates him and returns to Charles Stanley.[145]

Stein concedes that Charles Stanley cannot be a 'prime candidate' for 'Walter', for the simple reason that he was born in 1809. Despite the fact that this difficulty is insuperable, he attempts to make the other known facts of Stanley's life fit the picture, even adducing (to show that like 'Walter' he was a

traveller) the passport issued to a 'Charles H. Stanley' on 24 March 1862. But there is no proof that this was the same man.[146] Stein's final piece of 'evidence' concerns Fred, the narrator's cousin, whom 'Walter' tells us 'was killed in battle'. Stein assumes, first, that the reference is to either India (which seems more likely since Fred is posted there) or the Crimea,[147] and then, inexplicably, goes on to state categorically that he was 'killed in the Crimean War', a statement for which 'Walter' provides no justification whatsoever.[148] Could Fred have been a Stanley, Stein wonders? Might there have been Stanleys in the casualty lists of the Crimean War? Research shows that indeed there were. Of these, a certain David Stanley 'seems the most likely candidate to be "Cousin Fred"'. Stein himself is forced to admit that his reasoning here is weak in the extreme. 'Of course, all of this is merely circumstantial evidence, as there is a 50% chance that Cousin Fred's last name was *not* Stanley, even if Charles Stanley *was* the author of *MSL*. Yet, it is suggestive and supportive.'[149]

What we have here is not circumstantial evidence but a series of outlandish *non sequiturs*. Stein's draft ends with the following extraordinary paragraph:

The trail at this point leads to London. The best way of investigating it is perhaps to get into the early company records of Charles Stanley's Stock Brokerage Company. This I did not feel I could do (assuming the records still exist, which they may not) without either being dishonest about my aim, or else without revealing exactly why I wanted to examine their records. I felt that I could do neither ethically. I must leave this to others. Now that the trail is blazed, perhaps someone will follow it up, supplying additional documentation.[150]

Stein's case for Charles Stanley does not stand up to close scrutiny, and he himself cannot overcome the problem of his candidate's date of birth in 1809, at least eleven years before that of 'Walter'. There is no evidence that Stanley had literary

aspirations of any kind, whereas whoever wrote *My Secret Life* is a considerable author. It is impossible not to reach the conclusion that, if the latter really was an 'intimate friend' of William Overend (which is unlikely), Stein has got the wrong man.

Let us now turn to the circumstantial evidence which, added to that adduced by Legman, and by myself earlier in this chapter, convinces me that only Henry Spencer Ashbee could have written *My Secret Life*.

To begin with there are numerous broad similarities between 'Walter' and Ashbee not mentioned by Legman, and which taken together build up a considerable body of coincidence:

– As young men both are avid readers, Ashbee, as his diary shows, of plays, biography and history. It is noticeable that he seems to have no interest in fiction, contemporary or otherwise. 'Walter' tells us that 'before I had seen anyone frig I had been permitted to read novels, not a moment of my time when not at studies was I without them. My father used to select them for me at first, but soon left me to myself, and, now he was dead, I devoured what books I liked, hunting for the love passages.'[151] There is no indication in *My Secret Life*, however, that 'Walter' was any more familiar with contemporary fiction than Ashbee (there seems not to be a single allusion to Dickens, for example). Both work hard at being writers. 'Walter' at no point admits to this, but, as Marcus has indicated, the 'fancy' manner often adopted by the author shows clearly that he had literary aspirations.[152]

– Both were reared outside London within easy reach of the capital. 'Walter' gives no details, but the suggestion is that his village (only 'an hour's journey' from town)[153] and the school to which he goes at twelve, are west of the metropolis (this point will be developed further below). Ashbee's childhood, as we know, was spent in Hounslow; he was at Kensington Grammar School; and

when he married he settled in Spring Grove, Islington: there is a strong West London component in his early life. 'We had a very large playground; beyond it were fields, orchards and walks of large extent reserved for the use of the two head-masters' families,' 'Walter' recalls of his school.[154] A 'Map of the the Parish of St Mary Abbotts, Kensington' for 1846 shows that Kensington Square, where Ashbee's school was situated, abutted on a wide expanse of open fields. (The same map demonstrates that nearby Earl's Court was then a village completely surrounded by open space.)

– Both Ashbee and 'Walter' have an Anglican upbringing and then rebel against the strictures of Christianity. Both evince a particular dislike of Roman Catholic priests and the confessional.[155]

– The narrator's father goes abroad 'to look after some plantations, and after a year's absence came back and died'.[156] Ashbee's father apparently went to South America, the reason never being explained, and returned not long afterwards.

– 'Walter' does not attend university. Nor does Ashbee.

– 'I was passionately fond of dancing,' 'Walter' tells us.[157] Dancing was taught at Ashbee's school, and as we saw from a passage in his diary, he acquitted himself well in Seville.[158] In this connection it is interesting that when 'Walter' visits Rotterdam he makes a beeline for the 'dancing rooms' (admittedly more to pick up a woman than to dance).[159] Ashbee, when he visits the city for the first time in 1855, writes in his diary: 'There is little to see in Rotterdam [. . .] went into one or two dancing places.'[160]

– Both travel in essentially the same places in Europe (Belgium, Germany, France, Italy, Holland, Spain) and both visit the US and the East. Brussels is a 'well known town to me', we are told by 'Walter',[161] and it is interesting that, during one of his visits,

some other trippers he has fallen in with go off to see the battle site at Waterloo, just as Ashbee had done in 1854.[162] Paris for both is the second most important theatre of their activities.

– 'Walter' claims, as Ashbee does in his bibliographies, that it is no object of *his* 'to stimulate the passions'.[163] Yet, forgetting himself, he admits that re-reading his own 'diary' turns him on and even sets him masturbating.[164]

– Both Ashbee and 'Walter' take very seriously indeed the fact that they are 'gentlemen', and express irritation when the lower classes become too familiar, or fail to comply with their every wish. Their snobbery is cognate.

– 'Walter', like Ashbee, knows French very well, as the snatches of conversation reproduced in *My Secret Life* demonstrate conclusively. The author could have acquired his knowledge of French sexual terminology from erotic books, but not the language itself. Ashbee did reasonably well in French at Kensington Grammar School, continued with a native teacher in London, spent a few months in Paris getting the language up to scratch and thenceforth used it constantly. The French admired his ability at the language. It is surely no coincidence that 'Walter' gets his French spot on.[165]

– As regards other shared languages, 'Walter' says he speaks 'indifferent Italian',[166] which was probably true also of Ashbee. He tells us that he speaks only 'broken German' and, on another occasion, that his German is 'vile'.[167] In fact, though, his knowledge of colloquial German is much better than the author wants us to believe, to judge by one conversation with a prostitute which must have taken place in German.[168] Ashbee, we know, was fluent in German. Both admit to knowing only a few words of Russian (twenty in the case of Ashbee).[169] As regards Spanish, we will look at this more closely below.

– Both Ashbee and 'Walter' are good sailors. Ashbee boasts consistently about being the only passenger on board who doesn't get sick. No sea, no matter how rough, can prevent 'Walter' from getting to the lady's cabin and performing with his habitual proficiency.[170]

– Both 'Walter' and Ashbee move at great speed. Ashbee often finds dinner parties or evenings 'slow'. 'Walter' complains similarly on several occasions.

– Both are obsessive classifiers, Ashbee of erotic books, 'Walter' of vaginas. Where 'Walter' compares and notes the variations between female genitalia, Ashbee can write pages about the tiny differences between editions of one work. Both say again and again that they are describing only what they have handled personally. 'Walter' tends to sum up the qualities of a woman after describing his sex with her. In his travel diaries Ashbee habitually devotes some 'General Remarks' to the cities he has just visited. It may be added that both have a sharp eye for how much things cost, in the case of 'Walter' the 'things' include women: 'My prick was in the cunt of a French virgin, at a cost of two hundred pounds,'[171] etc.

– Both claim again and again that their only concern is truth, *the facts*. When 'Walter' says, 'This is a narrative of facts, not of opinions,'[172] we are reminded at once of the Ashbee of the bibliographies and *Travels in Tunisia*.

– Both enjoy billiards and dislike redheads.[173]

– Both love southern climes. 'I should be sorry to have to live in St Petersburg despite its many attractions, I yearn for the South, or any rate for a climate where the extremes are not so terribly severe as they are here,' writes Ashbee in his diary in January 1874. We know, too, that he loved Spain. 'Then on my way to the

sweet south, to get the sun in the months it's denied us here, for a few days sojourn we stopped at ****,' we read in *My Secret Life*.[174] One is also reminded of the letter written by Ashbee on Christmas Day 1887 to Burton, then in Trieste: 'In spite of heavy food and comfort(?) we envy you who are free from fogs and no doubt see the sun occasionally.'

– The only time (I think) that 'Walter' uses the word 'poetry' is when, as we saw, he writes in the 'Preface' to the book, 'The poetry of copulation I have only experienced with a few women, which however neither prevented them nor me from calling a spade a spade.'[175] Ashbee only once employs the word 'poetry' meta-phorically, when as a young man in Spain he terms the dancing of a troupe of Andalusian girls 'the poetry of motion' (did he devise the conceit or borrow it?). The coincidence is striking.[176]

– 'Walter' appears ten years younger than he is: 'I . . . did not look within ten years of my age and (it must be said) was thought handsome.'[177] When one of his doxies asks him how old he is, he tells her 'one younger than I was'. The girl replies that she thought him 'ten years younger than that'.[178] Ralph Thomas, who met Ashbee in 1875 when the latter was forty-one, wrote, 'At this time he looked about thirty, but he always seemed younger than he was.'[179] Ashbee and 'Walter' both look ten years younger than they are, then. Again, the coincidence is considerable.

– Both are fond of using Latin tags to clinch their points. 'Walter' has recourse, for example, to *Tempus edax rerum* (Ovid, *Metamorphoses*, xv, 234); *nil desperandum*; *cui bono?*; *veni, vidi, vici*; *ex uno disce omnes* and *lusus naturae*.[180] We find Ashbee using, among others, *se miserum*; *ipse dixit*; *vox, et praeterea nihil*; *literatim et in extenso* and *ejusdem farinae*.

– The author of *My Secret Life* locates a pungent Peeping Tom sequence in the warehouse of an East London gun factory,

whence through a basement grating he spies on the erotic and urological activities taking place in the street above. There is a linen draper's shop near by.[181] We recall that Robert Ashbee was manager of a gunpowder works, and that as a young man Henry Spencer worked for Groucock, Copestakes, Moor and Co. in Bow Church Yard, on the edge of the East End. The firm were lace and sewed muslin manufacturers and, as his diary shows, Ashbee was constantly on duty in the warehouse in the early months of his apprenticeship.[182]

– 'Then occurred (and soon after the Franco-German war) one of the most singular of my experiences. I was at a great German city stopping there for the night only . . .'[183] 'Walter' does not usually give such an explicit clue as to the chronology of his narrative. The allusion places the episode in 1871 or shortly after. We know from Ashbee's diary (20 January 1888) that he was in Berlin at the conclusion of the same war: 'It is many years since I was in Berlin, I do not remember to have been there since the entrance of the troops after the Franco-German war, the city is much enlarged . . .' A mere coincidence?

– One day 'Walter' spies through a peep-hole on a couple of lovers copulating in an 'accommodation house'. They dally too long, and the girl realizes that she now needs an excuse for being late. Her companion calls for a newspaper:

He stood under the gas light and called over a list of plays. – 'Say you have been to the Lyceum, they play *Hamlet*.' 'Oh but I have seen that.' 'So much the better, you'll know all about it.' 'They will wonder why I went again.' 'You say that they took you.' – Then they laughed, and I gathered that the woman was supposed to be at the theatre.[184]

The 'portico' of the Lyceum was a popular gathering place for prostitutes at the time, as both *My Secret Life* and Mayhew's *London Labour and the London Poor* testify. The latter adds that

next door there was a coffee-house that doubled as a brothel (as London coffee-houses so often did then).[185] The actor Henry Irving had begun a long association with the Lyceum in 1871, and became its manager in 1878, with Ellen Terry as his leading lady.[186] Ashbee's diary shows that he visited the theatre several times, and saw *Hamlet*. On 12 December 1874 he wrote:

On Wednesday night I went with Elizabeth, Collins & wife to the Lyceum to see *Hamlet* – Irving took Hamlet, Chippendale Pollonius & Compton 1st Gravedigger, the two latter were not to be surpassed, but Irving, well as he undoubtedly sustains the part, came far short of my beau-ideal. He avoids points, & has succeeded wonderfully in doing away with his mannerisms, but altogether his performance, in spite of the excitement which it is causing, can not be ranked higher than a good average one. Miss Bateman as Ophelia was simply vilainous.

Ashbee saw the play performed again at the Lyceum a few years later. Irving was still in the lead role, but Ellen Terry now played Ophelia and the other actors were also different. Then, in 1883, he returned once more:

On Friday took Elizabeth & Frances to the Lyceum to see *Hamlet*, *which I have seen before with the same cast* [my italics].[187]

Years earlier Ashbee had claimed to have read *Hamlet* '100s of times'.[188] Clearly the play fascinated him. He sees it three times at the Lyceum. In *My Secret Life* it 'happens' that there is a production of the play on at the Lyceum which the girl in the brothel has seen before, just as Ashbee has. Is this not this a signal coincidence?

Hamlet is not the only Shakespearean referent in *My Secret Life*, it may be added. There is a brief, unascribed quotation from *Macbeth*: 'I might now "in my sear and yellow leaf", form some opinion of my own nature,' an older 'Walter' muses;[189] and Marcus points to what looks like a phallic parody of Portia's

speech to the court in *The Merchant of Venice*.[190] The author of *My Secret Life* and Ashbee share, among so many things, an evident admiration for Shakespeare.

– As regards possible similarities between the design of *My Secret Life* and Ashbee's openly or semi-openly published works, there is not much to go on apart from the massive indexes to which Legman has drawn our attention. An exception is the technique of providing a synopsis of contents at the head of each chapter that is shared by *My Secret Life* and *Travels in Tunisia*:

Earliest recollections. – An erotic nurse-maid. – Ladies abed. – My cock. – A frisky governess. – Cousin Fred. – Thoughts on pudenda. – A female pedlar. – Baudy pictures. – A naked baby.[191]

TUNISIA A GOOD FIELD FOR STUDY – DIFFICULTIES OF TRAVELLING – THE 'COMPAGNIE TRANSLATLANTIQUE' – INCONVENIENCE OF PORTS – BAD ROADS – WANT OF ACCOMMODATION – NO FOOD – NO AMUSEMENTS – SCENERY – INFORMATION DIFFICULT TO OBTAIN – A TUNISIAN TOWN DESCRIBED – CHARACTER OF THE ARABS – CRUELTY TO ANIMALS – RESULTS OF ARAB RULE IN NORTH AFRICA.[192]

While the similarity is considerable, it cannot however be taken as conclusive, since the device was fairly common practice at the time.

– When examining the British Library's set of *My Secret Life* in 1978 I was fascinated to discover, as I held up some of the pages to the light, that one of the watermarks showed bees flying around a honeycomb flanked by a floral motif, with the words VAN GELDER ZONEN clearly visible. Bees! Ashbee! I thought. He could have chosen paper with a watermark that alluded to his name, thereby leaving a generous clue for future researchers! A second watermark carried the legend CONCORDIA RES PARVAE CRESCUNT (roughly, 'All things are possible through friendship'). When I discovered a few months later that this was the

motto of the Merchant Taylors Company in the City of London, my excitement increased. Ashbee, I knew, belonged to the Armourers and the Curriers. Perhaps he was also a member of the Merchant Taylors, and chose this paper, along with the other one, on account of its allusive watermark? But no, the Clerk of the Company assured me that Henry Spencer Ashbee did not figure in their records.[193] Was I imagining things? Not necessarily. If Ashbee really was the author of *My Secret Life*, one can well picture him choosing paper with watermarks that might hint at or bear upon some aspect of his life, secret or otherwise. He was a man well respected in the City, with many contacts there. Might he not have known people at the Merchant Taylors?

– Ashbee's diaries reveal him, unexpectedly in so precise a man, as a very erratic speller (some of his howlers have already been reproduced in the quotations). He is particularly weak on double consonants: ennacted, accademic, acustomed, briliant, siting (for sitting), afability, envellope, embelished, acomplish, exagerated, oposite, dilligence – his pages are strewn with such forms. A full list of his blunders in other regards would fill pages. Exicrable, basmly (for balmy), assend (for ascend), scrive (for scribe), paraphanalia, riggling (for wriggling), archaiologist, archetecture, Biron (for Byron), clowds, discernable, Profit (for Prophet!), delapidated, sacristie, jucey (for juicy), eliceted, anhielated (for annihilated), frollicked, hauty (for haughty), wheapons (for weapons), firtility, rye (for wry), immence, lucious (for luscious), medow (for meadow), seen (for scene), ours (for hours), pealing (for peeling), nocked (for knocked), raised (to the ground), parteo (for patio), seperate, rediculous, wofully, discription, peeks (for peaks), preist, primative, virmin, sacraficed, seam (for seem), creeking (for creaking), cespools, peice, Devenshire, Shelly (for Shelley), theives, vestage, draging (for dragging), labourious, dinasty, dye (for die), decrepid, edefice, climing (for

climbing) . . . he simply cannot be trusted. If Ashbee wrote *My Secret Life* – and this is the point – one might expect to find some pattern of shared orthographical oddities to emerge from a comparison of the diaries and the book, since the author was probably the only person who read the proofs of the latter and might not have noticed his own slips. Without electronic versions of the journals and of the first edition of *My Secret Life*, a comprehensive check is impractical.[194] It can be shown, none the less, that there are some noticeable similarities between them.

For example, 'Walter' habitually spells 'ate' as 'eat':

Sally and I together cooked the sausages, and <u>eat</u> them in the kitchen.

The girl <u>eat</u> them with pleasure, Champagne she drank, first remarking that she ought perhaps never to drink a glass of wine or spirits, as long as she lived.

We <u>eat</u>, drank and got more erotic.

We <u>eat</u> and drank with joy and baudy expectations, both of us.[195]

Ashbee uses 'eat' for 'ate' the only time I have come across the word in the diaries:

He <u>eat</u> & drank as if he had not partaken of a good meal for several days.[196]

Both Ashbee and the author of *My Secret Life* are hesitant about words ending in –ent, often opting for –ant, as in 'independant' and 'dependant'.[197]

With only the occasional exception, 'Walter' uses 'lewed' for 'lewd', and 'lewedness' for 'lewdness'. Both words, thus spelt, are ubiquitous in *My Secret Life*. 'Lewd' occurs only two or three times in Ashbee's diaries, where it is spelt conventionally ('lewdness' does not appear). Such infrequency makes a valid comparison impossible. 'Walter' uses 'baudy' for 'bawdy' throughout, but the word does not crop up in the Ashbee diaries.

'Lay' for 'lie', and 'laying' for 'lying' occur throughout *My Secret Life*. There appears to be some similar confusion in Ashbee, who on one occasion writes, 'The way from the Bungalow lays through Jeypore'.[198]

'Walter' habitually uses 'letch', Pisanus Fraxi 'lech'. But in the list of errata appended to the *Catena Librorum Tacendorum*, Ashbee corrects 'letcher'[199] to 'lecher',[200] which suggests that his instinct might have been to write 'letch' for 'lech', as 'Walter' does.

It is odd to find the latter often using the word 'lapunar' for brothel. This is a misspelling of the Spanish word 'lupanar'. The fact that 'Walter' has such frequent recourse to it might suggest Ashbee, but the latter does not use it in the diaries, however, so that, once again, comparison is impossible.

Without exception Ashbee misspells vegetation as 'vegitation' in the diaries, and vegetables as 'vegitables'. 'Vegetation' appears only once in *My Secret Life*, and is spelt thus;[201] 'vegetable' and 'vegitable' occur once each. There is some hesitation, then.[202] Both authors fall foul of the word 'colonnade'. Ashbee's diary registers 'collonade',[203] 'collonades',[204] 'colonnade'[205] and 'colonade'.[206] In *My Secret Life* we find 'colonade'.[207]

Ashbee is always unsure about double p's ('aparent', 'apropriate', 'disapointing', 'tripple', etc.) and is consistently wrong-footed by the verb 'worship', using the forms 'worshiped',[208] 'worshiping'[209] and 'worshipers'.[210] The author of *My Secret Life* writes 'worshiped'.[211]

Both also use the spelling 'omlette'.[212]

The author of *My Secret Life* consistently confuses 'wet' and 'whet':

I had not felt such a bum since Mary's (already told of), and it so <u>wetted</u> my appetite that I struck a bargain for a fuck.

The woman always said or did just enough to <u>wet</u> my appetite for knowing or seeing a little more.

Jenny now described her sister's first night, and her sister's form, and rather <u>wetted</u> my lust for her sister.

Her lovely naked arms, and plump legs, now showing, her dress being off, <u>wetted</u> my appetite.

Then night and day was a woman with all her harlot's cunning, <u>wetting</u> the girl's appetite for sexual pleasure.[213]

The only time the word 'whet' appears in Ashbee's diaries it usurps 'wet' – the coincidence is striking:

A first class English steamer was high & dry on land, having been on shore at high water, so that when we saw her, a cart might have been driven round her without <u>whetting</u> the wheels.[214]

My hunch is that electronic exploration of the diaries and *My Secret Life* would throw up more orthographical similarities.

Some of the coincidences set out over the last eleven pages are remarkable. Others less so. Taken as a whole, and added to those indicated by Legman, I believe that they form an impressive array of circumstantial evidence in favour of Ashbee's authorship of *My Secret Life*. But there is more to come.

Ashbee, we know, was an authority on flagellation, devoting an inordinate deal of space to the subject in his three bibliographies (as the French reviewers pointed out). Noticing in the *Index Librorum Prohibitorum* a volume entitled *The Adventures of Sir Henry Loveall*, published by William Dugdale, Pisanus Fraxi comments, 'One or two flagellation scenes occur, as in every English erotic work, but they are not made too prominent.'[215] This could be a description of the attention paid to the subject by 'Walter'. The first reference comes late in the book, when 'Walter' tells us, 'At that time with all my knowledge, I was singularly ignorant of the effects of flagellation, of the heat, lust, and physical enjoyment that may be generated by judicious bum whacking, flogging, and

birching.'[216] His curiosity now aroused, two hundred pages later he consults some of his prostitute friends on the matter. Yes, they all know about it. One of them has been flogged by a woman 'for a lady's delectation', the birch drawing blood. 'No man was present, it was a lady's letch, and the lady was masked,' reports 'Walter', adding, 'This story I did not then believe, but I do now.'[217] One of the main characteristics of Ashbee's discussion of flagellation in the bibliographies is the attempt to establish, against all the odds, that women enjoy beating as much, or more than, men. The scene with the masked lady adduced by 'Walter' fits this pattern.

Camille, one of the narrator's favourite whores, shows him the implements with which she beats her male clients. So does Nelly L**l*e. Still not convinced that beating can be a turn-on, 'Walter' submits to a brief experimental session at the hands of the latter. After a few strokes of the birch he asks her to leave off – it hurts too much and, moreover, no erection seems to be forthcoming. Nelly tells him of a woman who, half an hour after being birched by a man, 'grew wild with lust, the birching heated her buttocks, and then the heat flew to her cunt, and she frigged herself half a dozen times till exhausted'. 'If this be true,' concedes a now less sceptical 'Walter', 'it shows that birching does stimulate both prick and cunt to action.'[218]

'Walter' later witnesses for himself two birching rituals enacted in a London brothel run by an 'abbess' who is an 'expert' in catering to this 'letch'. The author now shows himself particularly perceptive about the infantile, 'pregenital' nature of the flagellant fantasy. The first client is wearing a woman's dress, which is tucked up to the waist 'showing his naked rump and thighs', but he retains his male socks and boots (intimations of Freud's 'polymorphous perverse child'). A woman's cap is 'tied carefully round his face to hide his whiskers'. He kneels on a large chair at the foot of a bed, bending over the latter to receive his 'punishment':

'Be a good boy or Miss Yellow (as I shall call her) will whip you hard,' said the abbess. – 'Oh – no – no – pray don't,' he whispered in reply. He spoke always in whispers. Then he said H. was lovely and wanted to see her cunt, which she refused. He never turned round during this but remained kneeling. Then after childish talk between him and the abbess (he always in whispers), 'Now she shall whip you, you naughty boy,' said the abbess – and 'swish' the rod descended heavily upon his rump.[219]

The second client is similarly addressed before being castigated: 'She talked some nonsense to him, about her being the governess and correcting him, to which he made no reply.'[220]

For Steven Marcus, these few pages 'put the literature of flagellation out of the running'.[221] This is true. Not even the flagellation scene in *Fanny Hill* (the novel so admired by both 'Walter' and Ashbee) can match them for psychological insight. The author knows far more about the subject than 'Walter' professes to do. Ashbee again fills the bill.

'Walter' professes to have copulated with well over a thousand prostitutes, in a wide variety of brothels situated in London, Paris and numerous other locations in Europe and further afield. These houses are never described in detail (although on occasion 'Walter' makes a pretence of doing so), and the author could have gleaned most or much of whatever knowledge he has of prostitution from his reading of erotica, from accounts appearing in the newspapers, and, in particular, from the chapter on the subject (largely the work of Bracebridge Hemyng) in Mayhew's *London Labour and the London Poor*. The fact that both the latter and *My Secret Life* mention the same London haunts frequented by harlots (Argyle Rooms, Cremorne, the Assembly Rooms in Holborn, the portico of the Lyceum Theatre, the brothel in James Street, the Burlington Arcade, Oxendon Street, Exeter Street, Haymarket, etc.) could simply be an accurate

reflection of the situation existing at the time, of course. But the similarity between the prostitutes' life histories reported by Mayhew and some of the conversations proposed by 'Walter' is so patent that it is hard to deny the influence of the former. Take the suitably loquacious Irishwoman interviewed in Bluegate Fields:

She was intensely civil to the inspector, who had once convicted her for allowing three women to sleep in one bed, and she was fined five pounds, all which she told us with the most tedious circumstantiality, vowing, as 'shure as the Almighty God was sitting on his throne', she did it out of charity, or she wished she might never speak no more. 'These gals', she said, 'comes to me in the night and swears (as I knows to be true) they has no place where to put their heads, and foxes they has holes, likewise birds of the air, which it's a mortial [*sic*] shame as they is better provided for and against than them that's flesh and blood Christians. And one night I let one in, when having no bed you see empty I bundled them in together. Police they came and I was fined five pounds, which I borrowed from Mrs Wilson what lives close to – five golden sovereigns, as I'm alive, and they took them all, which I've paid back two bob a week since, and I don't owe no one soul not a brass farthing, which it's all as thrue as Christ's holiness, let alone his blessed gospel . . . I've got three or four poor gals into the refuge, and I'll get Chaney Emm, as shure as the Almighty God's sitting on his throne.' (This was a favourite expression of hers.)²²²

Hemyng enjoys trying to reproduce the accents, dialectal usages or foreign syntax of the women interviewed (particularly memorable in his conversation with a German woman – 'Now I talk the English well, as well as any, and I go with the British sailor').²²³ 'Walter', too, has an acute ear for dialogue, and gets some good conversational mileage out of his Irish whores. 'Big-eyed Betsy Johnson', for example, is a laugh a minute:

She was always lascivious. – 'Your fucking is delicious, me dear. You still do it well.' – On my preparing to leave. 'Why sure, and you're not

going after doing it once, and all these years since I've seen you? – I recollect you, when I had to tell you you had done enough for your money. – Ah, I'm older, but sugar me if you go yet,' – said she, clutching hold of my prick. So we fucked again, and again, for I could not resist her.[224]

The 'light-haired bitch' just arrived in London is also good craic:

'You've a fine leg,' said I beginning. – With strong Irish brogue which I can't imitate in writing, nor indeed any way, she said, 'Sure and there isn't a foiner in all the town, won't your cock stand for shure if you see a little higher,' and she pulled up her clothes to her knees in the dark street. – I can't bear Irish women, having found them liars and thieves, and did not like her manner. – 'Com long.' 'No, I'm poor and can't to night, but here is a glass of wine for you.' 'Och! to the Divil with the cash – shure and we won't quarrel about that – com – shure an I loike the looks of you – I'm close by – com.' I followed her and she went at such a pace, as if either the police were after her, or that she was frightened of shitting herself. We entered a house and a comfortable room with a good fire. – A large trunk was on the floor. – Said she, 'Shure and I've not been here an hour and not unpacked – I've been a week coming from Dublin – It's God's truth – may I go to the biggest hell if I've been fucked for a week.' All this rapidly in answer to my questions, and some without my questions. – Then she pulled out my prick. – 'It's not stiff – wait a second and it'll be stiff enough, damned if I don't feel as if I'd forgotten what a man is,' and in a violent hurry, she tore off her things till she was start-naked, boots and stockings excepted, apostrophizing her parts from time to time. – 'There's a pair of thighs – haven't I a foine shape – not a foiner by Jasus, and there, feel my bubbs – look at my small waist – and with such a large rump.' – By that time she was naked whilst I had only taken my hat off. – Then she grabbed at my prick again (she had pulled it out), then threw herself at the edge of the bed, and opening her thighs, 'Put it up me darling bhoy, fuck me chunt – look at the hair on it, it's foine shure, ah! I envy the pleasure yer prick will have in it me bhoy – fuck – com on – fuck.'[225]

One would expect 'Walter' not to mention *London Labour*

and the London Poor – why should he? – but it is interesting that Ashbee never does so in his three bibliographies, despite the large amount of space devoted to prostitution. If he is the author of *My Secret Life*, his silence concerning Mayhew makes sense – he wanted to cover his literary traces. Moreover, the unacknowledged influence of Mayhew is further evidence that the book is largely fiction, not true autobiography. Which is not to say that the author did not have some personal experiences of brothels and their inmates. He probably did.

Towards the end of his chronicle 'Walter' sets off on 'a longish sea voyage' which takes him to an unidentified 'Oriental city', whose hinterland he also visits.[226] His account is concordant at several points with Ashbee's diary of his trips to Algeria and Tunisia. 'Walter' refers to a *café chantant* in the 'Oriental city', an indication of French administration. In 1883 Ashbee visits two 'Caffés chantants' in Blida, finding them 'curious' and 'the groups of Arabs at the different tables most picturesque'.[227] Ashbee is struck by the verdure of Algiers and the 'prolific vegitation' of nearby Cherchel.[228] 'Walter' notes, among the delights of the 'Oriental city', its 'vegetation'.[229] Another parallel is the reference by both authors to belly dances. Ashbee saw one performed at Biskra in 1883. 'It resembles the nauch of India,' he wrote in his diary, 'but is more gross & indecent.'[230] 'Walter' visits a brothel in the 'Oriental city' where two prostitutes perform, naked, their 'national dances'.[231] Among the headings to the chapter containing this episode we find the facetious indication: 'Terpsichorean bum-vibrating whores'.[232] Earlier 'Walter' had referred to a 'demirep' dancing girl picked up outside the Argyle Rooms as 'the terpsichorean harlot'.[233] In Ashbee's Indian diary, in 1881, he refers to the 'terpsecorian movements' of two nauch girls.[234] It would not occur to most writers to apply such a highfalutin term (from Terpsichore, the Muse of Dancing)

in such a context. Only a most unlikely coincidence would have led to their appearance in both texts.

Then there is the intriguing question of London's loop lines. 'Walter' narrates the beginning of one of his adventures as follows:

Towards the end of February, on a dirty but warmish night for that month, I visited an old relative in the suburbs, and went there by a loop line of railway which had not been opened long. I met there a little adventure, being I suppose always on the look out and unable to resist a grope of a warm cunt, whenever I got the opportunity of groping comfortably.

The station in the suburb led out of a wide long road about a tenth of a mile from a main metropolitan thoroughfare. On my return I found I was three-quarters of an hour too early, so loitered about the road, smoking and thinking. I noticed at length two women, unmistakably harlots of a middling class. Quite in my youth I had many times fucked in that very road when there were only oil lamps there and against fences enclosing fields and strawberry grounds. There were more houses about the road now, yet on both sides of the station road and viaduct, there were still large fields, and from the road which led up to the station was another – just before reaching it – which passed *under* the viaduct, connecting with a farm road and was altogether between fields, and led to a farm house.

After a time chatting, I gave the women a shilling apiece to feel their cunts, tho this was in the main road. Then said one, – 'Why don't you have me? Let's go on the other side of the viaduct and nobody will see us – we are very often done there –.' There I went with one, promising another shilling for an uninterrupted grope, it seemed a pleasant way of passing the time. I soon stood besides her having passed into the farm road, the night was quite dark, not a light was in that road, but a little light was shed down from the station platform above our heads.[235]

We saw earlier that one of the reasons why Ashbee settled with Elizabeth Lavy in Spring Grove in 1862 was almost certainly the double advantage it offered of being close to his father Robert

and on the loop line which, veering off from Barnes, had reached Isleworth in 1849 (and Hounslow in 1850), permitting rapid access to and from the City.[236] Is this the loop 'which had not been opened long' referred to by 'Walter'? Is the setting of the incident with the two harlots calqued on Spring Grove and Isleworth station? The line that reached Isleworth in 1849 was the first of the Victorian suburban railways known as 'loops'. It was followed by the Kingston (or Teddington) Loop in 1863/9; the Dartford Loop in 1866; the Hertford Loop in 1871 (as far as Enfield only, the rest was not completed until 1910/24); and, in 1892, the Catford Loop.[237] On the face of it the Hounslow Loop, the earliest, is our most likely candidate.

At Isleworth the loop crosses the main road on what can fairly be termed a 'viaduct', a fine bridge with three brick-built arches. The station, like that in *My Secret Life*, is as a result above the level of the road. A map of the area for 1865 shows that, while building hereabouts was then on the increase, stimulated by the arrival of the railway, there were still abundant open fields in the vicinity (see plate 16). The author of *My Secret Life* is careful not to identify the station closely, of course, and no doubt there are elements of imagination in his description of it. In theory the whole thing could be an invention. None the less the evocation corresponds so closely to Spring Grove and Isleworth station (there are no other 'viaducts' on the loop, moreover) that one feels the author is dropping a tiny hint for those who might one day care to investigate.

But we can take the matter further. 'Walter' tells us that 'quite as a youth' he had often copulated in the same road, 'when there were only oil lamps there and against fences enclosing fields and strawberry grounds before the area began to be developed'. The suggestion is that he lived near by. If not, why would he have been in these parts so frequently? Earlier in the book 'Walter' has informed us that he used to live 'on the western outskirts of

London where they were building on what had been and were still largely pleasant fields', and that the district was the scene of his youthful erotic exploits.[238] The nod, again, with the reference to houses overlooking open fields, is in the direction of Isleworth and Spring Grove.

If Henry Spencer Ashbee is indeed our author, we would expect to find some similarities of style, some shared 'tics', linking the novel and his other productions, particularly the diaries (composed at great speed and revised for publication only in the case of *Travels in Tunisia* and a few articles). Such similarities exist. Consider the following construction used frequently in Ashbee's diary:

A less martial set I never saw.

A less objectionable crowd as far as odour was concerned I was never in.

A more quiet, orderly, respectful & pleasant people I never saw.

A more utterly miserable place I never saw.

A more debased looking lot of men I never beheld.

A more complete instance of decay I have not yet witnessed.

A man so singularly unobservant I never met with.

A more tedious journey than this I never had.[239]

The author of *My Secret Life* has a liking for the same locution (or some variant of it):

A more superb form, more lovely white flesh, never was offered to my embraces.

Such a collection (at a baudy house) of lovely creatures of different nationalities I never saw before or since.

A more lovely creature I never embraced.

A more lustful, bawdier eye I never saw.

A more beautifully made woman I never saw.[240]

A mere coincidence in usage? Perhaps. But what about phrases such as the following from *My Secret Life*? (I deliberately provide a broad sample; the underlining is mine.)

Then I crawled on my knees, with fear that I was doing wrong, and pushed a little aside the curtains where they met at the bottom of the bed.

My godfather used to look at me and severely ask if I was up to tricks with the boys.

I met in the Strand one night Bessie, who put her arms round me.

I got out of bed, struck a light, and moved gently a wash-hand stand against the door.

I had now a little changed my opinion about the girl.

In fact, out of her I could squeeze no information.

By my investigations she was evidently taken unawares.

This incident was altogether due to throwing on the floor a lucifer, after she had lighted her cigarette.

But the gamahuching tho at first I avoided it, she often made me do.

The other slightly then turned around, quite closing her thighs.

So engrossed was he with the exercise, that when her pleasure was coming on, I pushed further open the door.

She also was not under such anxiety, and we had our frolics with increased pleasure.

We both washed – then at her cunt I looked more tranquilly, saw her naked form – and a lovely form she had.

'Fuck dear,' said she to him and began gently her share of the exercise.

I put this time my tongue in her mouth, her friend had never done that.

At the time agreed on <u>she in the cab was there</u>, we drove to the lodgings.

<u>I took another day with me a condom</u> tied on to a little bone tube.

The day after, <u>she with her parents departed</u> in a different direction from ours.

<u>Of photos I went out and bought another collection</u>.

Then asking him to wait, <u>I bought with her in the public house two bottles of sherry</u>.

I didn't mean it, <u>but savagely wanted to offend her</u>.

I put back <u>into my trowsers my prick</u>.

Her cunt <u>she speedily again washed</u>.[241]

Do not these sentences (and there are hundreds of similar ones) smack strongly, in their dislocated word order, *of German syntax*, particularly in the placing of the adverb? In 1862 Ashbee had married into the Lavys of Hamburg. When Ralph Thomas first visited the Ashbees at Upper Bedford Place in 1875, he found the entire family 'speaking English and German with equal ease'.[242] Ashbee's relationship with Hamburg and the German language was so intense that his English prose began to be affected. In the diary which fell silent in 1858, four years before his marriage, there is no trace of Germanic syntax, quite naturally. But when he takes it up again in 1873 we come across phrases such as the following, which almost exactly match those quoted from *My Secret Life* (again the underlining is mine):

The great artist is still a young man in the possession of all his powers both physical & mental, upright in carriage, quick in movement, ready & sprightly in conversation, <u>his face indeed retains still its beauty</u>, for the features are regular.

How fond he is of children, <u>he seems to be wanting always to be doing something for them</u>.

On the very top of one of the largest of these boulders, <u>on the top of the hill has a house been built</u>.

Letters of introduction worse than useless, produce a few polite words & invite to dine at best, generally waste of time, <u>never any one goes out with you & shows you round</u>.

Lastly <u>we ate copiously rambutan</u>, which I have already mentioned, but these were far more lucious & more pleasant.

They sleep much in the day, every one who can spare the time <u>taking regularly his siesta</u>.

Hergla was now in view which gave us, <u>who had also not tasted food</u>, new courage.

It appeared close <u>but other two hours were needed</u> to reach the stupendous edifice built by the emperor Gaudin.[243]

Nor are Ashbee's bibliographies (despite being proof-read by Ralph Thomas and another friend) entirely free from such constructions:

Albertine <u>tells chiefly her conquests</u> among her own sex.

He believes that a woman operating upon one of her own sex <u>experiences also pleasure and excitement</u> in the act.

She is dressed in a hat and feather, and <u>waves with her right hand a handkerchief to a ship</u>, visible through the open window.

I have elsewhere mentioned, under reserve, <u>balls of sodomites</u>.

He meets an old woman, <u>to whom he explains clearly his difficulty</u>.[244]

To clinch the matter, Ashbee himself became aware, in or about 1881, of the pressure of German on his syntax, and sought to correct the tendency. This is shown by three diary entries in which he reorganized the word order by placing a '1' and '2' beneath the terms to be inverted:

The roads around B. are abominable, full of holes & huge & large pro-
jecting pieces of rock which never have been levelled or cleared since
the roads were first made. [2] [1]

Music of the most determined & penetrating kind is continued
throughout the whole of the performances, flutes, fiddles, small drums,
cimbles, which becomes quite distracting, the phrase or utterance of
every actor being rounded off or rather drowned by a crash of noise
instrumental. [2]

[1]
He was for tolerance in every respect. Had any one *heard* him *ever*
speak with bitterness of Smith's murderers or of the persecution of the
Latter Day Saints? [245]

It seems to me that the presence of Germanic syntax in *My
Secret Life*, the bibliographies and the diaries is wellnigh con-
clusive evidence of Ashbee's authorship of the former. That he
tried to correct the tendency in the travel sections of the diaries,
which were intended for publication, made sense. But since *My
Secret Life* was anonymous, the author did not need to worry
himself overmuch about any such stylistic flaw.

Ashbee was particularly fond of Spain. If he is the author of *My
Secret Life* we would expect the book to contain some trace of
this affection. Not too much, though: an excessive familiarity
with the country on the part of 'Walter' might give the game
away. The first thing one notes is that, before the sole visit to
Spain recorded in the book, and before 'Walter' has copulated
with any female from that country, he expresses his appreciation
of Spanish women's gait. One of his whores, Nelly, 'had a beauti-
fully steady walk, like a Spanish woman's'; [246] and one night, in
the bar room of the Alhambra Theatre, in Leicester Square, he
notices a 'tall, finely shaped woman' who was 'as upright as a
dart, and moved with the grace of an Andalucian'. She turns out
not to be Spanish, however, although her lover is. He has taught

her many bawdy words in Castilian, which later she passes on to 'Walter'. Perhaps she is in the Alhambra because it is a fitting haunt for someone who feels an affinity with the passionate South.[247]

How does 'Walter' know that Andalusian women move with grace? There is no indication that he has ever met one. But Ashbee has, lots of them, and as we saw he was deeply impressed. One night back in 1858, he was invited to dinner in Seville. And as he sat down to write up his diary the word 'grace' sprang to his pen, as it does to that of the author of *My Secret Life*:

After the meal was over we had some dancing in which after being instructed by the young ladies there I joined & they also danced the Boleros of Andalucia. I was enchanted. The way they played the castinets & the grace they displayed in the dances pleased me beyond measure. They danced with a spirit & at the same time an artlessness only to be found in Spain.[248]

The chapter in which 'Walter' recounts his visit to Spain is extremely weak, and the author makes him misuse Spanish to the extent that some prostitutes are quoted as saying 'bono, bono' instead of 'bueno, bueno'. Again, if Ashbee is the author, this could have been a deliberate ploy to disguise his identity. A joke, in fact. 'Walter' sojourns in Madrid, Gibraltar, Seville and Cadiz, as Ashbee did, but also in Granada (where no visit by Henry Spencer is attested) and an unidentifiable locality represented by four asterisks and reputedly the hottest spot on the coast.

Of particular interest is the narrator's remark about Cadiz:

Then having tailed none of the so called lovely girls of C*d*z tho I felt one peripatetic's grummet on a moonlit evening – a cheap delight, what charm is in a cunt! – I sailed for home.[249]

The allusion to Byron's appreciation of the girls of Cadiz in

Childe Harold is unmistakable. On 31 October 1858 Ashbee had written in his diary:

'The lovely girls of Cadiz', sung by Byron are a race by no means extinct, & I think that more pretty women can be seen here in a week than in other towns in a month. There is something exceptional about them. Their eyes, hair, walk, dress, every thing about them is per se, everything is charming & attractive.

The broad similarity of the itinerary, the prominence given to Cadiz, the shared allusion to Bryon – surely, once again, the coincidences are too great to be accidental?

Bearing in mind that Ashbee is not only a student of Spain but a Cervantes scholar, let us turn finally to a locution that the author of *My Secret Life* found useful when he wished to convey the speed with which 'Walter' could get down to business when the pressure was on:

To rush downstairs, and open the door was the work of a minute.

To rush up to her and kiss her was instantaneous.

To put my fingers up to verify that, and look at them was the work of a moment.

To pull open the lips, to push up my finger, to frig it, smell it, then lick it was the work of a minute.

To look, to open the lips, and thrust my prick up her were the work of a minute.

To step inside, close the door, place my arms around her, and kiss her rapturously was the work of an instant.

To pull out my prick, drop my dressing-gown over it, let fall the clothes over Mary's posteriors was the work of an instant.

To strip the two and examine their cunts was an affair of five minutes.

To pull off my things, to help her off with hers partially, was the work of a minute.

To ring, get sal-volatile, spirits, was the work of a minute.

To pull it open, have a moment's glance at the red, kiss and feel her rapidly over, mount her, fuck and spend, was only an affair of two or three minutes.

To extinguish the light and get to the peep hole, was the work of a minute.[250]

In my view the repeated presence of this construction in *My Secret Life* (three partial usages also occur)[251] suggests strongly that the author was an attentive reader of Cervantes. For Cervantes, if he did not invent the formula, was apparently the first writer to put it into circulation. Early in *Don Quixote* (part I, chapter 8) we find the following sentence:

El decir esto, y el apretar la espada, y el cubrirse bien de su rodela, y el arremeter al vizcaíno, todo fue en un tiempo.[252]

Thomas Shelton, in the first complete English translation of the novel (1620), rendered the sentence thus:

The saying of these words, the griping fast of his Sword, the covering of himself well with his Buckler, and the assailing of the *Biscaine*, was done all in one instant.[253]

Charles Jarvis (1742) kept a pretty close eye on his predecessor:

The saying this, the drawing his sword, the covering himself well with his buckler, and falling furiously on the Biscainer, was all done in one moment.[254]

Thirteen years later Tobias Smollett established what was to be the canonical version of the locution in English:

To pronounce these words, to raise his sword, to secure himself with his target, and attack the Biscayan, was the work of one instant.[255]

In 1888 H. E. Watts refined a little further:

To say this, to raise his sword, to shelter himself well behind his buck-
ler, and to rush upon the Biscayan, was all the work of a moment.

'This is probably the first appearance of this familiar locution, of
so much use to novel writers from that time to this,' the translator
commented perceptively in a footnote.[256]

In *Don Quixote* the 'familiar locution' is used seven times, in
the *Exemplary Novels* four.[257] As Watts indicates, it did indeed
prove of much benefit to English novelists. In our own century
P. G. Wodehouse could not resist its lure:

To grab Comrade Butt by the neck and try to twist his head off was with
him the work of a moment.[258]

Ashbee, as the leading international authority on, and collec-
tor of, English translations of *Don Quixote* and the *Exemplary
Novels*, which are scrupulously listed in his lecture 'Some Books
about Cervantes',[259] must have been fully aware of the construc-
tion. While the author of *My Secret Life* could in theory have
borrowed it from a more contemporary source (from, say, Walter
Scott),[260] its recurrence in the book once again makes one think
of Ashbee, this time in his capacity as fervent admirer and
student of *Don Quixote*. We recall, moreover, that Ashbee was
little given to reading modern fiction.

The case for Ashbee's authorship of *My Secret Life* is entirely
circumstantial, it must be admitted: there is no trace of the
manuscript of the book, and no confirmatory written documen-
tation of any kind has come to light. Yet I believe that the weight
of the evidence accumulated in this chapter is such that his
authorship is incontestable.

It could be argued that, were Ashbee the author, a set of the
eleven volumes would have been found in his library at his death,

which apparently it was not. But this is a *non sequitur*: the author could have ensured that no such incriminatory evidence were left on the premises. (It is also possible to reason that he did retain a set, but that somebody appropriated or destroyed it before his books went to the British Museum.)

E. J. Dingwall, as we saw, was of the view that Ashbee could not have written *My Secret Life* because he lacked the imagination. But how much imagination was needed to do so? Not a great deal, I would suggest. The scenarios repeat themselves endlessly; the descriptions of foreplay and copulation undergo only minimal variation; there is but little evocation of mood or place; the episodes usually succeed one another without any chronological coherence – they could as a rule be rearranged and no one would notice any difference. 'How like this is to previous adventures,' 'Walter' comments on one occasion. That puts it in a nutshell.[261]

Another question arises. Did Ashbee have the *time* to write *My Secret Life*, living as he did at such a hectic pace? 'One must imagine Ashbee sitting down to write his erotic memoirs – if that is what *My Secret Life* may correctly be considered to be –' writes Gershon Legman, 'after having finished his more scholarly life-work with the publication of *Catena Librorum Absconditorum* in 1885.'[262] But Ashbee could never have written *My Secret Life* between 1885 and 1888, given what we know of his multiple activities during those years. My own belief is that he began work on the book in the 1860s and continued his labours during the 1870s and 1880s. This way he could certainly have done the job, writing at odd moments between other tasks, adding episodes, modifying . . . What he certainly did not have the time for was involvement with many hundreds of women. The secret life recorded in *My Secret Life* is that of sexual fantasy. Probably Ashbee handed over the bulk of the manuscript to the printer before setting off on his South American tour in 1888, the year

coinciding with that in which Carrington's 'rich, old English-man' summoned the 'well known bookseller and publisher' from Amsterdam to London. Internal evidence shows that the author of *My Secret Life* was still working on the book in the 1880s – the reference to Tommy Atkins in the Gibraltar sequence, for example, gives a *terminus a quo* of 1882.[263] It may well have been that once Ashbee had finished the *Catena* he began to polish in earnest the manuscript of *My Secret Life,* his eye now firmly on publication.

Steven Marcus's analysis of *My Secret Life* in *The Other Victorians* provides many useful insights into the mind of the author, but it is severely flawed because he believes that the book is true history. '*My Secret Life*', he concludes, 'is the record of a real life in which the pornographic, sexual fantasy was acted out.'[264] My view, on the contrary, is that *My Secret Life*, far from being the record of 'fantasies actively dramatized in reality', as Marcus says earlier,[265] is an account of those that were never dramatized other than in the author's mind and on the pages of his book. *My Secret Life* can thus be regarded as a fictional substitute for the full sexual life yearned for by the author, but unattainable. Commenting on the latter's good ear, his knack for reproducing speech, Marcus writes, 'If one were to persist in doubt over the authenticity of this kind of passage, the only alternative conclusion would be to say that we are confronted in this book by a remarkable novelistic talent.'[266] Remarkable? I don't think so. But talent certainly. The conversations reported in Ashbee's diary, particularly his American diary, some of which were quoted earlier, prove that he enjoyed taking note of regional accents and turns of speech.

Conceiving *My Secret Life* and writing it was exactly the sort of undertaking for which Ashbee was well suited. Bored with his conventional diary, I believe it suddenly dawned on him, as he moved deeper and deeper into the world of banned books in the 1860s, and began work on his bibliographies, that he could at the

same time embark on the most convincing fake erotic memoir of all time. One can imagine that it came as a relief to Ashbee to write fiction: his work as a bibliographer must often have seemed unbearably sterile. In writing *My Secret Life* he could let his hair down, and given the fact that the book was genuinely pseudo-nymous (unlike the bibliographies), he did not need to worry himself unduly about style. As a guide, there were the spurious memoirs he was busily collecting, classifying and analysing. Probably it was such books that gave him the idea of *My Secret Life* in the first place. A work such as Edward Sellon's *The Ups and Downs of Life*, which according to Pisanus Fraxi in the *Index Librorum Prohibitorum* is 'in truth the auto-biography of its author and artist',[267] but which Ashbee surely knew to be largely fiction. Using the same formula, he decided to go one better than Sellon, Davenport and all the other purveyors of what Pisanus Fraxi terms 'fantasy autobiographies'.

The result is impressive. *My Secret Life* constitutes a violent attack against Victorian hypocrisy and sexual repression, against the 'ultra-squeamishness and hyper-prudery' lamented by Pisanus Fraxi in his introduction to the *Index Librorum Prohibitorum*. The author of *My Secret Life* is outraged by the British refusal to call a spade a spade, to tell children the truth about their bodies (twice 'Walter' jeers at the parsley-bed theory of where babies come from).[268] *My Secret Life* is not an essay in pornography. It is an attempt to argue the case for uninhibited sex in a society in which 'this act of mighty power and eternal endowments' is termed 'foul, bestial, abominable!' and 'may not be mentioned or talked about':[269]

It seems to me, that both men and women may be straight, and fair in all they do, be as good and useful members of society as others, yet take their chief delight in carnal pleasures. I am sure that it is so with hundreds of thousands of men, in the middle and upper classes, who are good husbands and fathers, yet who don't put a half of their sperm into

their wives' cunts, and indulge in all the varieties, refinements, and eccentricities of lust habitually. But women can't act similarly without deteriorating.[270]

My Secret Life is ultimately a sad story. Sad, above all, for the author. No one with a reasonably happy affective life, it must be obvious, is going to spend years writing an obsessive, reiterative book like this. It is a tale told by someone who has not found erotic fulfilment, by someone for whom sex exists almost entirely in the head. The nostalgia for what might have been is present not only in the failed marriage which causes 'Walter' such misery (and from which the author liberates him after some fourteen years),[271] but also in the narrator's efforts to make us believe that behind the scenes, later in his life, there is a great love whom he betrays by his unremitting need to copulate with other women. 'I fell in love and was changed,' he tells us between square brackets as he allegedly revises his manuscript, 'yet my amorous frailty clung to me. – I loved deeply, truly, shall love to my dying hour, and, spite of my infidelity, would at any time have slain any one of my paramours rather than have given *her* pain.'[272] After the first mention of this woman, she disappears altogether for many hundreds of pages. When she resurfaces, we find 'Walter' asking, 'Am I in love with a gay woman again, when there is one woman whom I adore? It was true. I was really loving two women at the same time. I loved Jessie, tho I would have slain her for the other.'[273] A few pages later 'Walter' comments, 'I actually fretted after this woman, surprized and mad with myself at such a state of mind, still loving as I ever shall one woman to the last day of my life.'[274] There is no further allusion to the 'one woman'. Had 'Walter' really had such a relationship, one imagines that inter-course with an interminable succession of prostitutes would no longer have been necessary. The fiction is so imperfectly realized that one wonders if it does not reflect the failure in love of the author.

In this respect one is reminded forcibly of Steven Marcus's commentary on the main flagellation scene recorded by 'Walter': 'It shows us, as nothing else that I know does, the pathos of perversity, how deeply sad, how cheerless a condemnation it really is. It is more than a condemnation; it is – or was – an imprisonment for life.'[275] I have argued that Ashbee was a flagellomaniac, which is to argue that he was alienated from normal sexuality. Surely he can never have never confessed such a crippling 'letch' to Elizabeth Lavy, with whom any sexual relationship had probably petered out some time before their separation? We recall the Silver Wedding entry in his diary on 10 July 1887, an intimation of what was to come: 'One of the most unhappy days I ever spent, let me forget it. A visit to Paris of a week immediately afterwards.'

The author of *My Secret Life* was not a man of great imagination or literary talent. But he had an overriding ambition: to write a voluminous and convincing erotic chronicle that would help to liberate British society from its sexual misery, cant and hypocrisy. In this, as Legman says, he was a worthy predecessor of James Joyce, D. H. Lawrence and Henry Miller. I believe that the man who wrote *My Secret Life* was Henry Spencer Ashbee. If he didn't, who on earth did?

Henry Spencer Ashbee's Will

This is the last Will and Testament of me HENRY SPENCER ASHBEE of
119 and 120 London Wall in the City of London and of Fowlers Park
Hawkhurst in the County of Kent Esquire I REVOKE all former Wills by
me at any time heretofore made and declare this only to be my last Will
and Testament I APPOINT ARTHUR HERMANN LUDEWIG PETERSEN of
No. 119 and 120 London Wall aforesaid and EDWARD HENRY MONT-
AUBAN of No. 16 Queen Elizabeth Walk Stoke Newington in the
County of Middlesex to be the EXECUTORS and TRUSTEES of this my
Will and they and the survivor of them and the Executors and
Administrators of such Survivor or other the Trustees or Trustee for
the time being hereof are hereinafter called 'my Trustees' I BEQUEATH
to my daughter Frances Mary the Wife of Frederick George Langham
my Folio Bible containing the Family Pedigree I BEQUEATH to my
Cousin Edith Blaxland the sum of £1000 but if the said Edith Blaxland
shall be under age at the time of my decease then I DIRECT that such
sum of £1000 shall be paid to her Aunt Louisa Maud Ashbee to be
applied by her towards the maintenance education or advancement in
life of the said Edith Blaxland I BEQUEATH to Irene Montauban the
Sister of the said Edward Henry Montauban the sum of £1000 but if the
said Irene Montauban shall be under age at the time of my decease then
I DIRECT that such sum of £1000 shall be paid to her Mother Ellen
Mary Jane Montauban or if she is dead to the said Edward Henry
Montauban to be applied by her or him towards the maintenance edu-
cation or advancement in life of the said Irene Montauban I BEQUEATH
unto my Cousin Louisa Maud Ashbee the sum of £1000 absolutely and

I BEQUEATH all my carriages carts garden implements horses dogs cats poultry furniture and wine spirits household goods ornaments and curios not otherwise disposed of by this my Will and both at Fowlers and at No. 4 Grays Inn Square to my Cousin the said Louisa Maud Ashbee. I DEVISE unto and to the use of my said Cousin Louisa Maud Ashbee the brick grave situate in All Souls Cemetery Kensal Green in the County of Middlesex and Nod. 17075 which Grave formerly belonged to my Father Robert Ashbee I GIVE AND BEQUEATH unto the Trustees for the time being of the British Museum to be deposited and kept in the Print Room or other suitable Department there as the case may be all engravings in my possession framed or in portfolios not otherwise disposed of by this my Will or such of them as they may select I BEQUEATH to August Reick William Benjamin Maskell and Evan Macgregor Rogers the sum of £1000 each and to Arthur Atkins the sum of £500 if in my employ at the time of my decease but if any one or more of the four last mentioned Legatees shall not be employed in my business at the time of my decease then the Legacy to him or them is hereby revoked and shall be null and void I DECLARE that the Legacies to such of the four last mentioned persons as shall be employed in my business at the time of my death shall be paid only out of my capital in the said business and shall not be payable until 3 years after my death and the said Legatees shall not call upon my Trustees to pay and my Trustees shall not be liable to pay the said Legacies until the expiration of such period of three years but if the said Arthur Hermann Ludewig Petersen shall desire to pay the same at an earlier date he shall be at liberty to do so and in the meantime the said Arthur Hermann Ludewig Petersen shall pay to the said Legatees interest on their respective legacies half yearly at the rate of 5 per cent per annum from the day of my death I BEQUEATH to each of my male and female servants who shall have been more than two years in my service at the time of my death the sum of £100 in addition to any wages which may be due to them respectively at the date of my death I BEQUEATH all my antiquities and curiosities in glass earthenware metal and other material from Cyprus Egypt Peru and other countries or such of them as they may consider useful to the Trustees of the British Museum to be deposited and kept in the department of antiquities or other suitable

department there as the case may be and in the event of the Trustees of the British Museum rejecting the said curiosities and antiquities or any of them then I BEQUEATH the same or such of them as shall have been so rejected to the Trustees of the South Kensington Museum upon similar terms AND I DIRECT that any of the said antiquities and curiosities which may be rejected both by the Trustees of the British Museum and the Trustees of the South Kensington Museum shall sink into and form part of my residuary estate I BEQUEATH all my oil paintings and all my water colour drawings to the English Nation AND I DIRECT my Trustees to select some London Gallery – the National Gallery Trafalgar Square preferred or the Gallery at South Kensington and to allow the Trustees or Executive of either of these Galleries to take for the use and enjoyment of the English Nation for ever my said oil paintings and water colour drawings or such of them as the said Authorities shall consider suitable AND I DIRECT that any of my said oil paintings and water colour drawings which shall be refused by the said Authorities shall fall into and form part of my residuary estate I BEQUEATH my watch and chain and personal jewellery my ivory headed walking stick and my writing desk to my dear friend Charles Cordery Graham begging him to accept them as momentos [sic] of me I BEQUEATH unto the Bibliographical Society of London all copies whether in their possession or mine of my Iconography of Don Quixote and of any other book which I may at any time write for the said Society together with all engraved copper plates electros printers ornaments and all other things used to illustrate the said Iconography or such other book as aforesaid and together also with any impression or impressions which have been or may be struck off from such copper plates electros printers ornaments and other things as aforesaid. I BEQUEATH to James Fitzmaurice Kelly of 14 Palace Gardens Mansions London W. all my manuscripts or unpublished writings written on paper or cards. I beg him to examine them and should he deem them worthy of publication to cause them to be printed in any manner or form he may consider suitable with any omissions alterations or additions he may think fit either in my name alone or with his name conjointly as he may wish FURTHER I BEQUEATH to the said James Fitzmaurice Kelly the sum of £1000 as a partial equivalent for the trouble and loss of time

such examination will occasion him moreover I DIRECT my Executors in the event of James Fitzmaurice Kelly deciding to print my Manuscripts to pay the costs of such publication the sum not to exceed £500 I ALSO BEQUEATH to the said James Fitzmaurice Kelly all blocks or impressions which I may have already had made in order to illustrate my said writings Mr Fitzmaurice Kelly to decide as to the publication of my Manuscripts within twelve months after which time my Executors are not bound I BEQUEATH to my friend Alexander Graham 100 books or single volumes of books from my library but not sets of books such books or volumes to be by any one or more Authors and I beg him to keep and use the said books in memory of me I BEQUEATH all my books not hereby otherwise disposed of whether in my dwelling-house at Hawkhurst or in my Chambers at Gray's Inn unto the Trustees of the British Museum and I desire that they shall be called the 'Ashbee Collection' and that a small label bearing those two words shall be affixed to each volume I EMPOWER the Trustees of the British Museum at their discretion to distribute among any of the Public Libraries in the United Kingdom any books given to them by this my Will of which they already have a copy but if they wish to retain for any reason any copy of a book of which they have already a copy they are to be at liberty to do so I FURTHER AUTHORIZE them to destroy any book of which they already possess a copy and which they do not deem it expedient to send out of the Museum I DESIRE that in addition to the said label one of my bookplates shall be placed in every volume kept by the Trustees of the British Museum or sent out for the use of the General Public but not in those which they consider should be withheld from the General Public and to this end I FURTHER BEQUEATH to them the original plates of my said bookplates I BEQUEATH to the Arundel Club any engravings belonging to me at the said Club AND I DIRECT my Trustees to pay the sum of £500 per annum (provided for in manner hereinafter appearing) to the Trustees for the time being of the Deed of Separation dated the 30th day of January 1893 in the manner provided by such Deed in satisfaction of the covenant therein contained and from and after the decease or second marriage of my Wife whichever shall first happen. I DIRECT that my Trustees shall set apart out of my residuary Trust funds such a sum as will when invested in

securities authorised by Law for trust funds produce the yearly income of £312 and shall stand possessed of such yearly income IN TRUST to make to all or any of my daughters a weekly allowance of 40/- in case they or any one or more of them shall personally apply to my Trustees for the same such weekly allowance to commence from the date of such application or respective applications but my Trustees shall not pay to any of my said Daughters the sum of 40/- per week unless such personal application be made and they or she shall to the satisfaction of my Trustees prove that through accident sickness or other reasonable cause they or she are or is in indigent circumstances and unable to obtain a livelihood and that they or she are or is not living with my Son Charles Robert Ashbee and from and after the decease of one of my said daughters one third of the capital producing such yearly income of £312 shall fall into my residuary estate and from and after the decease of another of my said daughters another third part of the said capital shall fall into my residuary estate and from and after the decease of all my daughters the whole of the said capital shall fall into my residuary estate I DECLARE that the granting or withholding to all or any one or more of my said daughters of the said weekly allowance shall be in the absolute discretion of my Trustees and they shall if they think fit discontinue the said weekly allowances without being called upon to justify such discontinuance I BEQUEATH to the Worshipful Company of Curriers and to the Worshipful Company of Armourers and Brasiers the sum of £5000 each to be invested in such securities as the Master and Court of Assistance of such Companies respectively at the time of my death may select the revenue from such securities to be expended at the option of the Master and Court of such Companies respectively for the time being as to two thirds in Charity or works of public utility and as to the remaining one third for the benefit or hospitality of the respective Companies I BEQUEATH unto the said Worshipful Company of Armourers and Brasiers my Silver Table Ornament consisting of a Basket supported by 3 female figures and my Silver dish of Spanish make and bearing in the centre the Arms of the Marquis of Moscoso AND I BEQUEATH to the said Worshipful Company of Curriers the following silver articles my large kettle and stand my large Coffee pot my large milk jug my large cream jug and my large teapot AND I DIRECT

that all legacies whether pecuniary or specific bequeathed by this my Will except those bequeathed to the two city companies above mentioned shall be free of legacy duty AND with respect to the business carried on by me at Nos. 119 and 120 London Wall aforesaid in partnership with the said Arthur Hermann Ludewig Petersen I DIRECT my Trustees as soon as conveniently may be after my decease to adjust and settle all accounts and transactions relating to the said partnership business and to ascertain the amount of my capital and share of profits therein upon the day of my death I BEQUEATH unto the said Arthur Hermann Ludewig Petersen my share and interest in the said business including goodwill stock in trade and any chattels books engravings etc. which may be at my place of business No. 119 and 120 London Wall and in the Lease of the same premises but not including my capital and share of profits in such business which shall form part of my residuary estate I GIVE all the residue of my real and personal estate including my share of the profits of and my capital in the said business at 119 and 120 London Wall and my shares in the business in which I am interested in Paris unto my Trustees and UPON TRUST to sell call in and convert into money the same or such part thereof as shall not consist of money and out of the proceeds of such sale calling in and conversion and with and out of my ready money in the first place to pay my just debts crematory funeral and testamentary expenses and to invest the residue of such moneys upon securities authorised by law for the investment of trust funds AND to stand possessed of the said residuary trust moneys and the investments for the time being representing the same (hereinafter called the residuary trusts funds) upon the trusts following (that is to say) as to two equal fifth parts thereof IN TRUST to pay the income thereof to the said Arthur Hermann Ludewig Petersen during his life AND after his decease IN TRUST for all the children living at my death of my Daughter Frances Mary the Wife of Frederick George Langham who shall have attained or who shall attain the age of 21 years in equal shares and if there shall be only one such Child the whole to be IN TRUST for that one child AND as to two other equal fifth parts thereof IN TRUST to pay the income thereof to the said Louisa Maud Ashbee during her life and after her decease upon similar trusts in favor of the Children or Child living at my death of my said daughter Frances Mary

as are hereinbefore declared concerning the first mentioned two fifth shares after the death of the said Arthur Hermann Ludewig Petersen AND as to the remaining one fifth part of the residuary trust funds IN TRUST to pay the income thereof to the said Edward Henry Montauban during his life AND after his death upon similar trusts in favor of the Children or Child living at my death of my said daughter Frances Mary as are hereinbefore declared concerning the other parts of the residuary trust funds after the death of the said Arthur Hermann Ludewig Petersen and Louisa Maud Ashbee respectively PROVIDED nevertheless that during the minority of any Child of my said daughter my Trustees shall accumulate the income arising from his or her expectant share in the residuary trust funds by investing the same and the resulting income thereof in manner aforesaid to the intent that the accumulations shall be added to such expectant share and follow the destination thereof I DIRECT that the said Arthur Hermann Ludewig Petersen shall be at liberty to retain in his hands in the said business the sum of £10,000 during the joint lives of himself and my said Wife or until her second Marriage the interest on such sum of £10,000 to be applied by my Trustees in payment of the sum of 500 per annum so as aforesaid to be paid to the Trustee of the Deed of Separation hereinbefore mentioned AND I ALSO DIRECT that the said Arthur Hermann Ludewig Petersen shall not be called upon to pay to my Trustees the remainder of my capital in the said business carried on at No. 119 and 120 London Wall except by ten equal annual instalments the first of such instalments to be paid at the expiration of twelve calendar months after my decease PROVIDED ALWAYS that if the said Arthur Hermann Ludewig Petersen shall be desirous of paying the whole or any part of the said capital prior to the times hereinbefore appointed for payment thereof he shall be at liberty to do so in the meantime the said Arthur Hermann Ludewig Petersen shall pay to my Trustees interest on the unpaid balance of my said capital at the rate of 5 per cent per annum I DESIRE to be cremated in as inexpensive a manner as possible I do not wish any mourning worn for me or other demonstration made nor do I desire that any monument whatever be erected to my memory IN WITNESS whereof I have to this my last Will and Testament contained in [] sheets of paper set my hand this 28th day of June 1900.

SIGNED by the said Henry Spencer Ashbee the Testator as and for his last Will and Testament in the presence of us present at the same time who at his request in his presence and in the presence of each other have hereunto subscribed our names as Witnesses

Alfred Hardcastle
High Field Hawkhurst
J.P. (Kent)

L Weston Wigg
4 Clements Inn
Strand W.C.
Solicitor

References

ABBREVIATIONS USED IN THE REFERENCES

AD Unpublished diaries of Henry Spencer Ashbee

CLA Pisanus Fraxi, *Centuria Librorum Absconditorum*

CLT Pisanus Fraxi, *Catena Librorum Tacendorum*

GLA Guy Langham Archive

IDQ Ashbee, *An Iconography of Don Quixote, 1605–1895*

ILP Pisanus Fraxi, *Index Librorum Prohibitorum*

MSL *My Secret Life* (unless otherwise indicated by context, the 1966 Grove Press edition)

TT Ashbee, *Travels in Tunisia*

Unless otherwise stated, all periodical publications in English and French appeared respectively in London and Paris.

INTRODUCTION

1 Acton, *The Functions and Disorders of the Reproductive Organs*, 5th edn (1871), p. 21.

2 *The Education of Henry Adams* (1928), quoted in C. R. Ashbee, *'Grannie'*, p. 54.

3 Goncourts, *Journal*, 1887, vol. ii, p. 27.

4 Gibson, pp. 240–41. For some of Swinburne's efforts in the flagellant line, see ibid., Appendix C, pp. 320–28.

5 Hull Walton, p. 16.

6 Lovell, p. 620.

7 Quoted in Hull Walton, p. 32.

8 *The Swinburne Letters*, vol. i, p. 44; Pope-Hennessy (1951), pp. 127–8.

9 *The Swinburne Letters*, vol. i, p. 124.

10 From 'Hymn to Proserpine (after the Proclamation in Rome of the Christian Faith)'.

11 *The Poems of Algernon Charles Swinburne* (London, Chatto and Windus, 1911),
 vol. iv, p. 287.

1 THE MAKING OF AN EROTOMANIAC (1834–77)

1 The 1851 Census, in its account of Robert Ashbee's household in Whitton, states
 that his son Henry Spencer was born in 'Surry [*sic*] Blackfriars road'. This is con-
 firmed by information inserted in the Ashbee family Bible, according to which
 Henry Spencer was born in 'Blackfriars Road, London'. Frederick Boase (p. 178)
 goes further and specifies (without source) that the birth took place at number 24.
 I have not been able to find independent evidence for this. Peter Fryer (p. 3),
 following Boase, discovered that at 24 Blackfriars Road there was by 1833 an inn
 called The Rising Sun. According to the 1831 Census, number 24 was occupied
 by one Edward Grimmer, victualler. In *Robson's Directory* for 1832, the latter
 appears under the sign of The Rising Sun. (I am grateful to Stephen Humphrey,
 of the Local Studies Library, Southwark, for supplying the information contained
 in the previous two sentences.) In 1975, The Rising Sun at 24 Blackfriars Road
 was still in business, with striptease and 'topless go-go' as added attractions. No
 doubt Ashbee would have approved.

 For Ashbee's baptism, see 'Baptisms solemnized in the Parish of Boughton
 under the Blean in the County of Kent in the Year 1834', no. 1,040, Canterbury
 Cathedral Archives (my profuse thanks to my friend Ken Styan for obtaining and
 sending me a copy of this document).

2 C. R. Ashbee, *The Trivialities of Tom*, p. 9.

3 Ashbee family Bible.

4 C. R. Ashbee, *'Grannie'*, pp. 18–19; death certificate of Frances Elizabeth Ashbee;
 genealogical details in Ashbee family Bible.

5 C. R. Ashbee, *The Trivialities of Tom*, pp. 10–26.

6 Genealogical table in Ashbee family Bible; C. R. Ashbee, *'Grannie'*, pp. 18–19.

7 There was an explosion at the John Hall and Son works in 1841 (*The Times*,
 3 July 1841, p. 7). For the details of the mills at Faversham, my source is *Post Office
 Directory of London and Nine Counties; viz: Cambridgeshire, Norfolk, and Suffolk,
 with Essex, Hertfordshire, Kent, Middlesex, Surrey and Sussex* (1846),
 p. 884.

8 C. R. Ashbee, *'Grannie'*, pp. 19–20.

9 *The Times*, 13 March 1859, p. 8.

10 *AD*, 21 July 1854.

11 Boase, p. 178. My own researches have proved fruitless. According to the secretary
 of the Esher District Local History Society in 1977, Richard Haynes, at the time of
 Ashbee's boyhood there were in Esher a National School (for poor children) and
 three small private ones: 'William Blatch, a stationer, ran a day school, Jane Price
 had a boarding school, and the Revd Dr John Brown maintained an academy at
 his home, Albion House (now demolished). Almost certainly no record of any of

these three schools survives.' (Letter to the author, 18 November 1977.)

12 *AD*, 8 April 1882.

13 *Report of the Directors of the Kensington Proprietary Grammar School for the Year 1849*; *Post Office London Directory* (1852), p. 324.

14 Haig Brown, pp. 34–5.

15 Ibid., p. 35.

16 A comprehensive catalogue of the some 1,600 volumes in the library was printed in the Directors' Report for 1849. In succeeding years supplements were printed in the annual report.

17 Kensington School 'Order of Merit' lists (published quarterly), midsummer 1848 and 1850. Documentation sent to me in 1978 from the Central Library, The Royal Borough of Kensington and Chelsea, Phillimore Walk, London w8 7rx. My thanks to Mr Melvyn Barnes, the then Borough Librarian and Arts Officer, and Mrs P. K. Pratt, Co-ordinator of Reference and Information Services.

18 Ashbee, 'Don Quixote and British Art' (1900), p. 11.

19 Kensington School Annual Report, 1850.

20 Kensington School 'Order of Merit' lists, 1848–9.

21 *AD*, 13 January 1881.

22 *Post Office Directory of London and Nine Counties, viz: Cambridgeshire, Norfolk, and Suffolk, with Essex, Hertfordshire, Kent, Middlesex, Surrey and Sussex* (1846), p. 258.

23 *Post Office London Directory* (1850), p. 1,292; ibid. (1857).

24 *AD*, 23 July 1854.

25 *AD*, 29 July 1854.

26 *AD*, 1 August 1854.

27 *AD*, 30 July 1854.

28 *AD*, 4 August 1854.

29 *AD*, 1 August 1855.

30 *AD*, 29 September 1883.

31 Mayhew, vol. iv, between pp. 212 and 213.

32 *AD*, 17 October 1858.

33 *AD*, 31 October 1858.

34 *AD*, 20 and 25 August 1854.

35 *AD*, 31 October and 9 November 1858.

36 *AD*, 15 November 1858.

37 Ibid.

38 *The Times*, 15 March 1850.

39 Ibid., 13 March 1850, p. 8; 31 March 1859, p. 9; 4 April 1859, p. 8.

40 I am indebted to Mr Ken Styan for supplying me with certified copies of the respective birth certificates, in both of which Robert Ashbee is stated to be 'superintendent of powder mills'. In 1857 Frances Marion Purchase was resident at 14 Blenheim Street, in 1858 at 19 King Street.

41 Information contained in the Ashbee family Bible. How Edward Otto Charles
 Lavy met Marian Benjamin is not clear. They were married on 7 October 1837 at
 the parish church of St Luke, Middlesex, their wedding certificate describing him
 as a 'merchant, of 156 White Cross Road', which suggests that, since Marian is
 also stated to be resident at the same address, Edward Otto Charles was then
 living in London and perhaps working for her father. (Information from the
 wedding certificate obtained at Somerset House and summarized in a letter from
 Richard Ames-Lewis to Guy Langham, 22 February 1961; GLA.) When Edward
 Otto Charles Lavy and and Marian Benjamin moved to Hamburg we do not
 know.

42 Mayhew, vol. iv, p. 196.

43 C. R. Ashbee, 'Grannie', pp. 1–3.

44 Letter from one of the Ashbee relatives in Hamburg, Esther Craseman, to Guy
 Langham in 1960; GLA.

45 Boase, p. 178.

46 Crawford, pp. 1–3.

47 Certified copy of death entry of Frances Elizabeth Ashbee, General Register
 Office, London, 13 September 1977.

48 Letter to the author from local historian Margaret Lang, Isleworth, 7 October
 1977; Kelly's Middlesex (1862), p. 554, for the Davies properties at Spring Grove.

49 Letter to the author from Margaret Lang (see n. 48).

50 Ashbee family Bible.

51 Copy of Robert Ashbee's death certificate supplied by Somerset House.

52 C. R. Ashbee, 'Grannie', p. 18.

53 Will consulted at Probate Office, London.

54 Boase, p. 178.

55 Quoted in CLT, p. xlv, n. 65.

56 Ashbee, 'Octave Delepierre, LL.D.' (1879).

57 CLT, p. xlv; on p. 527, Pisanus Fraxi informs us that the work in question has
 thirty-five pages and contains 'bibliographical appreciations of thirty-two different
 works'.

58 Ashbee family Bible.

59 AD, 20 January 1888.

60 Ashbee family Bible.

61 Boase, p. 178.

62 Marcus, p. 72.

63 For an account of the work, see ILP, pp. 82–7.

64 AD, 11 March 1874.

65 W.H.K.W., 'The Late H. S. Ashbee', p. 129.

66 AD, 12 August 1875; CLA, pp. 326–45.

67 Mendes, p. 28.

68 AD, passim.

69 Pearsall, p. 474.

70 Marcus, p. 73.

71 *ILP*, pp. 249–56; *AD*, 12 November 1873.

72 *AD*, 25 July 1877.

73 Mendes, p. 3.

74 Fryer, p. 11.

75 Mendes, *passim*; *ILP*, p. 127. There is an account of Dugdale and his 'disgusting occupation' in Mayhew, vol. iv, pp. 267–8.

76 *CLT*, pp. xlvii–xlviii.

77 Noticed by Pisanus Fraxi in *ILP*, pp. 15–16; in his interleaved working copy of the *Index Librorum Prohibitorum*, preserved in the British Library, Ashbee inserted the following annotation opposite p. 15: 'The Adventures of a Schoolboy was written by James Campbell'. See also Mendes, pp. 347, 431.

78 *CLT*, p. 198.

79 Mendes, p. 347.

80 *ILP*, p. 436.

81 Legman (1966), p. xlix.

82 Quoted *CLT*, p. 197.

83 *The Swinburne Letters*, vol. ii, p. 32. Campbell has been misread as Capell. See Mendes, p. 215.

84 Ashbee, 'The Baffled Collector' (1891), n. 2.

85 *AD*, 25 September 1875.

86 *CLT*, pp. l–liii.

87 Mendes, p. 11.

88 Houghton Commonplace Books, Trinity College, Cambridge, 212 (1857–58–59–60), p. 160.

89 Goncourts' *Journal*, vol. v, p. 89.

90 Ibid., pp. 28–9; Gibson, pp. 243–4.

91 *CLT*, p. l.

92 Ibid., p. 188; Mendes, pp. 236–7.

93 Mendes, p. 237.

94 Paillet, p. 49.

95 *The Swinburne Letters*, vol. ii, pp. 19–20.

96 For the date of Ashbee's meeting with Paillet and Bégis, *AD*, 8 November 1873.

97 Ibid.

98 Paillet describes his first meeting at Hankey's with Ashbee in his obituary of the latter, published in the *Annuaire* of the Société des Amis des Livres, vol. xxii, no. 32 (1901), pp. 46–9.

99 C. R. Ashbee, *'Grannie'*, p. 31.

100 *ILP*, pp. xiv–xv.

101 Ralph Thomas, p. 121.

102 C. R. Ashbee, *The Trivialities of Tom*, p. 110.

103 Letter tipped into Ashbee's interleaved copy of the *Index Librorum Prohibitorum* in the British Library.

104 Crawford, pp. 6–7; C. R. Ashbee, *The Trivialities of Tom*, pp. 34–5.

105 C. R. Ashbee, *The Trivialities of Tom*, *passim*.

106 Ibid., pp. 93–4.

107 C. R. Ashbee, *'Grannie'*, pp. 31–2.

108 Kelly and Company's *The Post Office London Suburban Directory* (3rd edn, 1865), p. 573.

109 *AD*, 7 January 1876.

110 Ibid.

111 *AD*, 19 June 1876.

112 Mendes, pp. 28; 42, n. 1; 171; 192.

113 *ILP*, p. 434n.

114 *AD*, 26 May 1875; 24, 26, 27, 28, 30 October 1876.

115 *AD*, 18 September 1876.

116 Galitzin's collection was described in the *Catalogue du cabinet secret du Prince G**** (Brussels, 1887), which was 'stopped after only the first half of the alphabet had been published', according to Legman (1966), p. xxii.

117 *AD*, 22 October–1 November 1876.

118 *AD*, 5 January–15 April 1877, *passim*.

119 *ILP*, p. 536.

120 *AD*, 13 May 1877.

121 Ibid.

122 Ibid. For Delepierre's address, *AD*, 28 February 1875.

2 THE *INDEX LIBRORUM PROHIBITORUM* (1877)

1 'Speculator Morum', p. 2, no. 6, for the number of copies printed.

2 Farrell (May–June 1982), p. 43.

3 Juvenal, *The Sixteen Satires*, translated by Peter Green (Penguin, 3rd edn, 1998), p. 9.

4 *AD*, 10 April 1875.

5 *ILP*, pp. vii–viii.

6 *ILP*, pp. xvii–xviii.

7 *ILP*, p. xviii.

8 *ILP*, p. xxiv.

9 *ILP*, pp. xix–xx.

10 *ILP*, p. xxxii.

11 *ILP*, pp. xxxiii–xxxiv.

12 *ILP*, pp. xxxiv–xxxv.

13 *ILP*, pp. xxxv–xxxvi.

14 *ILP*, pp. xxxvii–xxxviii.

15 *ILP*, p. xxxviii.

16 *ILP*, pp.xxxviii–xxxix.
17 *ILP*, pp. xl–xlii.
18 Quoted by Mendes, p. 234.
19 For further details, see Gibson, pp. 194–232.
20 *ILP*, p. xlvi, n. 66.
21 *ILP*, pp. xlii–xliii.
22 Gibson, p. 252.
23 *ILP*, p. 398.
24 *ILP*, pp. xliii–xlv.
25 *ILP*, p. xlv.
26 *ILP*, pp. xlvi–xlvii.
27 Marcus, p. 61.
28 *ILP*, p. xlix.
29 *ILP*, p. lii.
30 *ILP*, p. lvi.
31 *ILP*, pp. lxviii–lxix.
32 *ILP*, p. lxx.
33 Marcus, p. 49.
34 *ILP*, pp. 106–7, 111, 125, 127, 249, 402.
35 *ILP*, pp. 16, 31, 43, 48, 110, 128, 142, 149, 195, 305, 435.
36 *ILP*, pp. 82–9.
37 *ILP*, pp. 175–7.
38 Reproduced by Lovell, p. 611, from W. G. Archer's introduction to the *Kama Sutra* (1963).
39 *ILP*, p. 283.
40 Quoted by Marcus, p. 32,
41 *ILP*, pp. 290–91.
42 *ILP*, p. 346.
43 *ILP*, pp. 400–401.
44 Krafft-Ebing, p. 101.
45 For a fuller discussion of Krafft-Ebing, and particularly of his findings on sexual flagellation, see Gibson, pp. 32–45. For the popularity of *Psychopathia Sexualis*, see Mendes, pp. 308–9, where an interesting comment by Aleister Crowley is reproduced. For Wilde, my source is Donald Thomas, vol. 3, p. xxix.

3 FROM THE *CENTURIA* TO THE *CATENA* (1877–85)

1 *Notes and Queries*, 18 August 1877, p. 136.
2 Crawford, p. 6.
3 *CLT*, pp. xlvii, xlix, 493–4.
4 *AD*, 7 November 1877.
5 *AD*, 21 December 1877.

6 *AD*, 9 February 1878.
7 Richard Ford, p. 131.
8 Brodie, p. 48.
9 Mendes, pp. 4 and 11.
10 *CLT*, p. 246; for the authorship, Mendes, pp. 2, 245, 432.
11 Fryer, p. 11; for date of foundation, Farrell (September–October 1982), p. 14.
12 Houghton Papers, Trinity College Library, Cambridge University.
13 *AD*, 8 December 1878.
14 C. R. Ashbee, *'Grannie'*, p. 55.
15 *CLA*, p. xvii.
16 *CLA*, pp. xxx–xxxi.
17 *CLA*, p. lv.
18 *CLA*, pp. 456–76.
19 *CLA*, pp. 456–7.
20 *CLA*, p. 458.
21 *CLA*, p. 459, note.
22 *CLA*, p. 461.
23 *AD*, 30 November 1879.
24 Paillet, p. 52.
25 Drujon, 'La Bibliographie en Angleterre. Étude sur deux ouvrages récemment parus à Londres' (1880), p. 14.
26 'French Literature', *Saturday Review*, 7 February 1880, pp. 194–6.
27 George Saintsbury, 'Le Livre', *Academy*, 7 February 1880, p. 104.
28 *AD*, 24 February 1880.
29 Fryer, p. 10. According to a list of useful contacts included by Ashbee in a letter to Houghton of 24 July 1880 (Houghton Papers, Trinity College Library, Cambridge), Drujon was at that time 'Chef de Cabinet du Préfet de Police, Bvd. du Palais'.
30 *AD*, 15 April 1880.
31 Houghton Papers, Trinity College Library, Cambridge.
32 Grego, vol. ii, p. 412.
33 Grego's allusion is listed, along with other references to the *Centuria*, in Ashbee's own copy of the work in the British Library.
34 *AD*, 26 April 1881.
35 Ashbee, 'The Metropolis of the Manchus' (1882), pp. 553–4.
36 *AD*, 18 January 1881.
37 *AD*, 11 June 1881, pp. 200, 212–13.
38 Langham, p. 201.
39 *AD*, 11 June 1881, pp. 213–14.
40 Mendes, p. 9.
41 Houghton Papers, Trinity College Library, Cambridge.
42 Ralph Thomas, 'The Late H. S. Ashbee', *Notes and Queries*, 18 August 1900, p. 121.

43 Brick vault no. 17075. Among the names on the tomb there is the inscription 'CHILD 1881'.

44 *AD*, 4 July 1881.

45 *AD*, 7 July 1881.

46 Octave Uzanne, 'Une Lettre de Londres sur les Bibliophiles Anglais', *Annuaire* of Société des Amis des Livres, 1881, pp. 32–3.

47 *CLT*, pp. lii–liii.

48 Houghton Papers, Trinity College Library, Cambridge.

49 Mendes, pp. 128, 237.

50 C. R. Ashbee Journals, Christmas Day 1901, King's College Library, Cambridge.

51 Ibid.

52 *AD*, 8–24 April 1882.

53 Certified copy of entry of death issued at the General Register Office, London, 21 April 1978.

54 *CLT*, p. 509.

55 *AD*, 13 August 1882.

56 *AD*, 15 August 1882.

57 *AD*, 21 August 1882.

58 *AD*, 4 August–3 September 1882, *passim*.

59 C. R. Ashbee, *'Grannie'*, pp. 34–5.

60 Crawford, p. 7.

61 Ibid.; C. R. Ashbee Journals, King's College Library, Cambridge.

62 *AD*, 10 November 1882.

63 *AD*, 26 September 1883.

64 *AD*, 8, 9, 12 December 1882; for Drujon's book, *CLA*, p. 485.

65 C. R. Ashbee, *'Grannie'*, p. 59.

66 *AD*, *passim*.

67 Lovell, pp. 610, 620–21.

68 Mendes, p. 25.

69 Ibid.

70 *CLT*, pp. 403–4.

71 Mendes, p. 25.

72 *AD*, 4 November 1883.

73 *AD*, 10 November 1883.

74 *AD*, 6 November 1883.

75 *AD*, 17 November 1883.

76 *AD*, 11 December 1883.

77 R.T., 'Notes on Curious and Uncommon Books', *Bibliographer*, vol. v (December 1883–May 1884), pp. 137–8.

78 E. H. Shebsa, 'The *Kama Sutra* of Vatsayayana'. Exact date of publication in the *Bibliographer* provided (p. 461) in the course of Ashbee's lengthy notice of the *Kama Sutra* in *CLT*, pp. 458–76.

79 *AD*, 4 April 1884.
80 Houghton Papers, Trinity College Library, Cambridge.
81 *AD*, 7 and 9 November 1884.
82 C. R. Ashbee Papers, King's College Library, Cambridge.
83 For the Tricotel manuscript, Farrell (September–October 1982), p. 22.
84 C. R. Ashbee Journals, 17 November 1884, King's College Library, Cambridge.
85 Ibid., 29 November 1884.
86 *AD*, 24 December 1884.
87 *AD*, 29 December 1884–12 January 1885.
88 *AD*, 6 January 1885.
89 *AD*, 7 January 1885.
90 *AD*, 7 February 1885.
91 *AD*, 21 June 1885.
92 Lovell, p. 686.
93 Ashbee, 'Une Traduction complète des *Mille et Une Nuits*' (1885).
94 C. R. Ashbee, *'Grannie'*, pp. 50–53.
95 Ashbee, *An Iconography of Don Quixote, 1605–1695*, p. ix.
96 *CLT*, pp. xxxix–xl.
97 Marcus, p. 50.
98 *CLT*, p. 254.
99 Mendes, pp. 4–6, 209.
100 *CLT*, p. 261.
101 Ibid.
102 *CLT*, pp. 264–5.
103 Mendes, p. 469.
104 *AD*, 28 November 1885.
105 *AD*, 19 November 1885, pp. 258–9.
106 *AD*, 17 November 1885.

4 THE LAST YEARS 1886–1900

1 Mendes, p. 144.
2 Ibid., pp. 24–5.
3 Ibid., p. 29.
4 Ibid.
5 Ibid., pp. 55–6.
6 Ibid., p. 25.
7 Farrell (September–October 1982), p. 15.
8 C. R. Ashbee Journals, King's College Library, Cambridge.
9 Crawford, p. 19.
10 C. R. Ashbee, *The Trivialities of Tom*, pp. 93–4.
11 Larousse *Grand dictionnaire universel du XIXe siècle*, vol. xvii (1886), p. 366.
12 Ashbee, 'Foreigners who have Written in English. Pierre Antoine Motteux' (1891),

pp. 262–3; *CLT*, pp. 404–8.

13 *AD*, 28 January–2 February 1886.

14 *AD*, 8 June 1887.

15 Langham, p. 306.

16 Letter from Janet Forbes to Guy Langham, dated 12 May [?1951]; GLA.

17 Crawford, p. 6.

18 *TT*, p. 205.

19 Kearney, no. 630, pp. 168–9; Mendes, p. 331. British Library, P.C. 30.g.8.

20 Mendes, pp. 172–3.

21 Richard Burton papers, Trinity College, Cambridge.

22 Ibid.

23 *Academy*, 16 June 1888.

24 *The Times*, 10 August 1888, p. 13.

25 *AD*, 14 and 25 January 1874, 15 February 1874, 8 September 1880.

26 C. R. Ashbee, *'Grannie'*, pp. 19–20.

27 Langham, p. 305.

28 Ashbee, *The Iconography of Don Quixote, 1605–1895*, p. 130.

29 Eugène Paillet, 'Travels in Tunisia', review of Ashbee and Graham's book published in the *Annuaire* of the Société des Amis des Livres, 1888, p. 61.

30 Kearney, no. 228, p. 112. British Library, P.C. 23.a.16.

31 Kearney, no. 609, p. 166. British Library, P.C. 31.i.17.

32 Certified copy of marriage entry of Frederick George Langham and Frances Mary Ashbee, supplied by the General Register Office, London, 13 September 1977.

33 For the dates of death of Bellamy and Hodgson, Mendes, p. 11.

34 Lovell, pp. 730–32.

35 *Le Livre moderne*, vol. ii (1890), pp. 157–8.

36 C. R. Ashbee papers, King's College Library, Cambridge.

37 My thanks, once again, to Felicity Ashbee, who over the years has repeatedly told me about her father's inability to talk about Henry Spencer.

38 C. R. Ashbee, *'Grannie'*, pp. 58–62.

39 Langham, pp. 306–7.

40 Ibid., p. 307.

41 Certified copy of Montauban's entry of birth, given at the General Register Office, London, 15 March 1978.

42 Letter from Janet Forbes to Guy Langham; GLA.

43 Croom Johnson, pp. 1, 6; certified copy of Montauban's entry of death, given at the General Register Office, London, 21 April 1978.

44 Langham, p. 307.

45 *ILP*, p. xli.

46 'A Bookworm', 'Bookworms of Yesterday and Today. Mr. Henry Spencer Ashbee', *Bookworm*, vol. ii (1889), p. 258.

47 C. R. Ashbee, 'An Error of the Poet Gray', *Notes and Queries*,

19 April 1884, p. 306.

48 Letter from Janet Forbes to Guy Langham; GLA.

49 Letter from Janet Forbes to Guy Langham, '22nd' [?February 1951]; GLA.

50 Ibid.

51 Letter dated 21 October 1960; GLA.

52 Crawford, p. 72.

53 Langham, p. 307.

54 I am grateful to my friend Ken Styan for his attempt to locate a copy of the Deed of Separation at the Public Record Office, Kew. Since no trace of it seems to exist there, we can probably conclude that it was a purely private deed with no intervention by the courts. Felicity Ashbee has never seen a copy of the document. Perhaps Ashbee's was destroyed by his trustees at his death, and Elizabeth Lavy's by Charles at hers (in 1919).

55 Langham, p. 307.

56 Crawford, p. 72.

57 C. R. Ashbee, 'Grannie', p. 60.

58 Draft letter to the author from Guy Langham, 25 June 1977.

59 Mendes, pp. 28, 251, notes that in Ashbee's copy of *The Marchioness's Amorous Pastimes and Some Other Merry Tales* (BL P.C. 31.f.33) Ashbee has written, 'Maheu/Bruxelles 1893'.

60 Ashbee, 'Some Books about Cervantes' (1898), p. 13.

61 *IDQ*, p. ix.

62 William Entwistle, 'Fitzmaurice-Kelly, James', in *Dictionary of National Biography* (1922–1930), pp. 309–11.

63 Ibid.

64 Fitzmaurice-Kelly, *Revue Hispanique*, vol. v (1987), pp. 93–5.

65 Ibid.

66 Langham, pp. 314–15.

67 Certified copy of marriage entry of Louisa Maud Ashbee and William Turner Clarke, 12 June 1906, supplied by the General Register Office, London, 10 March 1978; certified copy of death entry of Edward Ashbee, supplied by the General Register Office, London, 21 April 1978; draft of letter from Guy Langham to Gerald Fothergill, 7 April 1962; GLA.

68 Letter from Gerald Fothergill to Guy Langham, 9 April 1962; GLA.

69 Diary of Ashbee's neighbour at Hawkhurst, Major Henry Fothergill; GLA.

70 Guy Langham's notes on the Fothergill diaries; GLA.

71 Letter, in German, from Oswald Barber to Guy Langham, Hamburg, 26 April 1949; GLA. Quoted in translation in Langham, pp. 315–16.

72 Boase, p. 178.

73 Communication to the author from the present Secretary of the Spanish Royal Academy, Don Víctor García de la Concha, 16 November 1998.

74 Archive of the Real Academia Española de la Lengua, Madrid.
75 Legman (1966), p. xxiii.
76 Lemonnyer, vol. i, pp. 525–6.
77 Ibid., vol. ii, p. 654.
78 Drujon, 'La Bibliographie en Angleterre. Étude sur deux ouvrages récemment parus à Londres' (1880).
79 Legman (1966), p. li.
80 Bloch, *Englische Sittengeschichte* (1912), vol. ii, p. 502, quoted in Legman (1966), p. xxvii.
81 Legman (1966), p. li.
82 Ashbee, 'Some Books about Cervantes', p. 33; H.S.A., 'A Member of the University of Cambridge'.
83 'J.C.', 'Henry Spencer Ashbee', *L'Intermédiaire des chercheurs et curieux*, 10 December 1897, p. 720.
84 'X.', 'Henry Spencer Ashbee', ibid., 10 March 1898, p. 356.
85 Crawford, pp. 79, 82.
86 Ashbee, 'Some Books about Cervantes', *passim*.
87 T.S. [Thomas Seccombe], p. 80.
88 Ralph Thomas, p. 122.
89 Paillet, p. 51.
90 *Notes and Queries*, 18 August 1900, p. 121.
91 Ashbee, 'Don Quixote and British Art' (1900), *passim*.
92 Certified copy of Ashbee's entry of death, given at the General Register Office, London, 13 September 1977.
93 W.H.K.W., 'The Late H. S. Ashbee', *Ex Libris Journal*, vol. x (1900), pp. 127–9.
94 Press-mark Cerv. Cᵃ 39 nº 11.
95 *Transactions of the Bibliographical Society*, vol. vi (1900–1902), p. 4.
96 *Ex Libris Journal*, vol. x (1900), p. 2.
97 Details in the Ashbee family Bible.
98 Ibid.
99 Ralph Thomas in *Notes and Queries*, 22 December 1900, pp. 494–5.
100 *The Times*, 1 August 1900, p. 7.
101 *Athenaeum*, no. 3,797 (4 August 1900), p. 156.
102 *Notes and Queries*, 18 August 1900, pp. 121–2; Lemonnyer, vol. i, p. 526.
103 T. Cann Hughes, *Notes and Queries*, 1 September 1900, p. 176.
104 *Notes and Queries*, 1 September 1900, p. 176.
105 Ibid., 22 December 1900, p. 494.
106 Letter from Janet Forbes to Guy Langham, 15 January [?1950]; GLA.
107 *Daily News*, 26 September 1900.
108 Cross, p. 206.
109 Ibid.

110 Quotation taken from Mendes, p. 466.

111 Mendes, pp. 466–7.

112 Ibid., p. 466.

113 Copy of document kindly furnished to the author by Dr David Clements of the British Museum's Department of Printed Books, 28 September 1977.

114 Mendes, pp. 466–7.

115 C. R. Ashbee Journals, King's College Library, Cambridge.

116 Copies of documents kindly sent to the author by Dr David Clements of the British Museum's Department of Printed Books, 28 September 1977.

117 *Daily Chronicle*, 2 October 1900, p. 3.

118 'The Victoria and Albert Museum', *Standard*, 9 November 1900, p. 7.

119 *Notes and Queries*, 3 November 1900, p. 358.

120 Ibid., 22 December 1900, p. 495.

121 Conversation with Guy Langham, Evesham, Worcestershire, July 1977.

122 Mary Ashbee quoted in a letter from Janet Forbes to Guy Langham, 21 November [?1950]; GLA.

123 Letter from Christie's to Guy Langham, 29 March 1962, GLA; letter to the author from Christie's, 4 October 1977.

124 T.S., pp. 79–80.

125 W.H.K.W., pp. 127–9.

126 *Proceedings of the Society of Antiquarians*, 23 April 1901, p. 340.

127 *Transactions of the Bibliographical Society*, vol. vi (1900–1902), p. 2.

128 Boase, pp. 178–9; Mendes, p. 21.

129 Ashbee, 'Les Auteurs–Amateurs anglais' (1883), p. 45.

130 *ILP*, pp. xvii.

131 Fryer, p. 11.

5 ASHBEE AND *MY SECRET LIFE*

1 Kronhausen, vol.i, p. 4, note.

2 Farrell (July–August 1982), p. 3.

3 Review of the 1966 Grove Press edition of *My Secret Life*, *New York Times Book Review*, 1 January 1967.

4 Legman (1962), p. 51.

5 Vernon Symonds, in a communication to Alex Craig quoted in Legman (1966), p. xlvi.

6 Mendes, pp. 31–2. Legman (1966), p. xlv, gives slightly different dates: Carrington 'dominated the English-language field from about 1895 to 1917'.

7 Mendes, p. 309.

8 Quoted in Hyde, p. 177.

9 Legman (1966), p. xxxv. According to Peter Mendes, Carrington 'seems to have begun offering the 11 volumes for sale *c.* 1897–98'. No convincing evidence has

been found, however, that this happened before 1901.

10 [Carrington], p. 42. I am grateful to the Kinsey Institute for Research in Sex, Gender, and Reproduction, Indiana University, Bloomington, for providing me with a photocopy of the relevant pages of this rare document.

11 I am grateful to the Kinsey Institute for Research in Sex, Gender, and Reproduction, Indiana University, Bloomington, for providing me with a photocopy of this priceless publication.

12 The most detailed physical description of *My Secret Life*, accompanied by acute comments on its printing, is that given by Mendes, pp. 161–6.

13 Report sent to the author on 16 February 1978 by Dr David Clements, Department of Printed Books, British Library.

14 *MSL*, p. 2,315.

15 Peter Mendes, private communication to the author, 1999.

16 [Carrington], pp. 35–6.

17 Ibid., pp. 36–58.

18 Legman (1966), p. xlvii.

19 Donald Thomas, vol. i, p. xxiii.

20 *MSL*, p. 1,725.

21 *MSL*, p. 1,960.

22 Mendes, pp. 12–13.

23 Ibid., pp. 28, 165.

24 Kearney, *passim*.

25 Mendes, pp. 33, 165, 323.

26 Ibid., p. 165.

27 Marcus, p. 84.

28 *MSL*, p. 5.

29 *MSL*, pp. 354–5.

30 *MSL*, pp. 421, 443, 443–4, 805.

31 *MSL*, p. 1,636.

32 *MSL*, p. 7.

33 *MSL*, pp. 362, 882.

34 *MSL*, pp. 1,027, 1,120, 1,194, 1,195, 1,655, 1,273, 1,801.

35 *MSL*, p. 1,504.

36 *MSL*, p. 1,636.

37 *MSL*, pp. 443–4.

38 *MSL*, pp. 899, 912, 944, 1,437.

39 *MSL*, p. 7.

40 Ibid.

41 Stein, pp. 14–15; *CLT*, pp. 60–91.

42 *CLT*, p. 91.

43 *CLT*, p. 87.

44 *MSL*, pp. 124, 180–81, 183, 225, 583, 586–8, 589, 595, 2,026.

45 *MSL*, pp. 9–10.
46 *MSL*, pp. 17, 37 (twice), 42, 43, 66; C. R. Ashbee records in *'Grannie'*, pp. 40–41, that his mother called his father 'Harry'; in his letters to Guy Langham, Oswald Barber shows that the Hamburg side of the family referred to Ashbee as 'Onkel Harry' (GLA).
47 *MSL*, p. 948.
48 *MSL*, p. 1,918.
49 Original edition of *My Secret Life*, vol. i, p. 44, wrongly transcribed in *MSL*, p. 29.
50 *MSL*, p. 453.
51 *MSL*, p. 2,277. This is the only time 'Walter' uses the term.
52 *MSL*, p. 11.
53 *MSL*, p. 2,248.
54 *MSL*, p. 2,074.
55 *MSL*, p. 2,259.
56 *MSL*, p. 2,269.
57 *MSL*, pp. 1,114, 1,599, 2,269, 2,295.
58 *MSL*, pp. 1,013, 1,684.
59 For 'smutty chorus', *MSL*, p. 60. This version of the song comes on p. 697. There are others, with slight variants, at pp. 150, 152, 317–18, 481, 1,180 and 2,112.
60 *MSL*, p. 1,198.
61 *MSL*, p. 1,523.
62 *MSL*, p. 2,124.
63 *MSL*, p. 2,067.
64 *MSL*, pp. 903, 939, 1,020, etc.
65 *MSL*, p. 2,017.
66 *MSL*, p. 1,760.
67 *MSL*, p. 2,008.
68 *MSL*, p. 361.
69 *MSL*, p. 2,087.
70 *MSL*, p. 189.
71 *MSL*, p. 2,093.
72 *MSL*, p. 1,770.
73 *MSL*, p. 1,208.
74 *MSL*, p. 1,383.
75 *MSL*, p. 1,226.
76 *MSL*, pp. 1,481–95.
77 *MSL*, pp. 270, 274, etc.
78 *MSL*, p. 960.
79 *MSL*, p. 1,906.
80 *MSL*, p. 966.
81 *MSL*, pp. 734, 811, 1,062, 1,303, 2,291.
82 *MSL*, p. 1,054.

83 *MSL*, p. 1,006.
84 *MSL*, p. 1,225; earlier reference, p. 583.
85 *MSL*, pp. 819–20, 1,099, 1,127, 1,233, 1,915, 2,262.
86 *MSL*, p. 379.
87 *MSL*, p. 2,005.
88 *MSL*, pp. 401, 1,190.
89 *MSL*, p. 1,058.
90 *MSL*, p. 2,123.
91 *MSL*, p. 7.
92 *MSL*, p. 837.
93 *MSL*, p. 2,251.
94 *MSL*, p. 1,368.
95 *MSL*, p. 1,724.
96 *MSL*, p. 1,775.
97 *MSL*, p. 1,773.
98 *MSL*, p. 894.
99 *Pall Mall Gazette*, 6, 7, 8, 10 July 1885. For the impact of the articles in France, see Praz, pp. 467–70.
100 *MSL*, p. 2,125.
101 *MSL*, p. 2,062.
102 *MSL*, p. 1,147.
103 Quoted by Trudgill, p. 139.
104 *MSL*, p. 1,550.
105 *MSL*, pp. 1,642–3, 2,084, 2,192, 2,270.
106 *MSL*, p. 1,016.
107 *MSL*, p. 902.
108 *MSL*, pp. 2,070, 640.
109 *MSL*, pp. 1,379, 2,275.
110 *MSL*, p. 971.
111 *MSL*, p. 227.
112 *MSL*, p. 657.
113 *MSL*, p. 1,252.
114 *ILP*, pp. 82–9.
115 *ILP*, pp. 175–7.
116 *ILP*, p. xvii.
117 *MSL*, pp. 127, 1,957, 1,990.
118 *MSL*, p. 1,800.
119 *MSL*, p. 1,714.
120 *MSL*, p. 1,777.
121 *MSL*, p. 1,879.
122 *MSL*, p. 2,280.
123 *MSL*, p. 970.

124 *MSL*, pp. 509, 1,621, 1,661, 1,314, 1,782, 1,870, 2,116.

125 *MSL*, p. 1,834.

126 *MSL*, pp, 968, 1,611, 1,658, 1,786, 1,904–5.

127 For other reference to the saltiness of the fluid, *MSL*, pp. 892, 968, 1,403, 1,464, 1,501, 1,553, 1,573, 1,638, 1,660, 1,723, 1,785, 1,834, 1,859, 2,065.

128 *MSL*, pp. 927, 939, 944, 734, 1,340, 2,262.

129 *MSL*, pp. 1,231, 2,090, 2,278.

130 *MSL*, pp. 1,013, 1,048, 1,264.

131 *MSL*, pp. 1,288–90, 1,300.

132 Legman (1966), pp. xlvii–xlviii.

133 *ILP*, pp. 379–80.

134 Legman (1966), pp. liii–liv.

135 Ibid., p. lix; letter from E. J. Dingwall to Guy Langham, January 1967 (GLA).

136 Legman (1966), p. xliv.

137 Letter to the author from Gordon Stein, 11 July 1978. Stein's first letter to me is dated 17 June of the same year.

138 I am most grateful to Peter Mendes for supplying me with a copy of this draft, which is entitled 'The Authorship of *My Secret Life*'. Subsequently Patrick Kearnan kindly sent me his copy of another, slightly less complete draft.

139 Stein, pp. 19–24.

140 *MSL*, p. 346.

141 Stein, pp. 32–3.

142 *MSL*, p. 354.

143 Letter to the author from Peter Mendes, 12 August 1999.

144 Stein, pp. 34–7.

145 Ibid., p. 35.

146 Ibid., pp. 41–2.

147 Ibid., p. 27.

148 Ibid., p. 42.

149 Ibid., pp. 42–3.

150 Ibid., p. 43.

151 *MSL*, p. 35.

152 Marcus, p. 193.

153 *MSL*, p. 76.

154 *MSL*, pp. 33–4.

155 *AD*, *passim*; *MSL*, pp. 1,167–8, 1,584.

156 *MSL*, p. 32.

157 *MSL*, p. 35.

158 *AD*, 15 November 1858.

159 *MSL*, p. 1,177.

160 *AD*, 22 July 1855.

161 *MSL*, p. 1,577.

162 *MSL*, p. 1,181; *AD*, 31 July 1854.

163 *MSL*, p. 444.

164 *MSL*, p. 1,636.

165 See, for example, *MSL*, pp. 860, 877, 879, etc.

166 *MSL*, p. 1,106. See also p. 860.

167 *MSL*, pp. 1,087, 1,912.

168 *MSL*, p. 1,917.

169 *MSL*, p. 1,821; *AD*, 14-26 January 1874.

170 *MSL*, pp. 1,222-4.

171 *MSL*, p. 232.

172 *MSL*, p. 1,488.

173 For billiards, *MSL*, pp. 727, 925 and *AD*, *passim*; for the redheads, *MSL*, pp. 831, 847, 1,254, 2,223 and *AD*, 8 August 1854, in which Ashbee says that the only 'drawback' of his friend Aliston and his wife is that both have red hair.

174 *MSL*, p. 2,047.

175 *MSL*, p. 7.

176 *AD*, 17 October 1858.

177 *MSL*, p. 1,843.

178 *MSL*, p. 2,120.

179 Ralph Thomas, p. 121.

180 *MSL*, pp. 1,505, 1,935, 2,130, 1,984, 2,069, 2,190.

181 *MSL*, pp. 124-35.

182 *AD*, July–October 1854, *passim*.

183 *MSL*, p. 2,258.

184 *MSL*, p. 1,467.

185 *MSL*, pp. 418, 467; Mayhew, vol. iv, p. 238.

186 Banks, p. 216.

187 *AD*, 13 July 1883.

188 *AD*, 12 October 1854.

189 *MSL*, p. 1,388. The quotation, somewhat inaccurate, is from *Macbeth* v:iii.

190 Marcus, pp. 193-6.

191 *MSL*, p. 13.

192 *TT*, p. 1.

193 Letter to the author from J. M. Woodley, Clerk of the Merchant Taylors Company, 19 April 1978.

194 Neither the British Library nor the Kinsey Institute for Sex Research have done this as yet. The Grove Press edition is useless for the task since it regularizes (sporadically) the spelling of the original and adds new inconsistencies of its own.

195 *MSL*, pp. 736, 1,135, 1,426, 1,944.

196 *AD*, 12 November 1873.

197 'Independant' (*MSL*, vol. i, p. 373, emended by Grove to 'independent', p. 208; *AD*, 5 December 1880, 2 April 1881). 'Dependant' (*MSL*, vol. ii, p. 265, emended by

Grove to 'dependent', p. 362; *AD*, 2 April 1881). Ashbee also uses 'independance' (*AD*, 4 July 1881).

198 *AD*, 18 December 1880.

199 *CLT*, p. 315.

200 *CLT*, p. 594.

201 *MSL*, original edition, vol. x, p. 319.

202 'Vegetable' in *MSL*, original edition, vol. ii, ch. xxi (page not noted), Grove Press edition, p. 416; 'vegitable' in *MSL*, original edition, vol. vi, p. 201, silently emended by Grove Press, p. 1,189, to 'vegetable'. *AD* register 'vegitation' on 31 December 1880, 4 January 1881, 29 January 1881, 12 February 1881, 16 February 1881, 17 February 1881 (twice), 26 February 1881, 29 March 1881 (twice), 15 April 1881 (twice), 4 May 1881, 8 June 1881, 7 November 1883 (twice), 12 November 1885, 6 December 1885. 'Vegitables' is found on 5 November 1880, 15 February 1881, 'vegitarian' on 14 January 1881.

203 *AD*, 15 January 1881, 23 November 1883.

204 *AD*, 20 December 1880.

205 *AD*, 22 December 1880.

206 *AD*, 25 December 1880.

207 *MSL*, vol. ii, pp. 11, 234.

208 *AD*, 9 November 1856, 9 January 1881, 30 March 1881.

209 *AD*, 29 January 1881, 31 March 1881, 11 November 1883.

210 *AD*, 30 March 1881, 1 April 1881, 10 April 1881, 19 May 1881, 28 May 1881.

211 *MSL*, original edition, vol. viii, p. 135, respected by Grove, p. 1,589.

212 *MSL*, original edition, vol. i, p. 353, emended by Grove, p. 197, to 'omelette'; *AD*, 8 November 1883.

213 *MSL*, original edition, vol. i, p. 313, spelling respected by Grove, p. 174; vol. ii, p. 284, emended by Grove to 'whet', p. 373; vol. iii, p. 318, respected by Grove, p. 693; vol. vi, p. 35, emended by Grove to 'whetted', p. 1,096; vol. viii, p. 168, emended by Grove to 'whetting', p. 1,607.

214 *AD*, 3 May 1881.

215 *ILP*, p. 23.

216 *MSL*, p. 1,641.

217 *MSL*, p. 1,864.

218 *MSL*, pp. 1,864–5.

219 *MSL*, p. 2,196.

220 *MSL*, p. 2,242.

221 Marcus, p. 127.

222 Mayhew, vol. iv, pp. 232–3.

223 Ibid., p. 230.

224 *MSL*, p. 1,149.

225 *MSL*, p. 1,647.

226 *MSL*, pp. 2,131–43.

227 *AD*, 6 November 1883.
228 *AD*, 7 November 1883.
229 *MSL*, p. 2,132.
230 *AD*, 17 November 1883.
231 *MSL*, p. 2,139.
232 *MSL*, p. 2,138.
233 *MSL*, p. 1,907.
234 *AD*, 16 December 1881.
235 *MSL*, pp. 2,057–8.
236 Dendy Marshall, pp. 110–11.
237 Letter to the author dated 9 June 1978 from R. M Robbins, CBE, then Managing
 Director (Railways) at London Transport.
238 *MSL*, p. 671.
239 *AD*, 12 February 1881, 11 March 1881, 16 March 1881, 22 April 1881, 26 April 1881,
 27 April 1881, 30 April 1881, 25 June 1881.
240 *MSL*, pp. 1,647, 1,821–2, 2,039, 2,153, 2,234.
241 *MSL*, pp. 17, 38, 492, 735, 834, 1,100, 1,212, 1,590, 1,832, 1,928–9, 1,947, 2,020,
 2,038, 2,105, 2,117, 2,120, 2,128, 2,139, 2,182, 2,220, 2,239, 2,249, 2,275.
242 Ralph Thomas, 'The Late H. S. Ashbee'.
243 *AD*, 15 February 1874, 3 March 1874, 8 December 1880, 20 December 1880,
 18 February 1881, 18 February 1881, 9 November 1885, 12 November 1885.
244 *ILP*, p. 237; *ILP*, p. 344; *CLA*, p. 375; *CLA*, p. 416; *CLP*, p. 370.
245 *AD*, 19 February 1881, 9 April 1881, 3 July 1881.
246 *MSL*, p. 1,680.
247 *MSL*, pp. 1,823–30.
248 *AD*, 15 November 1858.
249 *MSL*, p. 2,042.
250 *MSL*, pp. 68, 257, 271, 292, 385, 404, 417, 471, 538, 691, 824, 1,469.
251 *MSL*, pp. 176, 376, 651.
252 Cervantes, *Don Quijote de la Mancha*, texto y notas de Martín de Riquer
 (London, Harrap, 1950), p. 89.
253 Cervantes, *The History of Don-Quichote* (London, 1620), p. 58.
254 Cervantes, *The Life and Exploits of the Ingenious Gentleman Don Quixote de la
 Mancha* (London, 1742), p. 37.
255 Cervantes, *The History and Adventures of the Renowned Don Quixote* (London,
 1755), p. 43.
256 Cervantes, *Don Quixote*, translated by H. E. Watts (London, 1888), p. 120.
257 For *Don Quixote*, see edition specified in note 252, pp. 159, 274, 523, 644, 717, 914.
 The *Exemplary Novels* in which the construction appears, once in each case, are
 La fuerza de la sangre, *La ilustre fregona* and *El casamiento engañoso y El coloquio
 de los perros*.
258 P. G. Wodehouse, *The Inimitable Jeeves* (Harmondsworth, Penguin, 1978), p. 119.

259 Ashbee, 'Some Books about Cervantes' (1898), pp. 25, 27.
260 Scott, *Rokeby* (1813), vol. ii, ch. xxi: 'To wrench the sword from Wilfrid's hand [. . .] was but one moment's work.'
261 *MSL*, p. 1,792.
262 Legman (1966), pp. lv–lvi.
263 Marcus, pp. 88–9: 1882 was 'the year of the campaign in Egypt which brought forth that term'.
264 Ibid., p. 199.
265 Ibid., p. 186.
266 Ibid., p. 124.
267 *ILP*, pp. 379–80.
268 *MSL*, pp. 22, 370.
269 *MSL*, p. 1,621.
270 *MSL*, p. 1,250.
271 *MSL*, p. 1,192.
272 *MSL*, p. 1,388.
273 *MSL*, p. 1,757.
274 *MSL*, p. 1,765.
275 Marcus, p. 128.

Bibliography

Unless otherwise stated, all periodical publications in English and French appeared respectively in London and Paris.

BOOKS BY HENRY SPENCER ASHBEE

Index Librorum Prohibitorum: being Notes Bio- Biblio- Icono- graphical and Critical, on Curious and Uncommon Books. By PISANUS FRAXI. London, privately printed, 1877. Reprinted in monochrome facsimile by Charles Skilton Ltd, London, 1960. Ashbee's interleaved and annotated working copy, in two parts, is in the British Museum at P.C. 14.de.3. The manuscript is unknown.

Centuria Librorum Absconditorum: being Notes Bio- Biblio- Icono- graphical and Critical, on Curious and Uncommon Books. By PISANUS FRAXI. London, privately printed, 1879. Reprinted in monochrome facsimile by Charles Skilton Ltd, London, 1960. Ashbee's interleaved, extra-illustrated and annotated working copy, in two parts, is in the British Library at P.C. 14.de.4. The manuscript is unknown.

Catena Librorum Tacendorum: being Notes Bio- Biblio- Icono- graphical and Critical, on Curious and Uncommon Books. By PISANUS FRAXI. London, privately printed, 1885. Reprinted in monochrome facsimile by Charles Skilton Ltd, London, 1960. Ashbee's copy in the British Library is neither interleaved, annotated nor catalogued. It is currently kept in the Early Printed Collection offices. The manuscript is unknown.

Travels in Tunisia. With a Glossary, a Map, a Bibliography, and Fifty Illustrations, by Alexander Graham, F.R.I.B.A., and H. S. Ashbee, F.S.A, F.R.G.S., London, Dulau and Co., 1887.

A Bibliography of Tunisia from the Earliest Times to the End of 1888 (in two parts) including Utica and Carthage, the Punic Wars, the Roman Occupation, the Arab Conquest, the Expeditions of Louis IX. and Charles V. and the French Protectorate, by H. S. Ashbee, F.S.A., F.R.G.S., London, Dulau and Co., 1889.

BIBLIOGRAPHY

An Iconography of Don Quixote, 1605–1895, by H. S. Ashbee, F.S.A., London, printed
for the author at the University Press, Aberdeen, and issued by the Bibliographical
Society, July 1895.

THE ASHBEE DIARIES

Ashbee's manuscript diaries (*AD*), contained in four books, are today in the possession
of his granddaughter, Felicity Ashbee, as are the papers of the late Captain Guy Langham
(GLA).

ARTICLES BY HENRY SPENCER ASHBEE

In *Notes and Queries*

'"*London by Night*"', 11 October 1873, p. 287. Signed: H.S.A.

'Gilles de Laval, Seigneur de Retz', 22 November 1873, p. 417. Signed: H.S.A.

'"*The Fair Concubine; or, the Secret History of the Beautiful Vanella* . . ."', 10 January
1874, p. 28. Signed: H.S.A.

'"*The Relicks of a Saint* . . ."', 14 March 1874, p. 209. Signed: H.S.A.

'Etched Female Portraits', 4 April 1874, p. 269. Signed: H.S.A.

'"*Ecclesiastical Gallantry: or, The Mystery Unravelled* . . ."', 25 April 1874, p. 528.
Signed: H.S.A.

'Lowndes', 30 May 1874, pp. 436–7. Signed: H.S.A.

'Henry James Bellars, one of the cleverest fac-similists of modern times . . .', 11 July
1874, p. 28. Signed: H.S.A.

'"*Don Leon, a Poem by the late Lord Byron* . . ."', 15 August 1874, p. 129. Signed: H.S.A.

'"*Private History of the Court of England*"', 3 October 1874, p. 277. Signed: H.S.A.

'"*By-Ways of History. History of an Unreadable Book* . . ."', 23 January 1875, p. 68.
Signed: H.S.A.

'"*The Covent Garden Repository; or, Ranger's Packet of Whim, Frolick, and
Amusement*"', 13 February 1874, p. 128. Signed: H.S.A.

'Rowlandson', 13 March 1875, pp. 207–8. Signed: H.S.A.

'R. W. Buss', 20 March 1875, p. 228. Signed: H.S.A.

'"*The Toast*"', 27 March 1875, p. 247. Signed: H.S.A.

'"*Essay on Woman*"', 8 May 1875, p. 369. Signed: H.S.A.

'"*Justine*"', 22 May 1875, p. 408. Signed: Apis.

'"*The Toast*"', 22 May 1875, p. 418. Signed: H.S.A.

'Giuspanio Graglia published a complete edit. of Martial's *Epigrams* . . .', 29 May 1875.
Signed: Fraxinus.

['R. W. Buss'], 5 June 1875, p. 455. Signed: H.S.A.

'Cruikshanks', 17 July 1875, p. 55. Signed: H.S.A.

'"*Human Ordure, botanically considered* . . ."', 27 November 1875, p. 427. Signed: Apis.

'"*Essay on Woman*"', 4 December 1875, p. 450. Signed: H.S.A.

'"*Sodom: a Play, by the E. of R*", was printed . . .', 1 January 1876, p. 10. Signed: Fraxinus.

'Louise Lateau', 15 January 1876, p. 55. Signed: Apis.

'Louise Lateau', 26 February 1876. Signed: Apis.

'"Imperial"', 22 April 1876, pp. 325–6. Signed: Apis.

'"*The Rodiad*"', 21 October 1876, p. 336. Signed: Apis.

'"*The Crimes of the Clergy*"', 13 January 1877, p. 27. Signed: Apis.

'George Garrow: Mrs. Selina Upton', 3 February 1877, p. 88. Signed: Fraxinus.

'"*Ecclesiastical Gallantry; or, The Mystery Unravelled* . . ."', 10 February 1877, p. 107. Signed: Apis.

'"*Desultory Reading*"', 17 February 1877, p. 134. Signed: Apis.

'F. Josephus Pauwels', 3 March 1877, p. 169. Signed: Fraxinus.

'Mrs. Selina Upton: George Garrow', 31 March 1877, p. 256. Signed: Fraxinus.

'W. Benbow, the printer and publisher . . .', 28 April 1877, p. 329. Signed: Apis.

'Madame de Solms: Rattazzi: Loulé', 5 May 1877, p. 350. Signed: Fraxinus.

'Comic opera on the Rod', 5 May 1877, pp. 357–8. Signed: Fraxinus.

'"Essay on Woman"', 26 May 1877, p. 409. Signed: H.S.A.

'Madame de Solms', 26 May 1877, p. 417. Signed: Fraxinus.

'Lady Hamilton', 23 June 1877, p. 493. Signed: Apis.

['"Tableaux des Moeurs du Temps", &c.'] 'Only one copy is known to exist . . .', 14 July 1877, pp. 31–2. Signed: Apis.

'*A Sequel to Don Juan*', 21 July 1877, p. 59. Signed: Fraxinus.

['Tableaux des Moeurs du Temps'], 'Mr. J. Borrajo is in error . . .', 18 August 1877, p. 136. signed Apis.

'George Cruickshank', 9 February 1878, pp. 119–20. Signed: H. S. Ashbee, F.S.A.

'Bibliography in France', 23 March 1878, p. 224. Signed: H. S. Ashbee.

['The Earl of Barrymore'], 'The Barrymores consisted of three brothers . . .', 10 August 1878, p. 111. Signed: Apis.

'Louise Lateau', 7 September 1878, p. 186. Signed: Apis.

'"Medical Bibliography. A. and B. . . ."', 21 September 1878, p. 228. Signed: Apis.

'Flogging at Christ's Hospital', 19 October 1878, p. 309. Signed: Apis.

'"Medical Bibliography. A. and B."', 28 December 1878, p. 524. Signed: Apis.

'Lady Anne Hamilton and the "Secret History"', 1 February 1879, p. 98. Signed: H.S.A.

'Derivation of "Huguenot"', 8 February 1879, p. 117. Signed: H.S.A.

'"The Authentic Memoirs of the Countess de Barre [*sic*], the French King's Mistress . . ."', 17 May 1879, p. 387. Signed: Fraxinus.

'Parthenissa', 17 May 1879, p. 387. Signed: Apis.

'Octave Delepierre, LL.D.', 30 August 1879. Signed: H. S. Ashbee.

'The Misuse of English by French Writers', 8 November 1879, pp. 361–2. Signed: H. S. Ashbee.

'Louis XV', 6 December 1879, p. 455. Signed: Apis.

'Octave Delepierre', 3 January 1880, p. 24. Signed: H.S.A.

'The Misuse of English by French Writers', 3 January 1880, p. 24. Signed: Apis.

['A Biographical Society'], 10 January 1880, pp. 38–9. Signed: H. S. Ashbee.

'A Biographical Society', 17 January 1880, pp. 64–5. Signed: H. S. Ashbee.

'The History of Literary Forgeries', 17 January 1880, p. 65. Signed: H.S.A.

'Rabelais', 1 May 1880, pp. 349–51. Signed: H. S. Ashbee.

'Errors of Authors', 19 June 1880, pp. 490–91. Signed: H. S. Ashbee.

'Bolton Corney', 14 August 1880, pp. 123–4. Signed: H. S. Ashbee.

'Bolton Corney', 8 October 1881, pp. 291–2. Signed: H. S. Ashbee. (Reproduces letter to Ashbee from Bolton Glanvill Corney, Government Medical Officer, Fiji.)

'"Bastard-title" or "Half-title"', 29 April 1882, p. 326. Signed: Fraxinus.

'Mr. Pratt, 1783', 19 August 1882, p. 149. Signed: Apis.

'Books Written in Latin by Moderns', 9 September 1882, p. 207. Signed: H.S.A.

['Strange omissions'], 28 October 1882, p. 346. Signed: H.S.A.

['Followers of "N & Q"'], 'To the list already given should be added *Willis's Current Notes* . . .', 17 February 1883, p. 136. Signed: H. S. Ashbee.

'"Le Style c'est l'homme"', 17 March 1883, p. 218. Signed: H. S. Ashbee.

'Verses by Voltaire', 28 July 1883, p. 68, Signed: H.S.A.

'Molière Illustrated by English Artists', 16 February 1884, p. 129. Signed: H. S. Ashbee.

'King James's "Book of Sports"', 16 February 1884, pp. 133–4. Signed: Apis.

'Victor Hugo', 7 March 1885, pp. 183–4. Signed: H. S. Ashbee.

'Lord Strangford's Fragments', 18 April 1885, p. 309. Signed: Apis.

'Illustrations to "Don Quixote"', 22 August 1885, pp. 149–50. Signed: H.S.A.

'Tunisia', 2 January 1886, p. 7. Signed: H.S.A.

'Illustrations to "Don Quxiote" [*sic*]', 9 January 1886, p. 29. Signed: H.S.A.

'"Giornale degli Eruditi e dei Curiosi"', 19 June 1886, p. 487. Signed: H. S. Ashbee.

'Lunby on Tunisia', 16 October 1886, p. 307. Signed: H.S.A.

'Shakespeare or Burton?', 27 November 1886, p. 424. Signed: H. S. Ashbee.

'Authors of Books [on Tunisia] Wanted', 4 December 1886, p. 449. Signed: H.S.A.

'The Twelve Good Rules', 29 January 1887, p. 92. Signed: H. S. Ashbee.

'Heinel', 26 February 1887, p. 169. Signed: H.S.A.

'Is the Great Wall of China a Myth?', 27 August 1887, p. 167. Signed: H. S. Ashbee.

'Book Illustrating, by which I mean Grangerizing . . .', 19 January 1889, p. 47. Signed: H.S.A.

'"A Claire-voie" is an expression . . .', 4 May 1889, p. 347. Signed: H.S.A.

['Pope's Size'], 4 May 1889, pp. 351–2. Signed: H.S.A.

'Errors of Translation', 4 May 1889, p. 355. Signed: H.S.A.

'Beckford's "Vathek"', 25 May 1889, p. 413. Signed: H. S. Ashbee.

'"Straparola"', 30 November 1889, p. 433. Signed: H.S.A.

'Jean Paul Marat', 11 January 1890, p. 29. Signed: H. S. Ashbee.

'Quintin Craufurd and Madame *****', 4 October 1890, p. 268. Signed: H.S.A.

'Pictures from "Don Quixote"', 17 February 1892, p. 167. Signed: H. S. Ashbee.

'Earliest Advertisement of a Sale of Tea', 23 July 1892, p. 75. Signed: H. S. Ashbee.

'"Lost Books"', 30 July 1892, p. 94. Signed: H. S. Ashbee.

'"Don Quixote"', 27 August 1892, p. 166. Signed: H.S.A.

'A Member of the University of Cambridge', 24 December 1898, p. 508. Signed: H.S.A.

'"Iconography of Don Quixote"', 21 January 1899, p. 50. Signed: H. S. Ashbee, Fowlers, Hawkhurst, Kent.

In other periodicals

'Une Visite à la Bibliothèque de Tanjore', *Le Livre,* bibliographie rétrospective, vol. ii (December 1881), pp. 364-9. Reprinted by Impr. Quantin, Paris, 1882. Signed: 'H. S. Ashbee'.

Note to the above published in the following number of *Le Livre,* p. 390. Signed: H. S. Ashbee.

'A Ride to Peking', *St James's Magazine,* December 1881, pp. 458-68. Reprinted by W. Lindsey and Co., London, 1881. Signed: 'H. S. Ashbee'.

'A Dinner of French Bibliophiles', *Bibliographer,* May 1882, pp. 169-71. Reprinted London, May 1882. Signed: H. S. Ashbee.

['Pisanus Fraxi. - Quel est le bibliophile anglais qui sous ce pseudonyme . . .'], *L'Intermédiaire des chercheurs et curieux. (Correspondance littéraire, NOTES and QUERIES français),* Paris, no. 338 (10 June 1882). Signed: A.T.

['Andréa de Nerciat. - Quel es le nom de l'auteur de la *Bibliographie anecdotique et raisonnée de tous les ouvrages d'Andréa de Nerciat* . . .'], ibid. Signed: A.T.

['Pisanus Fraxi (xv, 322). - Ce pseudonyme signifie Henry Ashbee'], ibid., no. 339 (25 June 1882). Signed: (Athenaeum Club. London.) H.R.T.

['Andréa de Nerciat (xv, 322). - Le nom de l'auteur importe peu. La brochure émane des presses du sieur Sluys, autrement Vital-Puissant . . .'], ibid., no. 341 (25 July 1882). Signed: LE FOUILLEUR.

['Pisanus Fraxi (xv, 322, 378). - La personne à laquelle H.R.F. [*sic*] applique, par erreur, le pseudonyme en question . . .'], ibid. Signed: A MAN OF KENT.

['Il ne faut pas trop se fier aux titres des livres, surtout de ceux qui sont *"printed for private circulation"* . . .'], ibid. Signed: (New-York.) PENSYLVAN.

['H. S. Ashbee, Esq., riche négociant anglais de Londres, avec succursale à Paris . . .'], ibid., Signed: LE FOUILLEUR.

'A Sunday at Coney Island', *Temple Bar Magazine,* vol. lxv (1882), pp. 263-7. Reprinted by William Clowes and Sons, London, 1882. Signed: H. S. Ashbee.

'The Metropolis of the Manchus', *St James's Magazine,* April 1882, pp. 462-78, and May 1882, pp. 546-67. Reprinted, no indication of printer, 1882. Signed: H. S. Ashbee.

'Les Anglais qui ont écrit en Français. William Beckford', *Le Livre,* vol. iii (1882), pp. 381-8. Signed: H.-S. Ashbee.

'The Rest of *Don Juan*', *Bibliographer*, vol. iv (1883), pp. 25–8. Signed: H. S. Ashbee.

'Les Auteurs–Amateurs anglais', *Société des Amis des Livres, Annuaire*, vol. iv (1883), pp. 43–53. Signed: 'H. S. Ashbée' [*sic*].

'De quelques sociétés littéraires en Angleterre. The Index Society', *Le Livre*, vol. iv (1883), pp. 209–13. Signed: H. S. Ashbee.

'The *Kama Sutra* of Vatsyayana', *Bibliographer*, vol. v (1883–4), pp. 162–4. Signed: E. H. Shebsa [anagram of H. S. Ashbee].

'Bibliomania in 1883', ibid., 6 September 1884, pp. 182–3. Signed: H.S.A.

'Paul Lacroix', ibid., 1 November 1884, pp. 345–6. Signed: H. S. Ashbee.

'The First(?) Idea of the Penny Post', ibid., 15 November 1884, p. 386. Signed: H. S. Ashbee.

'John Ruskin', ibid., 29 November 1884, p. 438. Signed: H. S. Ashbee.

'Les Amis des Livres', ibid., vol. vi (1884), pp. 30–32. Signed: H. S. Ashbee, F.S.A.

'Une traduction complète des *Mille et Une Nuits*', *Le Livre: Bibliographie rétrospective*, vol. vi (1885), pp. 312–16. Signed: H. S. Ashbee. [A review of Richard Burton's translation, 'Benares', 1885.]

'Bibliotheca Arcana', *Le Livre: Bibliographie moderne*, vol. vi (10 October 1885). Signed: H. S. Ashbee.

'Les Anglais qui ont écrit en Français: quelques poètes modernes', *Société des Amis des Livres, Annuaire*, vol. vii (1886), pp. 57–69. Signed: H. S. Ashbee.

'Notice Biographique sur Monsieur Turner. Robert Samuel Turner, *Société des Amis des Livres, Annuaire*, vol. ix (1888), pp. 31–42. Signed: H. S. Ashbee.

'The Distributor of Prospectuses', in *Paris qui crie. Petits Métiers*. Notices par Albert Arnal. – Henry Spencer Ashbee. – Jules Claretie. – Abel Giraudeau. – Henry Houssaye. – Henri Meilhac. – Victor Mercier. – Eugène Paillet. – Jean Paillet. – Roger Portalis. – Eugène Rodrigues. Préface para Henri Beraldi. Dessins de Pierre Vidal, Paris, Les Amis des Livres, 1890, pp. 67–8. Signed: H.S.A.

'Frenchmen who have Written in English. I. – Voltaire', *Bookworm*, vol. iii (1890), pp. 73–5. Signed: H. S. Ashbee.

'Quelques Illustrateurs de Don Quichotte. Observations iconographiques', *Annales littéraires des bibliophiles contemporains pour 1890* (1891), pp. 61–74. Signed: 'H.-S. Ashbee'.

'Marat en Angleterre', ibid., pp. 169–99. Signed: H. S. Ashbee. Reprinted Paris, 1890.

'Les Anglais qui ont écrit en Français (1) Quintin Crauford', *Société des Amis des Livres, Annuaire*, vol. xii (1891), pp. 53–71. Signed: H. S. Ashbee. Offprint, 'Quintin Crauford', Paris, 1891, 23 pp. Signed: H. S. Ashbee.

'Foreigners who have Written in English. Octave Delepierre', *Bookworm*, vol. iv (1891), pp. 9–12. Signed: H. S. Ashbee.

'The Baffled Collector' [verse], ibid., p. 230. Signed: 'H. S. Ashbee'.

'Foreigners who have Written in English. Pierre Antoine Motteux', ibid., pp. 261–8. Signed: 'H. S. Ashbee'.

'Les Anglais qui ont écrit en Français. Sir Charles Hanbury Williams', *Société des Amis*

des Livres, Annuaire, vol. xiii (1892), pp. 33-7. Signed: H. S. Asbhée [*sic*].

'Berlin Ex Libris Society', *Ex Libris Journal*, vol. ii (1892), p. 120. Signed: H.S.A.

'A Plea for Book-Plates', ibid., vol. iii (1893), pp. 181-2. Signed: H. S. Ashbee.

'Les Anglais qui ont écrit en Français. Mela Britannicus', *Société des Amis des Livres, Annuaire*, vol. xiv (1893), pp. 37-64. Signed: H. S. Ashbee. Reprinted, Paris, 1893.

'Une Traduction hollandaise du Don Quichotte', *L'Intermédiaire des chercheurs et curieux*, 1893, col. 170. [Source: Ford and Lansing, p. 117.]

'The Iconography of "Don Quixote"', *Transactions of the Bibliographical Society*, vol. i (1892-3), pp. 123-43. Signed: H. S. Ashbee, F.S.A. [Lecture read to the Society on 20 March 1893.]

'*Hudibras*', *Annales Littéraires des bibliophiles contemporains pour 1893* (1894), pp. 71-8. Signed: H. S. Ashbee.

'Book-Plates of Celebrities', *Ex Libris Journal*, vol. iv (1894), pp. 103-5. Signed: H. S. Ashbee, F.S.A.

'*Ex-libris Zeitschrift*', ibid., vol.v (1896), p. 37. Signed: H. S. Ashbee.

'*Ex-libris Zeitschrift*, VII, No. 1, January, 1897', ibid., vol. vii (1897), pp. 37-8. Signed: H. S. Ashbee.

'In the first number, April, 1897, of the *Zeitschrift für Bücherfreunde* . . .', ibid., p. 70. Signed: H.S.A.

'*Ex-libris Zeitschrift* for April, 1897', ibid., pp. 86-7. Signed: H.S.A.

'*Ex-libris Zeitschrift* for July, 1897, contains . . .', ibid., pp. 117-18. Signed: H.S.A.

'Henry Spencer Ashbee', *L'Intermédiaire des chercheurs et curieux*, no. 791 (10 March 1898), cols. 356-7. Signed: 'X'.

'Some Books about Cervantes. *Read 21st November, 1898*', *Transactions of the Bibliographical Society*, vol. v (1898-1900), pp. 13-38. Signed: H. S. Ashbee. Reprinted by Blades, East and Blades, London, 1900, 30 pp. [Source: Ford and Lansing, p. 117.]

'Don Quixote and Pickwick', *Revue Hispanique*, vol. vii (1899), pp. 307-10. Signed: H. S. Ashbee.

'Don Quixote and British Art. A Paper Read in the Gallery of the Royal British Artists, April 28, 1900'. Printed for the author by Blades, East and Blades, 23 Abchurch Lane, EC, 'for private circulation' (1900), 49 pp. Signed: H. S. Ashbee, F.S.A., Corresponding Member of the Royal Academy of Madrid.

CONTEMPORARY REVIEWS OF (AND ALLUSIONS TO) ASHBEE'S WORKS

Index Librorum Prohibitorum

1 [Gustave Brunet], *Bulletin du Bibliophile*, vol. xliv (1877), pp. 422-7.

2 Fernand Drujon, 'La Bibliographie en Angleterre. Étude sur deux ouvrages récemment parus à Londres. I', *Le Livre: Bibliographie Ancienne* (1880), pp. 9-16.

3 George Saintsbury, 'Le Livre', *Academy*, 7 February 1880, p. 104. [An attack on

Drujon's review, see 2 above.]

4 'French Literature', *Saturday Review*, 7 February 1880, pp. 194–6. [An attack on Drujon's review, see 2 above.]

5 G. Brunet, *Cat. de . . . la bibliothèque de feu M. Michelet*, Paris, Adolphe Labitte, 1881, vol. ii, pp. 389–90, art. 3,391. [Source: Fryer, p. 227.]

6 R.T. [Ralph Thomas], '"Notes on Curious and Uncommon Books"', *Bibliographer*, vol. v (1883–4), pp. 137–8.

Centuria Librorum Absconditorum

1 B. [Gustave Brunet], *Bulletin du Bibliophile*, vol. xlvi (1879), pp. 437–9.

2 G. Brunet, *Catalogue de . . . la bibliothèque de feu M. Michelet*, Paris, Adolphe Labitte, 1881, vol. ii, pp. 389–90, art. 3,391. [Source: Fryer, p. 227.]

3 Fernand Drujon, 'La Bibliographie en Angleterre. Étude sur deux ouvrages récemment parus à Londres. II', *Le Livre: Bibliographie Ancienne* (1880), pp. 107–16.

4 Joseph Grego, *Rowlandson the Caricaturist*, London, Chatto and Windus, 1880, vol. ii, p. 412.

Catena Librorum Tacendorum

1 Phil.Min. [Philomneste Minimus, i.e. Fernand Drujon], *Le Livre: Bibliographie Moderne*, vol. vi (1885), pp. 575–8.

Travels in Tunisia

1 Richard F. Burton, in *Academy*, 16 June 1888, pp. 405–6. [Source: Fryer, and excerpts from reviews of *Travels in Tunisia* printed at the end of Ashbee's *An Iconography of Don Quixote*.]

2 C.A.C., in *American Architect and Building New*s, 30 June 1888, pp. 310–12. [Source: Fryer, and excerpts from reviews of *Travels in Tunisia* printed at the end of Ashbee's *An Iconography of Don Quixote*.]

3 B.-H.G., in *Le Livre: Bibliographie Moderne*, vol. ix (February 1888), p. 83.

4 Eugène Paillet, 'Travels in Tunisia', *Société des Amis des Livres, Annuaire*, vol. ix (1888), pp. 53–61.

5 Alfred Waterhouse, in *Journal of Proceedings of the Royal Institute of British Architects,* new series, vol. v (8 November 1888), p. 24. [Source: Fryer, and excerpts from reviews of *Travels in Tunisia* printed at the end of Ashbee's *An Iconography of Don Quixote*.]

6 *Athenaeum*, 28 January 1888, pp. 111–12. [Source: Fryer, and excerpts from reviews of *Travels in Tunisia* printed at the end of Ashbee's *An Iconography of Don Quixote*.]

7 *Builder*, 10 December 1887, pp. 795–6. [Source: Fryer, and excerpts from reviews of *Travels in Tunisia* printed at the end of Ashbee's *An Iconography of Don Quixote*.]

8 *Catholic Press*, vol. iii (1888), p. 61. [Source: Fryer, and excerpts from reviews of *Travels in Tunisia* printed at the end of Ashbee's *An Iconography of Don Quixote*.]

9 *Morning Post*, 25 January 1888, p. 2.
10 *Notes and Queries*, 7th series, vol. v (1888), pp. 78–9.
11 *St James's Gazette*, 24 March 1888, p. 7.
12 *Saturday Review*, 31 March 1888, p. 392.
13 'New Tourist Publications', *The Times*, 10 August 1888, p. 13.

A Bibliography of Tunis

1 Victor Chauvin, in *Centralblatt für Bibliothekswesen*, Leipzig, vol. vii (1890), pp. 432–9.
2 *Athenaeum*, no. 3528 (5 April 1890), p. 434. [Source: Fryer, p. 228.]
3 *Le Livre moderne*, vol. i (1890), p. 209.
4 *Notes and Queries*, 7th series, vol. ix (1890), pp. 159–60.

An Iconography of Don Quixote, 1605–1895

1 James Fitzmaurice-Kelly, *Revue Hispanique*, vol. v (1897), pp. 93–5.

OTHER PRINCIPAL PUBLICATIONS CONSULTED

Anon, *My Secret Life*, introduction by Gershon Legman, 2 vols. with continuous pagination (New York, Grove Press, 1966); the first open and unabridged publication of the book [*MSL*]

Acton, William, *The Functions and Disorders of the Reproductive Organs in Youth, Adult Age, and Advanced Life, Considered in their Physiological, Social, and Psychological Relations* (London, J. & A. Churchill, 1857)

– *The Functions and Disorders of the Reproductive Organs in Childhood, Youth, Adult Age, and Advanced Life, Considered in their Physiological, Social, and Moral Relations* (London, J. & A. Churchill, 5th edn, 1871)

– *Prostitution* [1857], edited, and with an introduction by Peter Fryer (London, MacGibbon and Kee, 1968)

Ashbee, C. R., *'Grannie': A Victorian Cameo* (Oxford University Press, 1939).

– *The Trivialities of Tom, being Reflections on a Victorian Boyhood*, typescript (1940–41)

Banks, F. R., *The Penguin Guide to London* (Harmondsworth, Penguin, 4th edn, 1968)

Bloch, Iwan, *Sexual Life in England Past and Present* (London, Francis Aldor, 1938); *and see* Dühren, Eugen

Boase, Frederick, 'Ashbee, Henry Spencer', *Modern English Biography*, vol. iv (1908), pp. 178–9

'Bookworm, A', 'Bookworms of Yesterday and To-day. Mr. Henry Spencer Ashbee', *Bookworm*, vol. ii (1889), pp. 257–61

Brame, Gloria G., William Brame and Jon Jacobs, *Different Loving. The World of Sexual Dominance and Submission* (London, Century, 1997)

Brodie, Fawn M., *The Devil Drives. A Life of Sir Richard Burton* (Harmondsworth, Penguin, 1971)

Brunet, Gustave, 'Octave Delepierre. Notice sur sa Vie et ses oeuvres', *Le Livre*, vol. i (1880), pp. 22–8

[Burton, Richard F.], *Catalogue of Valuable Books, Manuscripts & Autograph Letters of Sir Richard Francis Burton KCMG 1821–1890. Many recorded for the first time. Including a fine portrait in oils* (London, Spink & Son, 1976)

[Carrington, Charles], *Forbidden Books. Notes and Gossip on Tabooed Literature* by An Old Bibliophile, For the Author and his Friends (Paris, 1902)

Chesney, Kellow, *The Victorian Underworld* (Harmondsworth, Pelican, 1972 [1970])

Comfort, Alex, *The Anxiety Makers; Some Curious Preoccupations of the Medical Profession* (London, Panther, 1969 [1967])

Connolly, Cyril, *Enemies of Promise* (New York, Macmillan, 1948)

Coppens, Armand, *Memoirs of an Erotic Bookseller* (London, Luxor Press, 1969)

Crawford, Alan, *C. R. Ashbee. Architect, Designer & Romantic Socialist* (New Haven and London, Yale University Press, 1985)

Croom Johnson, Reginald Powell, *The Origin of Stowe School* (Ipswich and London, W. S. Cowell, 1953)

Cross, Paul James, 'The Private Case: A History', in P. R. Harris (ed.), *The Library of the British Museum. Retrospective Essays on the Department of Printed Books* (London, The British Museum, 1991), pp. 201–40

Demogeot, J. and Montucci, H., *De l'Enseignement secondaire en Angleterre et en Écosse. Rapport adressé à son Exc. M. le Ministre de l'Instruction Publique* (Paris, 1867)

Dendy Marshall, C. F., *A History of the Southern Railway Compiled from Various Sources* (London, The Southern Railway Company, Waterloo Station, 1926)

Dühren, Eugen [pseudonym of Iwan Bloch], *Das Geschectsleben in England. Mit besonderer Beziehung auf London*, 3 vols. (Berlin, 1901–3)

Farrell, Charles, 'Henry Spencer Ashbee, Bibliographer of "Curious Literature"', *American Book Collector*, May–June 1982, pp. 43–51

- 'A Curious and Uncommon Man. Henry Spencer Ashbee Reconsidered. The Man and the Bibliographer', *American Book Collector*, July–August 1982, pp. 2–18

- 'A Curious and Uncommon Man. Henry Spencer Ashbee Reconsidered. The Collector', *American Book Collector*, September–October 1982, pp. 11–23

Ford, Jeremiah D. M., and Ruth Lansing, *Cervantes: A Tentative Bibliography of His Works and of the Biographical and Critical Material Concerning Him* (Harvard University Press, 1931)

Ford, Richard, *A Hand-Book for Travellers in Spain, and Readers at Home*, 2 vols. (London, John Murray, 1845)

Freud, Sigmund, *Three Essays on Sexuality* (1905), in *Standard Edition of the Complete Psychological Works of Sigmund Freud* (London, Hogarth Press and the Institute of Psycho-Analysis, 1975), vol. vii, pp. 123–243

- '"A Child is Being Beaten." A Contribution to the Study of the Origin of Sexual Perversions' (1919), ibid., vol. xvii, pp. 176–204

Fryer, Peter (ed.), *The Forbidden Books of the Victorians. Henry Spencer Ashbee's bibliographies of erotica abridged and edited, with an introduction and notes* (London,

The Odyssey Press, 1970); the volume contains a useful, if slightly incomplete, 'Check-list of Ashbee's Works', which also lists the reviews of his books

Gibson, Ian, *The English Vice. Beating, Sex and Shame in Victorian England and After* (London, Duckworth, 1978)

Goncourt, Edmond de, and Jules de Goncourt, *Journal. Mémoires de la vie littéraire* . . ., edited by Robert Ricatte, 22 vols. (Monaco, 1877–96)

Grego, Joseph, *Rowlandson the Caricaturist* (London, Chatto and Windus, 1880)

Haig Brown, Harold E. (ed.), *William Haig Brown of Charterhouse. A Short Biographical Memoir*, written by some of his pupils and edited by his son (London, Macmillan, 1908)

Fraser Harrison, *The Dark Angels. Aspects of Victorian Sexuality* (London, Sheldon Press, 1977)

Henriques, Fernando, *Modern Sexuality* (London, Panther, 1969)

Hull Walton, Alan, introduction to *The Perfumed Garden of the Shaykh Nefzawi*, translated by Sir Richard Burton (London, Panther, 1963)

Hyde, H. Montgomery, *A History of Pornography* (London, Heinemann, 1964)

Kearney, Patrick J., *The Private Case. An Annotated Bibliography of the Private Case Erotica Collection in the British (Museum) Library*, with an introduction by G. Legman (London, Jay Landesman, 1981)

Krafft-Ebing, Richard von, *Psychopathia Sexualis, with Especial Reference to Contrary Sexual Instinct: A Medico-Legal Study*, authorized translation of the seventh enlarged and revised German edition by Charles Gilbert Chaddock MD (Philadelphia and London, The F. A. Davis Co., 1892)

Kronhausen, Eberhard and Phyllis Kronhausen (eds.), *Walter. The English Casanova. A Presentation of his Unique Memoirs 'My Secret Life'*, 2 vols. (London, Polybooks, 2nd reprint, 1967)

Langham, Guy, *Grandpapa at Hawkhurst*, unpublished edition of Henry Spencer Ashbee's diaries, with introduction, miscellaneous commentaries and an 'Afterthought'

Legman, Gershon, '"Pisanus Fraxi" and his Books', introduction to the reprint of Ashbee's three erotic bibliographies (New York, Jack Brussel, 1962), pp. 5–51

– Introduction to the Grove Press (1966) edition of Anon., *My Secret Life*, vol. i, pp. xxi–lxiii.

Lemonnyer, J., *Bibliographie des Ouvrages relatifs à l'amour, aux femmes, au mariage, et des livres facétieux, pantagruéliques, scatologiques, satyriques, etc., par M. le C. d'I**** [Jules Gay], quatrième édition, entièrement refondue, augmentée et mise à jour par J. Lemonnyer, Paris, J. Lemonnyer, Éditeur, Ch. Gillet, Libraire, vol. i, 1894; vol. ii, 1897; vol. iii, 1899; vol. iv, 1900

Lovell, Mary S., *A Rage to Live. A Biography of Richard and Isabel Burton* (London, Little, Brown and Company, 1998)

Lowndes, Sir Thomas, *see* 'Speculator Morum'

Marcus, Steven, *The Other Victorians. A Study of Sexuality and Pornography in Mid-Nineteenth-Century England* (London, Corgi, 1971)

Mayhew, Henry, *London Labour and the London Poor* [London, 1861–62]; facsimile reprint, 4 vols. (New York, Dover, 1968)

Mendes, Peter, *Clandestine Erotic Fiction in English 1800–1930. A Bibliographical Study* (Aldershot, Scolar Press, 1993; reprinted 1998)

Morris, Desmond, *The Naked Ape* (London, Corgi, 1969)

Paillet, Eugène, 'Ashbee (Henry-Spencer)', *Société des Amis des Livres, Annuaire*, XXIIe. année (1901), pp. 43–52.

Pearsall, Ronald, *The Worm in the Bud. The World of Victorian Sexuality* (Harmondsworth, Penguin, 1972)

Pope-Hennessy, James, *Monckton Milnes. The Years of Promise* (London, Constable, 1949)

– *Monckton Milnes. The Flight of Youth* (London, Constable, 1951)

Portalis, Baron Roger, 'Trois Bons livres', *Société des Amis des Livres, Annuaire*, 1883, pp. 25–41.

Praz, Mario, *The Romantic Agony* (London, Collins [Fontana Library], 1960)

Priestley, J. B., *Victoria's Heyday* (Harmondsworth, Penguin, 1974)

Rattray Taylor, G., *Sex in History* (London, Panther, 1965)

Roberts, W., 'French Booklovers' Societies', *Bookworm*, vol. ii (1889), pp. 253–6

Rousseau, Jean-Jacques, *The Confessions*, translated by J. M. Cohen (Harmondsworth, Penguin, 1954)

Shadwell, Thomas, *The Virtuoso*, edited by Majorie Hope Nicolson and David Stuard Rodes, London, Edward Arnold, 1966.

'Speculator Morum' [Sir Thomas Lowndes], *Bibliotheca Arcana seu Catalogus Librorum Pentralium, being Brief notices of books that have been secretly printed, prohibited by law, seized, anathematised, burnt or Bowdlerised* (London, George Redway, 1885); facsimile reprint (London, Charles Skilton Publishing Group, 1971)

Stein, Gordon, 'The Authorship of *My Secret Life*', 46-page typescript draft of an unpublished article

Swinburne, Charles Algernon, *The Swinburne Letters*, edited by Cecil Y. Lang, 6 vols. (New Haven and Oxford, Yale University Press, 1960–62)

T.S. [Thomas Seccombe], 'Ashbee, Henry Spencer', *Dictionary of National Biography* (1901), vol. xxii (supplement), pp. 79–80

Thomas, Donald, introduction to 'Walter', *My Secret Life*, 3 vols. (London, Arrow, 1994)

Thomas, Ralph, 'The Late H. S. Ashbee', *Notes and Queries*, 18 August 1900, pp. 121–2

Trudgill, Eric, *Madonnas and Magdalens. The Origins and Development of Victorian Sexual Attitudes* (London, Heinemann, 1976)

Uzanne, Octave, 'Une Lettre de Londres sur les bibliophiles anglais', *Société des Amis des Livres, Annuaire*, 1881, pp. 21–33

W.H.K.W., 'The Late H. S. Ashbee', *Ex Libris Journal*, vol. x (1900), pp. 127–9

'Y', *The Autobiography of an Englishman* (London, Paul Elek, 1975)

Young, Wayland, *Eros Denied* (London, Weidenfeld and Nicolson, 1964)

Acknowledgements

My thanks must go first and foremost to Felicity Ashbee, to whom this book is dedicated, for her extraordinary generosity and for the gift of her friendship. Not content to lend me her grandfather's diaries so that I could peruse them at leisure, she was always ready to answer my questions about her fascinating family and to suggest avenues of enquiry. I remember with deep pleasure our animated conversations and, among other sorties, an adventure-packed outing to the Ashbee homeland in Kent. Without her I could never have put this monograph together.

In second place must come another grandchild, the late Captain Guy Langham, son of Ashbee's daughter Frances Mary, whom I was privileged to meet in 1977 and who presented me with a copy of his unpublished selection from Henry Spencer's diaries, as well as other papers. These have been a great help to me.

Through Felicity Ashbee I met a relative, Ken Styan, who, as he delved into his family's history, discovered that, behind the scenes, Robert Ashbee, Henry Spencer's father, had run a second ménage in London. Ken accompanied Felicity Ashbee and me down to Kent and will, I am confident, remember with amusement a little mishap that befell us. Over the years he has furnished me with much Ashbee information, and it is a pleasure to express my gratitude to him here.

To Gershon Legman, alas no longer with us, I owe a huge debt, not only for his pioneer work on Ashbee and the latter's possible authorship of *My Secret Life*, but for his insistence that I press ahead with my investigation. Meeting him at his unconventional Valbonne home in 1977 was an occasion that neither I nor my family are likely ever to forget.

The work of Patrick Kearney, Peter Mendes and Peter Fryer has been vital to me, and I am further beholden to them for their patience in answering questions and supplying insights and documentation.

I am grateful to Alan Crawford, biographer of Charles Ashbee, Henry Spencer's son, for his helpful response to my periodical cries for assistance.

At the British Museum, Nicolas Barker, David Clements and, much more recently, John Goldfinch were extremely obliging.

My thanks are also due to the following: Bernard Adams, Melvyn Barnes, the Revd Richard Ames-Lewis, Andrea Cameron, David Chambers, Timothy D'Arch Smith, Nigel Dennis, Jonathan Gathorne-Hardy, Paul Hammond, Richard Haynes, Stephen Humphrey, Margaret Lang, Susan Matusak and Kath Pennavaria (Kinsey Institute for Research in Sex, Gender and Reproduction, Bloomington), Arthur Percival, R. M. Robbins, CBE (British Transport) and J. Woodley (Merchant Taylors Company).

Finally, the critical acumen of my wife, Carole Elliott, proved invaluable once again as I tried to find my way through the almost impenetrable tangle of truth and subterfuge that characterizes the secret world of Henry Spencer Ashbee.

IAN GIBSON
Restábal (Granada), Spain
9 October 2000

Index
